PRAISE FOR *FUTURE-READY RETAIL*

'Ibrahim perfectly catches the transition of retail from being a commodity to being a structural part of the experiential activation of one of the most sensitive layers of the beauty and quality of every city, being the ground level integrated with public spaces.'
Manfredi Catella, Founder and CEO, Coima SGR

'This book provides guidance and great examples from someone with a global view. A valuable read and not just for retail players, as learnings are instantly transferable to other sectors.'
Henrie W Kötter, CEO, ECE Work & Live

'This book sets out an optimistic new roadmap for retail, backed by dizzying insights on every page. Ibrahim is always worth listening to, and this is a book that should be read by anyone involved in, or interested in, how cities will evolve.'
Graeme Craig, Director Commercial Development, Transport for London

'Ibrahim always provokes and inspires. An essential read.'
Mark Robinson, Chair, UK Government's High Street Task Force

'When Ibrahim speaks, the industry listens, quotes and follows.'
Kajsa Hernell, Managing Director, Nordic Council of Shopping Centres

'A fascinating book with real insight and creative thinking on how our high streets and town centres can evolve into being, once again, the heart of our communities and the very best places for people to experience.'
Nesil Caliskan, Leader, Enfield Council

'This publication elevates the retail conversation and is a thoughtful contribution to shaping a future vision for our retail places, as Ibrahim truly understands the vital appetite we have for physical connectivity and community experiences. It's an essential reference book for all strategists and decision makers involved in retail or placemaking.'
Ailish Christian-West, Director of Real Estate, Get Living

'I recommend this book to anyone involved in a business that focuses or touches on retail environments. Ibrahim is a true thought leader and innovator and has assembled a great team to consider the future of retail from a wide range of perspectives. He provides insight into a complex and fast-moving industry. This book challenges the current narrative and will stimulate reflection and debate.'
Lawrence Hutchings, Chief Executive, Capital & Regional

'A provocative read about retailing environments, filled with practical insights for retail strategists. A must-read for anyone interested in the future of retail, how it will be shaped by rapidly changing consumer expectations and how that may impact the physical spaces of shopping malls and main streets.'
Christopher Nurko, Global Chief Innovation Officer, Interbrand

'Essential reading for anyone working in the retail and placemaking industries and who is interested in the future and seeking actionable insights.'
Anthea Harries, Head of Assets, King's Cross, Argent

'I've know Ibrahim for decades and love his forward thinking approach. His book is inspiring and enlightens about the future of retail and the shift in consumers. A must-read not only for retailers, but for everyone in commercial activities!'
Walter Seib, CEO, HMSHost International

'This is a perfect moment for a book like this. I view it as a map to chart a course for the future of our high streets out of the crisis caused by the pandemic and our changing relationship with retail.'
Mark Middleton, Group Managing Partner, Grimshaw Architects

'Thoroughly inspiring, enriching, and once more manifesting Ibrahim's vast experience and penetrating insights into the future of retail!'
Rudolf Sprüngli, Founder, RKSSC Strategy Consulting

Future-Ready Retail

*How to reimagine the customer experience,
rebuild retail spaces and reignite
our shopping malls and streets*

Ibrahim Ibrahim

KoganPage

Publisher's note

Every possible effort has been made to ensure that the information contained in this book is accurate at the time of going to press, and the publishers and author cannot accept responsibility for any errors or omissions, however caused. No responsibility for loss or damage occasioned to any person acting, or refraining from action, as a result of the material in this publication can be accepted by the editor, the publisher or the author.

First published in Great Britain and the United States in 2022 by Kogan Page Limited

2nd Floor, 45 Gee Street	8 W 38th Street, Suite 902	4737/23 Ansari Road
London	New York, NY 10018	Daryaganj
EC1V 3RS	USA	New Delhi 110002
United Kingdom		India
www.koganpage.com		

Kogan Page books are printed on paper from sustainable forests.

ISBNs

Hardback	978 1 3986 0336 3
Paperback	978 1 3986 0334 9
Ebook	978 1 3986 0335 6

British Library Cataloguing-in-Publication Data
A CIP record for this book is available from the British Library.

Library of Congress Cataloging-in-Publication Data
Names: Ibrahim, Ibrahim (Designer), author.
Title: Future-ready retail: how to reimagine the customer experience,
    rebuild retail spaces and reignite our shopping malls and streets / Ibrahim Ibrahim.
Description: London; New York, NY: Kogan Page, 2022. | Includes
    bibliographical references and index.
Identifiers: LCCN 2022009074 (print) | LCCN 2022009075 (ebook) | ISBN
    9781398603349 (paperback) | ISBN 9781398603363 (hardback) | ISBN
    9781398603356 (ebook)
Subjects: LCSH: Retail trade. | Customer relations. | Branding (Marketing)
Classification: LCC HF5429 .I27 2022 (print) | LCC HF5429 (ebook) | DDC
    658.87–dc23/eng/20220303
LC record available at https://lccn.loc.gov/2022009074
LC ebook record available at https://lccn.loc.gov/2022009075

Typeset by Integra Software Services, Pondicherry
Print production managed by Jellyfish
Printed and bound by CPI Group (UK) Ltd, Croydon, CR0 4YY

To Six-Pack

CONTENTS

LIST OF FIGURES

ABOUT THE AUTHOR

Recognized as one of the world's foremost retail futurists, Ibrahim Ibrahim is a strategist and designer and the Managing Director of Portland Design, a sister company of Perkins & Will, the global architecture and design group. He is a board member of the UK Government's High Street Task Force, a member of ULI UK Infrastructure & Regeneration Council and an advisory panel member for the Centre for London Think Tank.

Ibrahim originally graduated as an aeronautical engineer and then gained a Master's degree in Industrial Design from the Royal College of Art and Imperial College London. He is a regular speaker at conferences globally and a frequent contributor to journals and trade press and has written a series of pieces for *The Economist* 'Insights'.

Over a career spanning more than 30 years Ibrahim has helped shape a broad range of projects covering retail, food, consumer brands, shopping centres, airports, train stations, mixed-use developments and urban regeneration. He has worked with some of the world's leading brands including Diageo, Nestlé, Mondelez, Lindt, Pernod Ricard, Bulthaup, Heathrow Airport, Dubai Airport, HS2, Grand Central Station NYC, British Land, TfL, Unibail-Rodamco-Westfield, Hammerson, L&G, Mubadala, ADNOC and Petronas.

Ibrahim's understanding of consumers' relationship with brands and their engagement with physical and digital environments lies at the heart of his work. This understanding is built through deep insights into the future of consumerism, retail and brands and their impact on our cities and high streets.

When Ibrahim is not overseeing the 'ideas-fuelled' studio at Portland Design he is normally with his family or in his workshop making sculpture and furniture, fiddling with classic cars or managing his family woodland.

ACKNOWLEDGEMENTS

I have been very fortunate throughout my life to have been able to learn from a lot of brilliant and generous people. The experiences and learning from the work we have done together and the conversations we have had over the years are reflected in the ideas and thoughts in this book.

My time at the Royal College of Art changed my life and proved to be the springboard to a fascinating and enriching career. I would like to thank Roger Butler and Tony Papaloizou for giving me my first opportunity in the early days and affording me the trust and confidence to pursue my own path.

I'm indebted to friends, colleagues, clients and partners I have shared experiences with, in particular to past and present colleagues at Portland Design and Perkins & Will. Thanks also to Lewis Allen for the years of provocation, insight, support, much laughter and puns! To the Morris brothers for their many years of support and friendship. And to Rodney Fitch who was an inspiration, but sadly is no longer with us.

Without the love and support of my parents Mustafa and Celen, my siblings Hussein and Rahme, and my wider family I am sure my early life would have taken a very different course.

But my deepest and most heartfelt thanks and appreciation go to my incredible wife Tomris and boys Denizer and Koral, and their respective partners Zehra and Ellena. They have given me unending and unquestioned support, inspiration, laughter and the deepest love and happiness anyone could wish for.

Without their support and sacrifices throughout the years this book and many other things in my life would not have been possible. For that I am forever grateful.

ABOUT THE CONTRIBUTORS

I have been delighted with the input of the 12 contributors to my book, and believe they have enriched the book with more diversity of opinion and insight. I have outlined below a brief biography of each contributor.

NICK BRACKENBURY

Nick is co-founder and CEO of NearSt, a retail tech start-up getting people back into high-street shops. He is building a future where shoppers can buy something from a nearby shop more easily than ordering it for delivery online. His company has been named The TechCrunch Europa's Hottest Retail Tech Start-up, an Industry Leader by London Tech Week, and he has been invited to speak on the future of shopping at WIRED and The Next Web.

A former director on Ogilvy's pioneering digital platforms team, Nick helped build out the multi-award-winning agency's earliest digital experience capabilities, working with clients including Land Rover, Nestlé and BP's London 2012 Games sponsorship.

Outside of work Nick is an avid triathlete, has driven a three-wheeled mototaxi through the Andes mountains and been spectacularly lost driving a 20-year-old car through the Mongolian wilderness.

BURAK CAPLI

Burak is the co-founder and CEO of Radius Tech, a London-based consumer intelligence provider that focuses on introducing disruptive data-driven technologies specifically for managing and operating commercial real estate. Radius aims to identify the gaps and define the opportunities in the market that arise from the misalignment between new-generation consumer expectations, real-estate asset operators and investors.

From the age of 19, Burak has been involved in cutting-edge innovations, from the first commercialized 3D chocolate printer to representing InnovateUK and the Department of International Trade as part of a trade and innovation envoy to India. He also contributed to Transport for London's Modernisation of the Four Line (4LM) where he analysed passenger behaviour in response to safety measures, paving his way to utilizing data insights for understanding human behaviour.

At its core Burak's work harmonizes the virtues of big data, artificial intelligence and human intuition while building upon an in-depth understanding of social media and the dynamics of human interaction.

ELISA CECILLI

Elisa was born and raised in Italy and after completing a BA in Economics and an MA in Arts and Culture Management in 2007 she moved to Canada to work as an academic researcher in the knowledge-based economy.

In 2010 she settled in London to build a career in strategic insights and took up a role as an in-house futurist for innovation consultancy GDR Creative Intelligence, Perkins & Will-owned design firm Portland Design and global agency Wunderman Thompson Intelligence.

Elisa has very broad knowledge and insight; she connects the dots between emerging technologies, major societal changes and consumer behaviours. In her work she uses a mix of qualitative and creative research activities, from stakeholder and expert interviews to design sprints and future scenarios. By designing and leading research programmes from Los Angeles to Tokyo, she helps clients identify new opportunities, market scenarios and change drivers.

In 2014 Elisa was part of the *MIT Technology Review*'s annual list of the top 10 Innovators Under 35 in Italy for her award-winning publication STREAM! magazine. In 2016 she started working as an independent consultant for the likes of Samsung, LinkedIn, Capgemini, Mastercard, Nike, Red Bull and Saïd Business School, among others.

KORAL IBRAHIM

Koral is the founder and Managing Director of the social media and digital design agency, The Ready House. Previously he has held positions in some of the world's leading digital, branding and advertising agencies including Cubo, FutureBrand and Mother London. He has managed global marketing and new business departments, with a focus on placemaking, tech, fashion and hospitality.

Koral has a real passion for launching brands from the ground up, and reinventing established brands to keep them relevant and at the forefront of their sector. He set up The Ready House to realize this passion, and with the view to changing and disrupting the out-dated consultancy model.

Koral and his team at TRH work with clients through a unique collaborative process to help brands step up to the challenges that this ever-changing, increasingly 'phygital' world presents.

NARAIN JASHANMAL

Narain is currently the Director of Social Commerce at Facebook Reality Labs, building new ways to shop for Oculus VR, Portal communications hardware and Ray-Ban Stories. He's been at Facebook since 2014 and previously led teams in commerce partnerships, product marketing and ad sales.

Prior to Facebook, Narain worked at his family business, the Jashanmal Group, for 10 years in various roles across operations, strategy and leadership. He is a graduate of New York University's Tisch School of the Arts from where he holds a BFA in Screenwriting and directed a feature film, *Refuge,* in 2002.

He is interested in the role that technology plays in the lives of both individuals and society, where computing goes now that it's ubiquitous, interior architecture and design and photography.

VIVIENNE KING

Vivienne has over 30 years' leadership experience in the real-estate industry.

She is a former CEO of Revo, the membership organization supporting the retail and leisure property market; of Soho Housing

Association and Soho Ltd, a retail property business in Central London; co-founder of Real Estate Balance, campaigning for equality diversity and inclusion; and over 20 years in the senior team at the Crown Estate.

Vivienne is now a consultant, NED and board advisor, and is a well-recognized voice in commercial real estate, speaking out on a wide range of issues

ALEX MCCULLOCH

Alex is a director at CACI, one of the world's leading consumer and demographic data analytics, location intelligence and customer marketing solutions businesses. Alex heads up proposition and innovation at CACI.

During a career spent working with occupiers and owners of space, Alex has developed a deep understanding of people and place that is fundamentally grounded in the consumer: where they go, what they do, how they shop, what they want and, crucially, why they make the decisions they do. With this insight Alex has advised the largest developers in Europe on investment, asset management and strategy, delivering informed insight that supports decision-making.

A regular speaker at conferences and contributor to trade journals Alex is a thought leader who is driving the industry forward by doing amazing things with data.

JAG MINHAS

Jag is the founder and CEO of Sensing Feeling, a fast-growing SME building smart visual sensing products for real-world spaces powered by computer vision and AI machine learning.

Jag is a prolific business innovator, digital services practitioner and inventor, has over 25 years of experience in technology innovation and product development with a deep understanding of Internet of Things technologies and how they can be used to transform customer experiences across multiple industry sectors.

MARK ROBINSON

Mark is a high-profile leader in the worlds of retail property and placemaking, a position recognized with his appointment to lead the government's High Street Task Force in July 2020, following his role as Revo President in 2019.

Over nearly three decades Mark has worked in all aspects of the industry as an advisor, investor/developer and occupier. In 2008 he co-founded Ellandi, a business currently undertaking over 30 projects in the UK with a value in excess of £1.5 billion. In 2016 Ellandi won Property Entrepreneurs of the Year at the Property Awards and were shortlisted for the Retail Property Company of the Year award by *Estates Gazette*. Most recently Ellandi won the inaugural *Estates Gazette* Rewire award, recognizing its commitment to leading diversity and inclusivity in the built environment industry.

Mark is a passionate advocate of the role of community in repurposing and shaping the purpose of our future places in response to the challenges and opportunities presented by the current market.

HERCULANO RODRIGUEZ

Herculano is currently Managing Director, Digital Strategy at THG's Ingenuity. As Ingenuity's digital strategy lead he is responsible for helping to create winning strategies for our retailers and brands.

He has nearly two decades of experience in retail strategy and consumer insight, working with leading international retailers and brands to develop commercial insights to inform finance, marketing and strategic planning.

Herculano is passionate about strategic innovation and technology driving the future of retail, and is helping clients deploy practical applications to help to unlock value and transform businesses. Over the past few years, he has led board-level engagements to embed customer insight and analytics to drive value from the merging of the physical and digital retail environments.

Before THG, Herculano was an Associate Director, Accenture's Retail Strategy practice and has held roles at CACI and Kantar.

MUSTAFA TAHIR

Mustafa has developed a broad range of experience across e-commerce, marketing and management consulting, his journey having covered commercial and strategic customer-facing roles working with global brands at organizations such as Google, Publicis Sapient and DigitasLBi.

Through this time, he has delivered numerous end-to-end digital lead projects across a range of functions, as well as helping businesses to design and transform the teams and processes required to support these initiatives.

Based in London, he currently leads an Experience Design function at Salesforce that leads their clients in executing adventurous digital transformation plans focused around delivering best-in-class customer experiences

JACQUELINE WELBERS

Jacqueline is passionate about developing people and companies by linking purpose and people.

She believes that 'People who are linked to the purpose of the company will be much happier and the results of the company will be much better – not only financially.'

Educated as an interior architect, photographer and marketeer, Jacqueline worked in strategic positions in several organizations. Inspired by Ingvar Kamprad, founder of IKEA, she started her own company Lovelyday, linking purpose and people in the 1990s.

Jacqueline looks at organizational development from different perspectives and has an unconventional way of working with organizations.

Introduction

For years I have been fortunate enough to be invited to write for numerous publications and speak at countless conferences and to journalists around the world on the future of retail and how it will impact our shopping centres, high streets and main streets.

When I started writing this book, the first thing I did was to re-read many of the articles I had written and the interviews I had given. What struck me was that on the one hand many of the challenges still remain, but on the other I have been amazed at the speed at which new challenges confront us.

So in writing this book I was aware that any thoughts and ideas existed in a snapshot of time. I was also aware that this is a very complex subject and a rapidly moving feast. I also thought that there are many other opinions and insights that could make such a book richer, whether those opinions aligned with my own or not.

For this reason, I thought that it would enhance the book and make it more insightful for my readers if I invited contributors to share their thoughts and opinions along with my own and the sources I researched. And luckily Chris Cudmore at Kogan Page, the publisher of this book, agreed with me!

After much thought and many conversations, I identified 12 amazing professionals to each write a piece on their specific area of expertise. To varying degrees, I have worked with all 12 of my contributors. Each one has vast experience and immense talent, and each is highly regarded in their respective spheres for work.

I hope you find their pieces insightful and feel, as I do, that they add great value to my book.

Many of our shopping centres, high streets and main streets are suffering from a pandemic of mediocrity, of 'cookie-cutter' shops that have lost their relevance to communities and consumers.

There is a sense of urgency and no time to waste in addressing the dichotomy between the dependency on physical retail, and its decline. Shopping centres, high streets and main streets must be repurposed by shifting the emphasis from a place for people to just *buy* stuff to a place for communities to *do* stuff.

The way forward is to invest in repurposing them into connected and localized 'blended places'. It will be critical to develop strategies to seamlessly bring together places for shopping, eating, drinking and entertainment with places for living, working, learning, well-being, creating and making things, and community activities and amenities.

To deliver this shift, a 'place curation' approach is essential that transcends 'leasing boxes'.

The internet has taken business away from physical retail. But I passionately believe the internet will not kill shopping centres, high streets and main streets; it will liberate them!

Releasing our shopping centres, high streets and main streets from the shackles of 'vanilla' retail that has lost its relevance to communities and consumers, and imbuing them with a truly authentic 'spirit of place' will involve a mix of unique experiences that align with communities and reflect the true essence of the place.

We are entering an era where people demand genuine value and experiences that deliver on the one hand convenience, simplicity and speed, and on the other surprise, newness and serendipity. Our aim should be to create places that are *serendipity machines* to build anticipation, engagement, sharing, repeat visits and a true sense of belonging.

I genuinely believe that there is a case for optimism if we embrace this thinking and these ideas to deliver new and relevant places and experiences, driven not by the demands of real estate, but by the true expectations and desires of citizens, consumers and communities. That is, the human truths.

01

Entropy, retail and defining the place experience

The future of retail

Consumer expectations are changing faster than many businesses can adapt. It is not so much a survival of the fittest as the survival of the most agile, and those that can adapt to the fast-moving retail landscape will prosper. We are living in an era of Retail Darwinism. To respond to this paradigm retail businesses must make the shift from being a responsive business to being a predictive one.

We live in a VUCA world, one that is full of *vulnerability, uncertainty, complexity* and is *ambiguous*.[1] In this world places and brands must build resilience through predictive strategies and embedded flexibility to ensure they can adapt to a rapidly changing landscape in order to remain Future Ready.

Today's changes in retail are not cyclical, they are structural, and the consumer has changed forever. And retail has been going through existential challenges at warp speed. The changes are not necessarily driven by new technologies or the latest new trends in design. The changes that retail is experiencing are more fundamental and far reaching. Retail's future is being shaped by the rapidly changing relationship consumers have with brands, places and with each other.

FUTURE-READY NOTE

Shift from a responsive business to a predictive business.

As a retail business, whether you own multiple shopping centres or stores, or have thousands of square metres of inflexible bricks and mortar, how can you develop the agility to adapt at the speed at which consumers are changing, particularly as more of them are shopping on platforms that maybe didn't exist even six months ago? Such businesses need to set up systems, processes and teams to research future trends and gain insight into future consumer behaviour and expectations. To imagine future scenarios and craft the stories that define how consumers may engage with brands and places and what role they will play in their lives.

The 'do nothing' strategy is not an option. And fiddling around the edges with updated assortments, new promotions, slightly nicer interior design and architecture won't cut it.

The time has come to rethink and reimagine the role that high streets, shopping centres or stores play in consumers' lives and their communities. How do they add value beyond 'stuff' and short-term commercial returns.

In the following chapters I'll be exploring these and many more themes.

Decline in retail

Disruption in retail has many facets, the most critical of which is the disruption in the retail 'food chain'. The manufacturer–distributor–wholesaler–retailer supply chain has been broken. Manufacturers are selling directly to consumers. Brands are selling direct to consumers while missing out third-party retailers such as department stores. E-tailers are selling direct to consumers. Consumers are selling directly to their peers.

Here we should note Jeff Bezos's comment, 'Your margin is my opportunity.'[2] The implication seems to be that Amazon's lower prices are delivered by removing the costs added by the wholesaler in the supply chain.

If true, it should send shivers through the bodies of brands with a high cost base. In saying that, Jeff Bezos was being very open. Amazon has the opportunity to learn about customer preferences through the data it captures, and to leverage this to sell its own products. This is no different to what the grocery sector has been doing for years, except in terms of the scale, speed of response and accuracy of Amazon's data capture operation.

Covering up the problems

Retail as we know it has been in gradual decline over the past two decades or so. However, as Mark Pilkington pointed out in his book *Retail Therapy*, there have been three factors that have plastered over the problems and anaesthetized businesses in the sector.[3]

The first is the explosion of international franchising which has allowed brands and retailers to grow, particularly in Russia, the Middle East and Asia, while hiding the structural issues in other markets. In some cases the 'cookie-cutter' roll-out of franchise stores has meant the watering down of the concept and a compromise of the brand DNA through the service proposition. The growth of international franchising has also led to clone shopping centres and high streets, where in any given city each shopping centre has the same stores, making them devoid of any unique sense of place.

The second factor that Mark Pilkington describes is private equity investments that have driven brands and retailers to invest in their stores and marketing. However, the private equity 'quick buck' strategy has saddled retailers with immense debt that has partly caused their problems in the downturn.

The third factor he describes is the dotcom bust in 2000. This made traditional retailers complacent and led them to underestimate the threat of e-commerce, as they assumed it was just a fad or not significant enough to challenge their market. This complacency led to them being slow to develop their e-commerce and digital experiences. And where they did, the digital experience often amounted to a digital catalogue of products. Being slow to invest in their digital offers gave the opportunity for the new 'digital first' players to establish their brands and capture market share. Although slow at first, this first-mover advantage is now paying back.

Retail entropy

At a more fundamental level, it is *entropy* that is causing the decline of physical retail. As Steven Pinker pointed out in his book *Enlightenment Now,* the second law of thermodynamics states that in an isolated system (one that is not interacting with its environment) entropy never decreases.[4] These systems inexorably become less structured, less organized, less able to accomplish interesting and compelling outcomes, until they slide into an equilibrium of grey, tepid, homogeneous monotony and stay there. That is entropy.

This is what we are seeing in retail. Hermetically sealed, dreary, clone shopping centres and high streets are fast becoming irrelevant and are dying due to a disconnection with their communities, the public realm and surrounding streetscapes. Disconnection also takes the form of a lack of new ideas from outside the retail sphere to respond to the rapidly changing expectations of their audience. So, if we look at the situation through this lens, we can see the structural demise of retail is partly due to 'retail entropy'.

For shopping centres and high streets to avoid 'retail entropy' they must be reconnected to their communities and to the urban streetscape, be more permeable, open and connected to the public realm through activations such as events, markets and participatory community activities. In the future, shopping centres and high streets must kick their dependency on transactional retail and bring together a mix of brands, amenities, 'non-retail' uses and experiences that attract new audiences and animate the public spaces. To bring the life back to our shopping centres and high streets we must deliver constant refreshment, newness and surprise. This is achieved through engagement with the needs of our communities and customers.

The place experience

Retail real estate, including shopping centres and high streets, can no longer rely on leasing boxes and collecting rent. Retail is no longer about real estate; it's now about *content,* the curation of blended commercial offers and compelling experiences, of which leasing is a by-product.

> **FUTURE-READY NOTE**
>
> Retail is no longer driven by real estate. It's now about content.

This is true 'placemaking', which is defined as the process of creating quality places where people want to live, work, play and learn.

For too long placemaking has been driven by architecture, where the focus on shapes on a plan and the form of buildings determine the approach. Architecture does not make place. The process of placemaking must focus on a deep understanding of people and communities, those who will be engaging with the place, their journeys and missions at different parts of the day, week, month and seasons.

> **FUTURE-READY NOTE**
>
> Architecture does not make place.

So, the human experience must be front and centre of all decisions in creating places. Architecture that is not human-centric is irrelevant and will not deliver future-ready places.

The process

The process of placemaking has five steps.

STEP ONE: CULTURE

The first is *culture*, and involves deep research and analysis of key cultural and consumer trends that will impact users' behaviour and expectations. We must undertake deep research into their communities and the role that retail plays in their day-to-day lives. Using ethnographic research methods allows us to explore and reveal the human truths that drive behaviour. And through observation we can often understand the motivation and behaviour of people that they may not necessarily be aware of themselves or be able to articulate.

Ethnography allows us to explore culture from the point of view of people's day-to-day lives. It involves the analysis of behaviour of people in a given social situation and understanding of behaviour from their own interpretation. Critically, ethnography allows us to understand our audiences in their local contexts and all the elements that influence their behaviour. A critical part of this research is social media and influencer mapping which gives us insight into what brands, places and interests our audience are engaging with at a very granular level

Of course we can also gain insight into culture through other quantitative and qualitative research methods, through surveys, focus groups and one-to-one interviews.

STEP TWO: PEOPLE

The second step is *people*. Understanding the community and our audience as specific groups is essential if we are to deliver relevant offers and experiences. From the insights and 'human truths' that the ethnographic research has revealed we can now define and analyse our audiences' profiles, needs and desires. It is important that the profiles are not just bland statistics. We must craft the stories of our audiences' lives, priorities and the things that create emotional connection while understanding what part a shopping centre or high street plays. We can then map their journeys and missions in relation to a shopping centre or high street which we can feed into the experience masterplan in Step Four.

STEP THREE: PLACE

Defining the vision and ambition for the place will give us the building blocks in order to craft the *place* story. We start with interrogating and understanding the origins of the place, its history, unique experiences and people. We then explore the attributes of a place, its location, unique features, its community, connectivity and the physical built environment. In order to define the place personality, values and positioning we interrogate how the place brand speaks, looks, thinks and behaves, and the values that underpin these. From this we can define its positioning in its own right and also in comparison to competitive places. And although it is difficult, ideally we would also define what is referred to as 'one word equity'. This is the one word that describes very succinctly the essence of the place and experience.

From this very rich content and insight we can begin to define the place vision, the 'North Star', i.e. the key idea that helps guide the future. When the vision is right, it reflects and supports all strategies, differentiates them from competitors, resonates with stakeholders, energizes and inspires employees and partners, and drives all communication.

In parallel with defining the vision we also define the ambition. This is the narrative that describes what is to be achieved. The critical difference between the vision and the ambition is that the vision is an idea that can be imagined and may or may not be achieved. The ambition, however, is a defined aim that is measurable and has milestones.

STEP FOUR: SPACE

The fourth step is *space*. Translating the above into the 'experience masterplan', with the right mix of experiences and amenities and identifying the synergies between them, with a focus on the connectivity of different districts and public realm. The experience masterplan defines the *connective tissue* that binds the experiences, activates the public realm and imbues it with an authentic spirit of place and a sense of belonging.

FUTURE-READY NOTE

The connective tissue of blended experiences creates authentic place.

STEP FIVE: DESIGN

Then, and only then, should the *design* of the buildings and public spaces come into the picture, with the architecture and public realm design based on the 'strategic platform' established in the first four steps. The approach that drives the creation of successful and future-ready places therefore comes more from anthropology than it does from architecture. Understanding people and culture is the bedrock on which authentic and future-ready places are created. The design of the built environment is a by-product of this understanding.

> **FUTURE-READY NOTE**
>
> Placemaking is about people and places, not buildings and spaces.

Notes

1 Vuca-World. Leadership Skills & Strategies, 2021, www.vuca-world.org (archived at https://perma.cc/7L7W-3G25)

2 Marketplace Pulse. The cost of 'Your margin is my opportunity', 2020, www.marketplacepulse.com/articles/the-cost-of-your-margin-is-my-opportunity (archived at https://perma.cc/49DQ-MP2H)

3 M Pilkington (2019) *Retail Therapy: Why the retail industry is broken – and what can be done to fix it,* Bloomsbury, London

4 S Pinker (2018) *Enlightenment Now: The case for reason, science, humanism and progress,* Allen Lane, London

02

A new audience

Demographic segmentation

Traditionally, brands have segmented consumers on the basis of demographics. These demographics make generalizations about individual consumers and their particular habits, desires, wants, needs, expectations and values. Demographic segmentation is based on factors such as age, income, marital status, gender, culture or education. This is the most traditional form of segmentation used by many brands.

There are broadly four types of demographic segmentation as outlined by Mark Pilkington in his book *Retail Therapy*.[1]

Baby boomers

Baby boomers (born 1945 to 1965): the youngest boomers are now in their mid-fifties, the eldest in their mid-seventies. They make up about half of all spending growth over the past decade compared to other generations. There are two reasons for this. Firstly, increased life expectancy means there are more consumers over 60. Secondly, baby boomers compared to previous generations are retiring later, so have more income to spend.

Generation X

Generation X (born 1965 to 1980): many Gen Xers have high spending power as they occupy high-paying jobs. Globally Gen X represents the majority of business leadership – about two-thirds of CEOs of Fortune 500 companies are currently Gen Xers. Across all generations, Gen X has the highest brand loyalty.

Generation Y

Generation Y (born 1980 to 1995): also referred to as Millennials, the oldest of them are now around 40 years of age. Gen Yers are predicted to be the most powerful consumers in the coming years. They have a disproportionate influence on brands and retail, they tend to be more mobile savvy, more demanding and educated to a higher degree than previous generations. They have grown up with technology and the mobile device has always been an integral part of their lives. They are natural with social media and online payments.

Unlike previous generations, Gen Y has a tendency to not respond to retailers pushing products through messaging. They prefer authentic experiences and brand representatives who understand and have knowledge of the product or service. Again, unlike previous generations they like to be involved with the brand and prefer dialogue to monologue communications.

Some 72 per cent of Gen Yers would like to increase their spending on experiences rather than physical things, pointing to a move away from materialism and a growing demand for real-life experiences. Around 69 per cent of Millennials experience FOMO (the fear of missing out). As more experiences are broadcast across social media they are driven to attend events, participate and share, due to this fear.[2]

Generation Z

Generation Z (born 1995 to 2012): also referred to as post-Millennials or Centennials. Those that are of working age are used to working in a freelance capacity in the gig economy, whether it's by choice or not.

Gen Zers are digital natives; technology and the mobile device are part of their DNA. The mobile device is their 'remote control for life'. Many of them do not remember a time before the internet, which has become the generic platform for all their interactions with brands and retailers.

Some 67 per cent of Gen Zers believe websites will have the data to determine what they want to buy before they interact with the website.[3] They have very little patience and will not even wait even five seconds for a YouTube video to buffer. They are also very happy to create content and share with their network and with brands and retailers.

Blurring the lines

There is a potential danger in demographic segmentation. Naturally, generations influence each other. In particular we are seeing Generation Z, with its natural engagement with technology and mobile devices, influencing other generations in the way it engages with brands and with each other. This is blurring the lines marked out by demographic segmentation and so we are seeing common behaviours across these generations, really putting into question the whole basis of segmenting the audience through a crude demographic model.

I have personal experience of this. I am almost 60 and I have two sons: one is 31 and the other 27 years old. As consumers it seems that all three of us behave in very similar ways. We shop in similar shops, eat in similar restaurants and go on holiday to similar places. We drive similar cars and the clothes we wear are not very different. There are some differences, particularly when it comes to our choices of TV programmes, films and apps. But the similarities that I have with my two sons are very different to those that I have with my father. In respect to brand engagement, there has been a seismic shift in just one generation.

Geographic segmentation

Brands also use geographic segmentation which divides the audience based on their country, state, postcode, district or neighbourhood. The

Nike by Melrose store in LA is the first neighbourhood-specific Nike Live concept store built for and inspired by local NikePlus members.[4] It offers city-specific styles, all of which are determined by Nike digital commerce data (buying patterns, app usage and engagement) to serve local NikePlus members exactly what they want, when they want it. That means new apparel, footwear and accessories (all specific to local customer needs rather than Nike's broader seasonal priorities) will fill the store on a bi-weekly basis and sometimes even exclusively.

Psychographic segmentation

To respond to the blurring of the lines between generations we first need to consider psychographic segmentation, which looks deeper into who the person is. Psychographic segmentation considers all aspects of a consumer's behaviour, interests, hobbies, opinions and values, and how to appeal to these.

> **FUTURE-READY NOTE**
>
> Shift from demographic segmentation to interest- and behaviour-based segmentation.

Outdoor clothing company **Patagonia** does this very well. It targets audiences who share their brand's ethos and beliefs around sustainability and circularity. This was really well illustrated through Patagonia's 'Don't Buy This Jacket' campaign. The message was intended to encourage people to consider the effect of consumerism on the environment and purchase only what they need. The campaign was part of Patagonia's wider 'Common Thread' initiative which was set up to ask people to buy only what they need, repair what wears out to lengthen its life and recycle everything else.[5]

Although this approach might have seemed risky, it helped build a strong community of people who respond to the brand's values and its products. It had the impact of changing Patagonia's customers' behaviour by encouraging them to make more thoughtful purchases.

Toms Shoes is another brand that engages with its consumer based on their values. It is driven by the fact that almost a billion people across the planet do not have access to clean safe drinking water. In some countries just $5 can give a single person clean water for five years. As a brand whose values of doing good are part of its DNA, it decided to support the charity Water which is dedicated to bringing clean and safe drinking water to people in developing countries. Toms committed to match each individual $5 donation made to Water, up to $10,000, to fund important water projects in areas most in need. Although it does not relate to the product directly, this action aligns to the values of their customers. And it demonstrates how increasingly consumers from multiple demographics are united by turning to brands for their beliefs and actions as well as their products and services.

Generation C

Taking a psychographic approach to segmentation blurs the boundaries of the different demographic consumer segments, and shows a commonality of behaviour. This cross-boundary, segmentation-busting consumer is referred to as 'Generation C'. And it's this shift from demographic segmentation to interest- and behaviour-based segmentation that defines Gen C.

Gen C describes an audience that blurs the lines and breaks the silos of demographic segmentation. Defined below are the seven Cs of Generation C. As you read through them it will become clear how brands such as Nike, Apple, Patagonia and others deliver many of these demands.

1. CONTROL

First and foremost, Gen C's key demand is to be in *control*. Their expectation is that places and experiences will be designed to be intuitive and simple. They expect all brands that they engage with to be transparent and honest, and if they are not, they will be found out. Being in control also means that they demand what they want, how they want, when they want, and the freedom to be able to change their mind.

2. CONVENIENCE

Generation C lead busy, complex and transient lives. They demand experiences that are frictionless and *convenient*. In order to meet the expectations of Generation C, brands must analyse every touchpoint of their customer journey and deliver hyper-convenient experiences devoid of complexity.

In physical retail, queues at the till contribute significantly to inconvenience. Research of UK shoppers indicates that 89 per cent of shoppers have left a store as a result of a long queue;[6] more worryingly, 65 per cent of these shoppers admit to visiting a rival store straight afterwards to get what they need. People's expectations have been shaped by their experiences of shopping in the virtual world, meaning they now have little to no patience when it comes to queuing.

Hointer of Seattle, the men's jeans shop, is a great example of a brand that understands the importance of hyper-convenience and simplicity.[7] The store allows customers to shop quickly with the help of their smartphone. By downloading the Hointer app the shopper can try on clothes and place them in a virtual shopping cart. The jeans are suspended from cables within the store each of which has a tag with a QR or NFC (near field communication) code. The clothes in the customer's shopping cart arrive in the dressing room via a chute within 30 seconds. A specific dressing room number on the app directs the shopper. If the clothes don't fit, the shopper can request a different pair on their phone, while the clothes that don't fit are removed from the shoppers' virtual shopping cart. The jeans can be purchased while the shopper is still in the fitting room by swiping a credit/debit card on a card reader in the fitting room.

There are no sales staff in the store needed to replenish shelves of racks. The store behaves like a 'walk-in vending machine' delivering a frictionless experiences with all complexities stripped out. The Hointer store is exactly the type of simple, seamless and speedy experience that responds to Gen C's fast-paced, complex life.

3. CONNECTED

Generation C is of course constantly *connected* and will increasingly engage with brands that have a seamless physical/digital offer. **Made.com** is a great example of a retailer that delivers a truly integrated physical/

digital experience. Their showrooms have examples of the pieces they sell in their range but the actual transaction by the customer is undertaken on computers within the store. The customer can take an iPad from a rack in the store and scan a QR code on each product, and then receive information on the product and fabrics and finishes that are available. The actual transaction is then performed digitally. Of course the customer can purchase products in the conventional way via the Made.com website either on their own computer, their mobile device or as described above within the Made.com showroom.

4. COLLABORATION

Generation C seek brands that encourage *collaboration* where they are made to feel like a partner and influence the voice of the brand and be part of its universe. They demand the ability to shape a brand, to have an influence on the type of experience being offered. They see their experience with a brand as a two-way relationship that goes beyond transaction, and they will only allow brands into their lives that demonstrate true value beyond selling them stuff. They turn to brands that connect them to like-minded people.

A good example of a brand that delivers true value beyond just selling stuff is the athleisure brand **Sweaty Betty**. The brand has evolved from a content-based online community and is now an omnichannel brand with a network of stores that are often seen by their customers as a place to meet like-minded people, to participate in workouts and share opinions and ideas. Sweaty Betty is a brand with opinions and has supported a range of social issues and organizations

5. CO-CREATION

Gen C want to shape the future of a brand's products and services. They want to be part of a *co-creation* process and influence the design of its products and services.

FUTURE-READY NOTE

Brands are not created. They are co-created.

Unilever is a good example of a business that encourages its customers to participate in the design of its products. As one of the world's largest FMCG firms, with over 400 brands used by over 2.5 billion people in 190 countries, Unilever has a pool of customers with whom it co-creates products, actively looking for product solutions, ideas and suggestions. It achieves this through its Open Innovation platform.[8] Using this platform, Unilever encourages customers to submit ideas that the firm may adopt. If a suggestion is successful, the customer can be offered a commercial contract for their solution, as well as professional recognition.

The response to the Unilever Open Innovation platform has been strong, with over 60 per cent of Unilever's research projects involving external collaboration.[9] The company's approach to co-creation reflects the value of open innovation and shows the potential uses of crowdsourcing to solve problems and create new product ideas.

As Gen C increasingly demand customized products they will turn to brands that give them the opportunity to be creative and input into the design process.

In 2018, **IKEA** launched 'Co-Create IKEA', a digital platform encouraging customers and fans to develop new products. If a suggestion for furniture or product design is successful, IKEA may agree to invest in its future. IKEA has received thousands of customer suggestions. Participants are eligible for cash rewards if their ideas work and are selected. Additionally, IKEA provides resources like test labs and prototype shops to help customers develop and fine-tune their suggestions. Co-creation helps IKEA in product innovation, allowing it to gain value from useful design insights. This creates real market advantages for the company and builds a community of dedicated customers that transcends demographics by appealing to the universal Gen C demand for co-creation.

Lego is another company that takes customer co-creation seriously and draws immense value from it. Lego has a fresh approach to customer co-creation for product development. Since 2004, it has received suggestions from over 1 million people, with fans voting on the most popular ideas. In return for contributing a winning idea, the creator can give final approval for the end product, be recognized on all packaging and marketing, and even earn a percentage of product sales. Lego's commitment to co-creation has helped lift revenue. And its commitment to customer co-creation shows how this kind of collaboration can help create new communities of fans around the world. This initiative has also driven media coverage and strengthened customer loyalty.

DeWalt, one of the world's leading manufacturers of power tools, has built an 'Insights Community' where customers contribute product development ideas. Since its establishment, the Insight Community has grown to include more than 12,000 users who contribute a valuable range of product suggestions. DeWalt seeks customers' ideas in product design and development, packaging and website usability. The Insight Community also helps create improvements to DeWalt's products. The Community hasn't just been entertaining for customers – it's also meant big savings for DeWalt. It is estimated that the Insight Community has saved DeWalt almost $6 million in research costs.[10]

DHL, the world's largest courier company, shows how customer co-creation can be applied to services as well as products. DHL hosts workshops with customers to find creative solutions and improve customer experience. Customers are invited to talk to DHL employees and brainstorm new initiatives. One idea to emerge from the workshops was the 'Parcelopter' drone used for deliveries of parcels. Up to 2017, DHL had held over 6,000 co-creation sessions with customers. Its co-creation efforts have helped customer satisfaction scores to rise over 80 per cent, generating higher client retention as a result.

6. COMMUNITIES

Gen C builds *communities* that mirror their interests and passions. And they become loyal to brands that have communities of interest at their heart. Brands respond to this specific need by creating places and experiences that bring the fans of the brand together. These places transcend the idea of a shop. They are more akin to community centres, sometimes referred to as 'branded habitats'.

7. CONSCIENCE

Most critically, Generation C has a *conscience*. They will gravitate towards brands and places that demonstrate added value in their lives and the wider world with actionable purpose.

According to research by IBM:

> 57 per cent of consumers are willing to change their purchasing habits to help reduce negative environmental impact. And 71 per cent of those surveyed who indicated that traceability is very important are willing to pay a premium for brands that provide it.[11]

Twelve traits of Gen C

In summary, we can see that Generation C wants to be part of a place or brand community. They want to shape it, and they care about the role it plays in their life and the wider world. These desires are expressed in the following traits:

1 They value freedom and choice in their life.
2 They demand transparency and scrutinize everything: there is no hiding place for brands.
3 They like to share their experiences physically and digitally.
4 They demand honesty, openness and integrity from brands.
5 They love customizing and personalizing.
6 They like informality and seek entertainment and play in work, education and leisure.
7 They want wellness to be imbued in all experiences and places.
8 They are commitment-phobes and promiscuous to brands.
9 They are digital nomads: they work, shop, learn and play anywhere, anytime.
10 They are globally connected and constantly engaged with brands and each other.
11 They are impatient and expect everything to happen at lighting speed.
12 They expect constant newness, surprise and innovation.

> **FUTURE-READY NOTE**
>
> Generation C represents not a demographic but a set of values and an attitude.

The new consumer

The marketing Ps

In marketing we were taught about the five Ps: product, price, place, promotion and people. I always thought that these five Ps were too business focused; for a business to be customer obsessed it must redefine these five Ps to reflect that. So:

- *Product* is customer value and not just the product that is produced.
- *Price* is customer cost and not just about the pricing strategy of a brand; this cost is beyond a monetary cost – it also represents the cost of time and inconvenience.
- *Place* should emphasize the customer experience and not the brand's distribution channels.
- *Promotion* is about emotional connection and can no longer be the brand talking *to* or (even worse) *at* customers, but must be a dialogue with customers.
- *People* should focus on customers as advocates of the brand and not just the people who work for the brand.

In addition to the five Ps we must add two further Ps: purpose and planet. Consumers are increasingly turning to brands with a clear *purpose* that relates to their lives and the wider world.

And for *planet*, brands must have a clear environmental, social and governance (ESG) strategy that defines its actions in relation to environmental and economic sustainability.

Status

At its core, consumerism is about one thing – status. In the past, consumers craved the status that a logo conferred on them, or the status of putting an expensive bottle of whisky on the table for their guests to see.

Now the nature of status is changing. As millions of consumers around the world can afford branded products for which they pay a premium, the status in purely owning that product and showing it off is diminishing.

We are seeing a shift from 'status symbols' to 'status skills', where the real status is now in understanding the product, the stories that underpin it and the skills and connoisseurship that are associated with it. Owning and showing off the expensive bottle of Scotch is no longer sufficient. The status is gained in being able to tell the brand stories; the history, the tasting notes, the region of Scotland in which it was produced. Hence, we are seeing an explosion of 'craft brands' and specialist independent retailers, many of which are being targeted for acquisition by multinationals.

FUTURE-READY NOTE

From status symbols to status skills.

A good example of this is the **T2** tea brand. Established in Melbourne, Australia, T2 has taken the traditional area of tea, and presented it in an accessible retail format where the service proposition includes a wide range of tea rituals performed by associates with a deep knowledge of the origins of the teas and the stories behind them. After their initial expansion abroad T2 was acquired by Unilever.

Audiences

Forward-thinking retailers refer to their customers as 'audiences', as those retailers increasingly behave like media brands with everchanging content. Brian Solis referred to 'Audiences of Audiences', whereby retailers should identify their brand champions in order to engage with the champions' audiences in turn.[12]

Trust

There has been a huge shift in audiences' relationship with brands. Trust in brands is waning. According to the global communications firm Edelman only 34 per cent of consumers trust the brands they purchase from.[13] For 81 per cent of the report's 16,000 respondents (spread across eight countries) trust is a deal breaker or a deciding factor in their purchase decisions.

The respondents ranked other deciding factors, with quality at 85 per cent, convenience at 84 per cent, value at 84 per cent and ingredients at 82 per cent. The study also revealed that of all the consumers who trust a brand, only 53 per cent would be the first to buy from their trusted businesses. Only 21 per cent of respondents reported that the brands they buy from have society's best interests in mind.

For a brand, future trust and success will depend on its ability to emotionally connect with consumers, not just communicate. Message-based monologue marketing is dead, and increasingly consumers will ignore one-way communication. So, we are seeing a shift from marketing communication (MARCOMMS) to marketing connection (MARCONNS) where participation is the new consumption, as demonstrated by Lulu Lemon with their yoga classes and Rapha with their cycling fans watching screenings of Le Tour de France in the brand's 'Club Houses' in high streets.

FUTURE-READY NOTE

Participation is the new consumption.

Technology

We are entering a future world where, according to Gartner Research, one in three jobs will be converted to software, robots and smart machines by 2025.[14] Additionally, the World Economic Forum has suggested that 'children entering primary school today will ultimately end up working in completely new job types that don't yet exist'.

But, when it comes to retail, we must not fall into the trap of being obsessed by the latest fads in technology. To remain relevant, retail must put people first and develop strategies that put the human experience front and centre. The audience must be treated with a duty of care as citizens first, and not be taken for granted with the assumption that they are automatically consumers.

FUTURE-READY NOTE

Citizen first.

We can see six key trends emerging that are influencing our audience and will drive their future behaviour and expectations:

1 *Always-on culture:* as people are increasingly locked into complex, uncertain, busy and hyper-connected lifestyles they feel pressurized and the speed at which everyday decisions have to be made, combined with multiple activities, can be overwhelming.

2 *Experience hunters:* in developed economies people have embraced a culture where greater value is placed on the pursuit of unique, memorable experiences which are increasingly ephemeral and instantly shared digitally.

3 *Individual and expressive:* the pursuit of individualism has transformed single markets of millions into the 'long tail' of millions of single markets, where individuals demand hyper-personalized products and experiences, and have the desire to express themselves in a unique way.

4 *Mindful and playful:* busy and complex urban lifestyles have left people feeling uncertain, anxious and unfulfilled. People want to find solace and joy, they want to relax, recharge and reconnect by finding delight amidst the chaos.

5 *Open and collaborative:* people seek deeper meaning, are more emotionally open and crave authentic experiences and emotional connection. This has driven the demand for collaborative communities, and interest groups for like-minded people.

6 *Socially conscious:* consumers will increasingly turn to brands that have an authentic purpose and can add true value to their lives. What a brand stands for is just as important as what it sells, and consumers want to engage with brands that align with their own personal values, to become not merely a consumer but a fan, an advocate, a member.

These six trends are going to shape how our audience engages with brands and places in the future and will determine which brands succeed and which fail.

Correspondingly, there are six ways that brand and place experiences should evolve in order to meet the future expectations and desires of their audiences:

a *Escape the everyday:* to escape mundane routine people want to be surprised; they love serendipity, happy coincidences they never expected. They will turn to brands that go beyond selling them stuff, brands that deliver memorable moments in their day-to-day life, moments that can be shared and revisited.

b *Hyper-personalization:* the demand for personalized products and services will continue to increase. People want to feel like an individual not a clone, and so will seek products and services that meet their specific needs and desires at any given time.

c *Ritualization:* brands must evolve their service proposition into unique rituals that align to the values of the brand. Consumers will turn to brands that have authentic rituals that deliver multi-sensory, 'other-worldly' experiences.

d *Brand as community:* when engaging with brands consumers will want to feel a sense of belonging; not merely to buy from a brand but to join as a member, to share experiences with other like-minded members.

e *Time sensitive:* with the limited time they have consumers want maximum value from the time they spend with brands and places. Not only do they expect convenient and seamless experiences, but they also want those experiences to be enriching and worthwhile.

f *Blended experiences:* in future consumers will not distinguish between online and offline. Most online experiences will take place in a brand's physical space, and consumers will flip between online and offline instantly and continuously, and will expect brands to facilitate this with seamless and integrated experiences.

FUTURE-READY NOTE

The future of retail will not be about technology. It will be about anthropology.

Notes

1 M Pilkington (2019) *Retail Therapy: Why the retail industry is broken – and what can be done to fix it*, Bloomsbury, London

2 Eventbrite. Millennials: Fueling the Experience Economy, eventbrite-s3.s3. amazonaws.com/marketing/Millennials_Research/Gen_PR_Final.pdf (archived at https://perma.cc/JW7C-YJYA)

3 M E Dugan. For Generation Z the digital experience is the human experience, AdAge, 2019, adage.com/article/wp-engine/generation-z-digital-experience-human-experience/316487 (archived at https://perma.cc/7K74-JSKY)

4 S Campisi. Nike by Melrose, Los Angeles, Echochamber, 2021, echochamber. com/article/nike-by-melrose-los-angeles/ (archived at https://perma.cc/C3N7-8JFW)

5 J Allchin. Case study: Patagonia's 'Don't buy this jacket' campaign, *Marketing Week,* 2013, web.archive.org/web/20201127235120/https://www. marketingweek.com/case-study-patagonias-dont-buy-this-jacket-campaign/ (archived at https://perma.cc/3ZRW-U7NP)

6 D Nixdorf. Eliminate in-store queues – not revenues, RetailWeek, 2018, www. retail-week.com/retail-voice/eliminate-in-store-queues-not-revenues/7028926. article?authent=1 (archived at https://perma.cc/FSX2-UTRV)

7 Retail Innovation. US retailer Hointer uses robots to deliver your selections to the fitting room, 2013, retail-innovation.com/us-retailer-hointer-uses-robots-to-deliver-your-selections-to-the-fitting-room (archived at https://perma.cc/87KB-YQXF)

8 J Livescault. Customer co-creation examples: 12 companies doing it right, Braineet.com, www.braineet.com/blog/co-creation-examples (archived at https:// perma.cc/W7VL-F4LN)

9 Warc. Open innovation boosts Unilever, 2012, www.warc.com/
newsandopinion/news/open-innovation-boosts-unilever/30488 (archived at
https://perma.cc/PKC9-ECEN)

10 J Livescault. Customer co-creation examples: 12 companies doing it right,
Braineet.com, www.braineet.com/blog/co-creation-examples (archived at
https://perma.cc/W7VL-F4LN)

11 K Haller, J Lee and J Cheung. Meet the 2020 consumers driving change, IBM
Institute for Business Value, 2019, www.ibm.com/thought-leadership/institute-
business-value/report/consumer-2020 (archived at https://perma.cc/8XE6-
SUTP)

12 B Solis (2011) *The end of business as usual: Rewire the way you work to
succeed in the consumer revolution*, John Wiley & Sons, Inc, NJ

13 Edelman.com. Edelman Trust Barometer Special Report: In brands we trust,
2019, www.edelman.com/sites/g/files/aatuss191/files/2019-06/2019_edelman_
trust_barometer_special_report_in_brands_we_trust.pdf (archived at https://
perma.cc/7NB7-5CWR)

14 J Barajas. Smart robots will take over a third of jobs by 2025, Gartner says,
PBS NewsHour, 2014, www.pbs.org/newshour/economy/smart-robots-will-
take-third-jobs-2025-gartner-says (archived at https://perma.cc/8DWN-CM3Q)

03

A new customer journey

The new customer journey is 'elastic'. It is no longer confined to the physical store and is increasingly made up of engagement before, during and after the physical experience.

Brands must engage with consumers through a broad range of touch-points along their journey. These touchpoints are both internal and external to the brand. Internal platforms include the brand's e-commerce site; mobile apps; events; entertainment content; and a wide range of physical stores from flagships, local stores, shop-in-shops, pop-ups and sometimes even vending. External platforms include in-home and out-of-home media channels, social media plat-forms such as Instagram and Facebook; chat platforms such as WhatsApp and Messenger; video streaming sites such as YouTube and TikTok; third-party websites such as Amazon and eBay; and third-party retailers such as multi-brand stores.

The physical store represents one touchpoint along an increasingly complex journey. In the past, conventional and more recently digital media were primarily used to recruit customers to drive them either to online e-commerce sites or physical stores for transaction.

As more consumers transact online, whether through conventional e-commerce sites or on social media platforms, the physical store will become a touchpoint along the customer journey that will increasingly be used to recruit customers, to then drive them online for transaction. I expect we will also see that a larger proportion of transactions online will take place within the physical store.

> **FUTURE-READY NOTE**
>
> Prepare for more online transaction to take place within your physical stores.

Contrary to popular opinion, I strongly believe that the internet will not kill physical stores; it will liberate them! The physical store will find a new purpose and it will be the most important component of the customer journey. The physical store will be where the brand comes to life, where the rituals are played out and where people who share interests and passions will gather. The physical store has the potential to be the most powerful customer recruitment platform available to a brand and where the customers can develop an emotional connection to the brand; rather than just buying what it sells, they will be buying into what the brand believes. The physical store must be used to magnify the journey.

> **FUTURE-READY NOTE**
>
> The physical store must be used to magnify the journey.

> **FUTURE-READY NOTE**
>
> The internet will not kill stores, it will liberate them!

As we have seen, the new customer journey is getting more complicated and is blurring physical and digital touchpoints. In the future, consumers will not distinguish between physical and digital, between online and offline. They will flip between physical and digital experiences in milliseconds and expect a seamless journey that is frictionless and hyper-convenient, and mobile connectivity will be the glue that binds their journeys.

The customer mission

The type of customer journey depends on the mission that the customer is on. It is critical to understand these missions and to organize the physical store to respond to their behaviour, which in turn is driven by the mission. Broadly speaking there are three core shopper missions, each with a specific behavioural pattern: *find*, *discover* and *inspire*.

Find

The first is the *Find* mission whereby a shopper has a clear idea about what they want to buy. Having carried out all the research necessary, they have pre-planned their purchase. At the store they require very little service or information as they have knowledge or previous experience of the product. However, what they do require is a clear, simple and convenient journey to find the product with easy navigation, good communications and in the case of a physical store, clear sight lines. On a find mission the customer has a good understanding of price and just needs to know that they're not paying too much, however in some instances they are prepared to pay a premium for convenience. In short, they seek price reassurance. The customer also seeks brand authenticity, so more often than not the find mission will be for well-known brands with high levels of consumer trust.

Find shopping generally happens during regular visits to a store either online or offline. In the future, an increasing amount of this type of shopping will be through a voice platform such as Amazon's Alexa. It is thought that for brands this may represent an existential threat as the voice platform becomes the gatekeeper to the consumer, having the potential to block direct engagement with the consumer. This is becoming further pronounced as find shopping moves to a subscription model whereby the consumer does not physically spend time shopping for the product. Hence the find mission in future will be mostly unconscious shopping. This can be described as 'zero-click' shopping, where shopping becomes a utility. A good example of a subscription retail brand is the New York-based beauty and cosmetics brand **Birchbox**. It offers an online monthly subscription service where subscribing customers take monthly deliveries of a box of beauty products, which could include perfumes, skincare and other cosmetics products. At time of writing, a monthly subscription costs £13.95, a three-monthly is £30, six-monthly £60 and a yearly £110.

For brands to respond to the find mission, they may need to have a presence on voice platforms and treat them as they would a media platform. Brands should consider buying time on voice platforms in order to 'interrupt' the consumer habit of repeat purchases, to 'upsell' them.

For example, if a consumer repeatedly orders a brand of toothpaste on a voice platform, in order to keep the attention of the consumer, and also to upsell them, the brand could have a presence on the platform that reminds the consumer that a new version of the product has teeth-whitening properties. This will keep the brand front of mind.

FUTURE-READY NOTE

Voice platforms may become the gatekeepers to the consumer.

Discover

The second mission is the *Discover* mission. Here the shopper targets the specific category they want to shop. They like to browse the category, exploring the options and trying out the products. In the discover mission the shopper responds well to trialling, advice and customer service. Knowledgeable staff is a critical factor in the discover mission, as shoppers really want to engage with staff. During the discover mission shoppers respond well to stories that describe how to use a product or the role it may play for a particular occasion.

For example, if a shopper is looking to buy vodka, stories about cocktails, parties and instructions on how to make cocktails and the ingredients needed would be very beneficial in converting the sale.

Inspire

The third mission is *Inspire*. This is the most critical mission as it is the least price sensitive. Here the shopper does not necessarily have plans to shop for a specific item but is seeking ideas and inspiration. In the inspire mission consumers are most open-minded, whether they are at home browsing new trends online or just wanting to have fun and escape the everyday in the physical space. Often the inspire mission involves deeper human interaction and connection and is typified by very personalized experiences. To engage the shopper on an inspire mission it is critical to present new ideas, new ways of experiencing a product and most critically, surprises. It is novelty and inspirational ideas that engage the shopper on an inspire mission. Participatory experiences, learning and conviviality will encourage the inspire shopper to dwell and engage with products and services that capture their imagination. Transient and ephemeral experiences such as pop-ups capture the attention of a shopper on an inspire mission.

The **T2** tea brand is a great example of a store that can deliver on the 'find', 'discover' and 'inspire' missions. Their website delivers on the *find* mission. For the *discover* mission both the T2 website and store deliver an experience that allows the shopper to discover new teas and tastes, as well as all the accessories for making and serving tea. For the *inspire* mission the T2 shop is always surprising and new with constantly changing displays of teas and accessories. The shopper can learn about the many types and flavours of tea and the rituals of serving, and can gain a deeper knowledge of the origins of the teas, the leaf types and the farmers, locations and production process involved.

Another brand that delivers on the three missions is **Glossier**. Its simple and frictionless purchase process delivers very well on the *find* mission. The *discover* mission is delivered through great user reviews and product demonstrations. The *inspire* mission is delivered through an inspirational community; the experience centres on real people experiencing real life who show how they wear Glossier products and demonstrate them in action. Shoppers, or more accurately fans, are inspired with make-up ideas with new shade combinations, all in the context of a social experience.

In a very different context, *The Guardian* newspaper has recognized that it must deliver on the three missions. Its *find* mission is delivered through its Instagram feed whereby the reader can access small snippets and teasers of news very conveniently. The *discover* mission can be experienced through *The Guardian* website, or the physical newspaper where the reader can access more information or indeed discover new stories with its long-form journalism. Very interestingly, the *inspire* mission can be experienced through online or in real life (IRL) debates and classes with journalists and other thought leaders, all as part of the brand's subscription model.

The path to purchase

Within each mission there is a common 'path to purchase', involving five steps. The matrix in Table 3.1 indicates how each step in the path relates to each mission.

TABLE 3.1 The mission/path to purchase matrix

Path to Purchase	Mission		
	Find	Discover	Inspire
Explore	Straightforward – most convenient retailer	Plan and research category	Surprise encounters
Evaluation	Reassurance of price and brand authenticity	Gain experience via trialling/customer service	Identify whether surprises match needs and desires
Purchase	Simple and frictionless, usually online	Part of an overall solution, including add-ons	Involves related experiences
Experience	Familiar, no surprises	Discover new ways of using product	Involves lasting memories
Advocacy	Little advocacy – habit only	Active advocacy – leaving simple reviews, sharing on social media	Pronounced advocacy – leaving in-depth reviews, sharing on social media

Explore

The first step on the path to purchase is *Explore*. The explore stage is mostly about gathering ideas for purchase. The shopper will assemble an initial list of brands and retailers to consider.

Increasingly, Amazon is used as a product search engine, with 63 per cent of consumers worldwide starting their product search on Amazon; 48 per cent start their search on search engines; 33 per cent on retailer sites; 25 per cent on other marketplaces; 21 per cent on the website of the brand they want; 10 per cent on comparison sites; and 8 per cent on social media.[1]

The explore stage for the find mission is very straightforward; it's just finding out which is the most convenient retailer stocking the product. Indeed, the explore step is often omitted as the purchase is one of habit from the regular store visit. For the discover mission the explore stage is about pre-planning and researching the category, and for the inspire mission the explore stage is the surprise encounters the shopper has while dwelling in the physical or digital place. The behaviour of shoppers in the explore stage varies immensely:

- 91 per cent of 18- to 34-year-olds trust online reviews as much as personal recommendations, while 93 per cent of consumers say that online reviews influenced their purchase decisions[2]
- 42.6 minutes are spent in shops browsing, compared with 36.4 minutes on PCs and laptops[3]
- UK consumers spend 16 hours a week, or 832 hours a year, browsing online[4]

Evaluation

The second step on the path to purchase is *Evaluation*. Here the shopper gathers information from online and offline sources. Preferences and needs emerge as the shopper researches and compares prices and delivery options. Evaluation for the find mission is simply a reassurance of price and authenticity of brand. For the discover mission evaluation is influenced by the customer experience whether that be trialling products or customer service. For the inspire mission evaluation involves assessing how the surprises that are experienced meet the needs and desires.

The evaluation stage is characterized by consumers' use of both online and physical research, with 65 per cent of consumers looking up price comparisons on a mobile while in a physical store and 18 per cent of consumers leaving a store after consulting their mobile device and finding a product cheaper elsewhere.[5,6]

Purchase

The actual *Purchase* is the third step on the path where the shopper selects what to buy and whether to buy online and receive delivery or collect in-store, or indeed to buy in-store. For the find mission the purchase is very straightforward and often online; it needs to be simple and frictionless. For the discover mission the purchase would be part of an overall solution involving the main product and a series of accessories, for example, the purchase of a bottle of vodka and ingredients to make cocktails. For the inspire mission the purchase of the product would often also involve a related experience based on learning about the product or a social experience.

Experience

The fourth step on the path to purchase is the *Experience* of the product or service. An increasing number of shoppers are writing reviews about their satisfaction or dissatisfaction via social media or review sites; in fact, 30 per cent of consumers have posted product feedback online, with 56.7 per cent positive and just over 33 per cent negative.[7] If the shopper writes a review there is a likelihood they will begin to influence other shoppers who are at the discovery and evaluation stages on the path to purchase. For the find mission the experience is very familiar with no surprises. For the discover mission the experience is often new and involves discovering new ways of consuming the product. For the inspire mission, the experience often involves lasting memories of the rituals of the purchase.

Advocacy

The fifth and final step on the path to purchase is *Advocacy*. After owning the product, consumers decide whether or not to select the same product or brand again. As well as the price and performance of the product, customer service and experience play an important part in customers' loyalty. For the find mission there is very little advocacy as the purchase is one of habit. For the discover mission active advocacy can often involve leaving reviews or sharing the experience with friends and family. For the inspire mission advocacy is a lot more pronounced and could include more involved reviews and sharing on social media.

INDUSTRY EXPERT
Mustafa Tahir

To ensure future readiness, brands and retailers must have an intimate understanding of every step of their customers' journey before, during and after the physical store experience. Here, Mustafa Tahir from Salesforce explains the importance and benefits of a 'single view' of the customer journey.

If I asked you to take a moment to think of the last time you truly had a great experience with a company as a consumer, an experience that captured your mind, emotions, spirits, what were the things that made it so great for you?

When I work with businesses to help them overcome their own customer challenges, I get them to start by thinking of themselves as consumers. Almost without fail, I am inundated with endless examples of seamless shopping experiences online or in-store, excellent customer service in person or remotely, expectations around quality being exceeded and the occasional surprise that can add the cherry on top. And when I ask the opposite, to tell me about an awful experience you've had, the stories come at me two- or three-fold! I get the horror stories of disappearing orders, complex return processes to send back something that looks nothing like it did on the website, endlessly repeating personal details despite being a long-standing customer... the list goes on and on and on.

So if everyone at the clients that I work with clearly knows what makes a great customer experience, and what makes a downright awful one, why am I there in the first place to try and help improve the experience they provide for their own customers?

Let's start with the actor at the centre of this complicated conundrum – the customers themselves. Painting the picture of your typical customer journey – how they interact and shop with you – is an increasingly complex minefield of the digital and physical, where the way they interact with you moves across channels, leaving behind morsels of information about themselves as they go. Paths to purchase are rarely linear, with lines never being more blurred between the online and offline worlds, and are often overlapping. Endless information is now available for researching before buying, alongside the ability to start and end your purchase online or in-store as you so desire. With the unlimited choice available from the endless digital aisles, customers are becoming increasingly sensitive to pricing and service levels, which is acting to reduce long-term brand loyalty.

Parallel to the customer experience are the business units tasked with having to meet them at every touchpoint, delivering against their expectations or risk losing them to the next best option at the slightest hint of disappointment. Often a combination of commercial and IT teams to support these varied experiences requires a vast array of technology; think about the different platforms behind a website, a mobile app, social media, connectivity between warehouse and stores, and the challenge of bringing together all of the data your customers provide centrally. Behind each of these technologies may be different suppliers, service teams, development roadmaps, technology frameworks – a Frankenstein patchwork of touchpoints that are required to deliver, maintain and improve upon the experience your customers have with your business. Where the holy grail is often to build a 360-degree view of their customers, this landscape highlights the many obstacles that can stand in the way of collecting and connecting the data dots across these touchpoints, where the reality is often an incomplete view of the modern customer. Complicated customer, please meet complex business operations – a cat and mouse relationship with no sense of simplification in sight; a fragmented world of silos that is challenging to navigate and understand across businesses of all sizes and resources.

While this complexity behind the scenes continues to increase, consumers remain adept at finding their own path of least resistance, all the while maintaining the highest expectations from businesses in terms of experience. If you think about the apps that you choose to have on the first screen of your phone, maybe they are for your shopping needs, to connect with friends, arrange transport or stream your favourite series or podcast. The battle to be on the first page is being won by an array of businesses whose names I'm sure would roll off your tongue, that have been driven foremost by the customer-centric experience that they deliver from their founding. They have become so ubiquitous and their impact is so significant that the experience they give consumers influences expectations across ALL industries. In fact, 65 per cent of customers now compare buying experiences to Amazon, and 61 per cent of customers are more likely to buy from businesses that provide personalized services, just like you would have on your favourite streaming platform or retail website. Your customers are no longer being driven by just looking at your competition to demand what is best for them. Influences are coming from everywhere, at every swipe, click and scan, refactoring expectations across the board at ever increasing speeds.

This increasingly complex and competitive customer landscape has led to a hyper-paced giant game of catch-up. We can all think of the many long-established, traditional business models that were once considered bombproof that have already been made extinct by their modern, evolved equivalent, but for those that are surviving, the topic of digital transformation is rapidly moving up their agenda, and along with it, how they can shift towards becoming a customer-centric organization that can meet the expectations of the modern consumer.

The objective of shifting to a more customer-centric way of operation is to do business with your customer in a way that provides a positive experience before and after the sale in order to drive repeat business, customer loyalty and ultimately profits. However, it goes beyond just offering a good product or service, and at its core, shifts to focusing on the experience that is intended to deliver this. Integral to the success in delivering this is to ensure that this vision is shared across a business so that everyone knows how they contribute towards it. As a further factor, a study by Deloitte and Touche has shown that customer-centric companies are 60 per cent more profitable compared to those that did not have a focus on the customer.[8]

With so many ubiquitous references from across industries, it should surely be easy to cherry-pick the best-of-breed, bring these together and, with a moderate amount of resources and expenditure, seamlessly evolve to the future state of your business? And yet, in this drive towards customer centricity, research from McKinsey has shown that 70 per cent of companies are failing in their plans for transformation largely due to a resistance from employees and a lack of management support.[9] The consequential impact of this further leads to unclear plans, misalignment and further enforced silos across teams, skills gaps that are not identified, inability to execute, and ultimately drives cultural resistance to change.

And therein lies the crux – in the pursuit to deliver a better experience for their end consumers, businesses that adopt a traditional top-down approach to change are ignoring their own internal customer, their employees, who are not only responsible for delivering the future of the business, but are also those closest to what end consumers are experiencing today, and the challenges facing them in doing so. Whether an external consumer or internal customer, the transformation vision is less likely to succeed when it is built without an understanding of the experience as it is today, and instead relies on a limited set of executive-level perspectives that are cascaded downwards and then monitored for results.

Introducing the *Design Thinking* methodology can be a successful way for a brand to develop a customer-centric approach to transformation that helps meet the needs of the modern customer. Its main premise is to approach problems with a human-centred mindset, trying to understand the needs and wants of your brand from the perspective of your customers as a logical starting point when tackling complex projects and initiatives.

Firstly, businesses need to develop a common understanding of the customer experience and the end-to-end journey that they go through with your brand. Among the common challenges faced are entrenched departmental silos that only cater to a portion of the customer journey, and as a result lead to a fragmented experience being delivered. If there is no consensus view of the experiences that your customer goes through, you are already starting with a handicap when it comes to delivering initiatives that are intended to help achieve strategic business goals.

The intent of customer journey mapping is to involve a blended group of stakeholders to map out your brand experience following a typical customer life cycle, from building brand awareness and customer acquisition, through engagement and conversion, to retention and advocacy. The intention of this exercise would be to highlight the different interactions, considerations and actions a customer could take as they proceed through their life cycle with you, and what their corresponding touchpoint could be with your brand at each step. The end point of this activity will be the detailing on this journey blueprint from the external customer perspective, but contributed to by all of the internal participants that are key to delivering on this.

Complementary to this would be the use of customer personas, a research-based profile of a hypothetical customer type detailing their demographics and psychographics, for example an unknown new customer or loyal long-term customer. These profiles can be used by a brand as a layer over the blueprint customer journey to highlight points of differentiation per persona; for example, a new customer would have a different level of interaction at the brand awareness life cycle stage when compared to a long-standing loyal customer of your brand. Using this insight can be the first step towards delivering more relevant and less one-dimensional customer experiences based on needs, and can serve to develop a better understanding of who your customers are and their preferences.

With this journey blueprint in place, the next step for a brand is to map out how its technology stack overlays against the key touchpoints that have been detailed in the customer path. Which technologies are driving experiences and to what degree of success currently? What level of data are you capturing across the customer life cycle, and how well are you consolidating this in order to make it actionable to further improve the customer experience? Alongside mapping out current capability, this process also acts to identify experience gaps where a new solution could be implemented, or where potential upgrades or technology consolidation opportunities may exist.

This combined view of journeys and technology should highlight where the biggest opportunities and focus areas lie to improve the customer experience. Focusing on a creative process, this should act as the gateway for your stakeholders to collaborate on which new initiatives can deliver against specific business objectives and overcome the experience challenges you have identified.

In the same way that customer expectations are being influenced from all around, inspiration should come from anywhere and step outside of *how we do things today*. After that there needs to follow a process of ranking and prioritization based on customer impact and technical complexity. The objective should be to deliver features on an ongoing, incremental basis that can be deployed at speed, monitored and learnt from, rather than a long-term project that drops in one big bang that inevitably faces interminable delays. Challenge your business to deliver features and functionality that improve the experience of your customers at the same rate as that of their demands and expectations.

Bringing these plans to life requires a business to understand whether it has the right people, with the sufficient level of skills and capacity, to deliver on the initiatives that have been highlighted and prioritized. It is important to understand how the activities your teams are currently undertaking are aligned to the moments of value identified in your customer journey blueprint, and if time and resources are being used in the most effective way.

Here stakeholder interviews are a key tool to understand more about the day-to-day of those closest to the customer and to understand what the reality is for your business in the day-to-day. Being able to identify your biggest gaps and obstacles in your path to executing the right things should be a key output. Identifying problems such as broken processes, poor collaboration, missing critical skills or unclear priorities, and then planning to overcome these issues, are essential to transforming to a customer-centric operation. By really understanding what changes you need to make, and by leading with empathy to put people first, businesses can successfully transform their approach to their customers. Moving towards a shared customer-centric vision, built with an understanding of the current internal and external experience, businesses can become increasingly agile in making changes, in line with the changing consumer behaviours. Planning for and delivering successful change comes from starting with people, with your staff, your suppliers, your customers, and from understanding the world in their shoes. Leading with empathy means building a picture of all perspectives of the transformation you are trying to deliver, and answering the question of how they are currently delivering the customer experience. Establishing this context provides a lens through which you can prioritize against the goals of the business, while improving the customer experience in the most impactful way. This can also be married with the feasibility of what can be achieved through technology. By bringing people together to collaborate and share transparently, ownership significantly increases, and ideas can converge to dictate a clear path to the future with a shared vision that is developed together, seeking influence from all perspectives. Yes, the balance of viability and capability will bring some more traditional structure to this approach, but by fuelling ideas from the people involved, they can help transition a business to a more effective user-led operation, focused on getting the things done that have the greatest impact, working from the bottom up.

In the same way that today's consumer is increasingly influenced by experiences all around them to determine what is important and what they desire, businesses have a path to follow to ensure they are also taking in the breadth of experience across their own people to determine the best path to take in their customer-centric transformation journeys.

You've got to start with the customer experience, and work back towards the technology – not the other way round. (Steve Jobs[10])

When considering the regeneration of our high streets and the repurposing of our shopping centres we must ensure that we can deliver experiences that meet the needs of the three missions: Find, Explore and Inspire. Our high streets must be places where citizens have easy access to critical community amenities, services and goods for everyday life. Our high streets must also accommodate a wide range of shops, service providers, leisure and entertainment for citizens to discover experiences that make them happy and healthy and encourage them to connect with their community. The high street must also be a place of excitement and new experiences that enrich the lives of citizens. To bring the crowds back to our high streets we must respond to the inspire mission by delivering a range of experiences that create serendipity: happy coincidences that you never expected, bringing surprise and delight.

The following four chapters, Chapters 4 to 7, will describe the four pillars of Future Readiness: reinventing convenience, reconnecting to community, remaking place and repositioning value.

Notes

1 Statista. Online sources for product searches worldwide 2021, 2021, www. statista.com/statistics/1034209/global-product-search-online-sources/ (archived at https://perma.cc/JM4E-A66Y)

2 D Kaemingk. Online review stats to know in 2019, Qualtrics, 2020, www. qualtrics.com/blog/online-review-stats/ (archived at https://perma.cc/ 9VZ3-CCEX)

3 Webloyalty. The connected consumer, 2015, webloyaltycorporatecontent. s3.amazonaws.com/webloyalty__the_connected_consumer_report_ 2015_1425891143.pdf (archived at https://perma.cc/AC2F-K83P)

4 Propellernet. UK consumers now spend more time shopping online than socialising, ResponseSource Press Release Wire, 2019, pressreleases. responsesource.com/news/98850/uk-consumers-now-spend-more-time-shopping-online-than-socialising/ (archived at https://perma.cc/7XS9-EKZ4)

5 KPMG. 65% of consumers look up price comparisons on mobile while in a physical store, Transaction eCommerce Agency, 2019, transaction.agency/ ecommerce-statistics/65-of-consumers-look-up-price-comparisons-on-mobile-while-in-a-physical-store/ (archived at https://perma.cc/4QSE-FULP)

6 Digitas.com. Connected commerce, 2014, www.digitas.com/globalassets/ solutions/connected-commerce/2014/digitaslbiconnectedcommercesurvey_ short_040114_r4.pdf (archived at https://perma.cc/B459-M35F)

7 KPMG. The truth about customer loyalty, KPMG, 2019, home.kpmg/xx/en/ home/insights/2019/11/customer-loyalty-survey.html (archived at https:// perma.cc/J3RN-E8YR)

8 L Bedgood. Customer-focused companies are 60% more profitable. How do your strategies line up?, Business2Community, 2021, www.business2 community.com/customer-experience/customer-focused-companies-are-60- more-profitable-how-do-your-strategies-line-up-02383992 (archived at https:// perma.cc/DVK8-F6CB)

9 McKinsey & Company.) Why do most transformations fail? A conversation with Harry Robinson, 2019, www.mckinsey.com/business-functions/ transformation/our-insights/why-do-most-transformations-fail-a-conversation- with-harry-robinson (archived at https://perma.cc/PE7P-45SG)

10 W Lynx. 32 impactful customer experience quotes for leaders (in 2020), The Digital Savvy, 2020, thedigitalsavvy.com/32-customer-experience-quotes-for- leaders/ (archived at https://perma.cc/E5XM-9SN8)

04

Reinventing convenience

In order to reinvent convenience, brands need to respond to peoples' increasingly complex and busy lives. They must reinvent their approach to convenience in relation to their product and service offerings. Consumers live increasingly transient lives and in an 'always-on' culture. Many are digital nomads, constantly connected and seeking to work, shop and socialize wherever and whenever it is most convenient. And so they demand experiences that are easy, simple and frictionless, with minimum pain points.

This demand for hyper-convenience, for simplicity, is driving the expectations of many consumers. 'Nowness' is also a key expectation. Even waiting 5 seconds for a video to buffer is not acceptable. This drives a mindset and an expectation, where consumers demand speed and immediacy, with products and services responding to ever ever-busier and transient lives. Developing products and services that respond to the demands of 'just-in-time-living' is becoming more difficult: 'I want *what* I want, *how* I want it, *when* I want it and with zero hassle' is a complicated and costly demand to respond to for both brands and retailers.

The proliferation of online shopping has partly driven these consumers' expectations. Our demands for convenience and ease are conditioned by a world where we can read a review of a book and seconds later order it online with one click and expect it to be delivered the next day. Or where we will increasingly expect goods that we buy regularly to be automatically replenished as we use them.

The death of the queue

With this heightened expectation of convenience and ease, queuing will become anathema in consumers' lives. Queuing is a key cause of shoppers abandoning their basket or leaving the store. According to research by Qudini 26 per cent of customers who walk out of stores due to long waiting times and poor customer service will discontinue their purchase completely.[1] This costs British retailers £3.4 billion a year. According to the research, the average British retailer will lose 10 per cent of its footfall due to queues and waiting times for service. UK retailers in aggregate lose a total of £15 billion in potential sales each year due to walkouts from their stores. Qudini's research goes on to highlight that while some customers might turn to competitor stores or the internet to continue their purchase, on average 26 per cent of customers will discontinue their purchase journey entirely, costing the UK economy approximately £3.4 billion in potential revenue.

According to research by Intel and Box Technologies queuing has become one of the most off-putting factors when shopping.[2] The average shopping trip includes 20.2 minutes queuing time, during which 27 per cent of consumers get annoyed by fellow shoppers when queuing and 19 per cent of shoppers have had an argument with a partner or friend in a queue. Supermarkets, fashion stores and DIY stores are rated as having the longest queue lengths.

Some 38 per cent of consumers have previously abandoned their purchase as a result of long queues. After nine minutes consumers are likely to give up queuing and leave empty handed; however, 24 per cent will queue for less than five minutes before giving up; 86 per cent of shoppers will avoid a store if they deem the queue too long; and 70 per cent are less likely to return to the store if they experienced long waiting times on one occasion. Seven people is the 'queue tipping point'; any longer and shoppers won't join the line.

FUTURE-READY NOTE

Add value by stripping out complexity.

Too much choice kills choice

We have been conditioned to believe that choice is a good thing. It confirms our freedom, personal responsibility, autonomy and self-determination. According to Andy Crouch, the average adult makes around 35,000 decisions a day. And apparently, if you visit Tesco to buy tomato ketchup you could be faced with 28 choices.[3]

But as we live increasingly complex and accelerated lives, choice is becoming debilitating. Shopping in a supermarket with an abundance of choice can be confusing and off-putting. Supermarkets can have up to 50,000 products on their shelves. And Amazon have a mind-numbing number of choices. For example, if you type in the word 'hangers' into the Amazon search, you can have up to 200,000 choices.

In a famous study by US psychologist and professor of social theory Barry Schwartz, researchers observed the jam category of a store where they set up one display with six choices of jam and another with 24 choices. Of those exposed to the smaller selection, 30 per cent made a purchase, compared to only 3 per cent of those exposed to the larger selection. Schwartz termed this the 'Paradox of Choice'.[4]

The big fast-moving consumer goods (FMCG) firms are responding to new consumer expectations for more convenience and simpler experiences by reducing the number of product lines. It is reported that when Procter & Gamble, one of the world's leading consumer goods firms, cut its haircare product lines in the United States with fewer shapes, sizes, packages and formulas, meaning less choice for consumers, its market share grew.

If you walk into a Starbucks today you could potentially be faced with around six thousand different options made up of all the choice combinations. For example: brewed coffee (cappuccino, espresso, macchiato, latte, mocha, Americano, filter, iced coffee, cold brew, etc), cold brews (iced coffee, cold brew latte, Nitro latte, Nitro cold brew, vanilla iced coffee, cold brew, nitro cappuccino), teas (brewed, latte tea, matcha, shaken iced tea, iced tea latte, iced tea infusions, frozen iced tea), hot chocolates (classic, truffle deluxe), smoothies and frappuccinos (banana, raspberry, blueberry, mango and passion fruit, coffee frappuccino, cream frappuccino), toppings (chocolate, cinnamon, vanilla, etc), milk types (skimmed, semi-skimmed, full fat, oat, soya, cashew, almond, etc), sugar (none, white, brown, sweetener), coffee strength (extra shots, decaf), syrups (hazelnut, almond, vanilla, honey), cup sizes (short, tall, grande, venti hot, venti cold, trenta). And, of course there are many choices of food as well.

In an attempt to cope with this abundance of choice on a daily basis, we rely on 'heuristics' to make decisions. These can be described as mental shortcuts. Heuristics are decision-making tools that save effort by ignoring superfluous information. They can reduce and simplify the mental processing of cues and information that surround us. When we are trying to make a decision or choose from a series of options, we can turn to these mental shortcuts. One of the most effective forms of heuristics is branding, which gives us a shortcut to making a choice because a brand at its core is a 'trust mark'.

There are two main types of heuristics, the *availability* heuristic and the *representativeness heuristic:*

- The availability heuristic is when you make a choice based on how available examples of a similar type are in your mind. This is influenced by your memory of specific experiences and brands to which you've been exposed. And of course, both good and bad brand experiences will influence your choices.

- The representativeness heuristic is based on stereotyping. While availability has more to do with memory of specific experiences, representativeness has more to do with stereotyping that builds over time but is not necessarily factual beyond very generic assumptions or prejudices. Again, branding can build representativeness heuristics by creating associations to a product over time that become stereotypes. For example, Volvos are the safest cars on the road. Ben & Jerry's is a small cuddly ice cream firm run by two hip guys called Ben and Jerry. John Lewis is never undersold.

These two types of heuristic are very relevant as they determine *brand preferences.* Brands that develop ritualized experiences delivering convenience and delight become lodged in the memory and can counteract negative prejudices and assumptions.

Robots of convenience

As a response to the increasing demand for convenience, simplicity and speed, we will see the proliferation of automated services, autonomous shops and robotics. In many cases these new offers will, for example, allow us to pre-order food and drinks that will be prepared and ready just in time for the customer's arrival. This is a response to a demand for 'just-in-time' living.

An interesting example of this development is the **X-Robotics Robotic Pizza Maker**. The employee puts the dough onto a tray, chooses the toppings from a digital screen and the machine does the rest. The tray turns gradually to ensure an equal distribution of sauce, cheese and toppings. The X-Robotics Pizza Maker is capable of topping multiple pizzas simultaneously, and can churn out up to 150 pizzas per hour with a selection of 20 toppings and a variety of different pizza base sizes. Launched in September 2020, with 400 pre-orders, there are plans to have more than 50 locations in 2021.

The **Costa Coffee BaristaBot** (previously Briggo) sits among a new wave of standalone automated kiosks that are reinventing the vending machine. Designed for high-traffic areas, they make coffee on demand, and not in large batches that get thrown out because they've sat around for too long. These robot coffee baristas also reduce the use of milk and sugar because they are precisely dispensed by the robot. The BaristaBot looks like a very fancy vending machine. The customer cannot see the operations as they take place behind the façade of the machine, which is made up of a digital display and an area where the coffee is dispensed.

Another robotic barista is the **Café-X**. The Café-X, however , is a lot more theatrical than the BaristaBot. The set-up here is a glass-fronted kiosk behind which sits a robotic barista in the form of a robotic arm. The arm operates a coffee machine and after the coffee is dispensed into the cup the robotic arm picks up the cup and gives it a little shake before presenting it to the customer.

The DIY sector is also getting in on the robotics act. Lowe's, the North American DIY chain, has developed the **LoweBot**, an autonomous retail service robot. Using a 3D scanner, the LoweBot detects customers as they come into the store. After greeting them, it guides them around the store using smart laser sensors and helps them with product information. Customers can ask the LoweBot, in one of seven languages, to help them with what they're looking for. Along the way, the LoweBot displays location-based special offers and recommendations on its display screen. There is no downloading of the store app needed. LoweBots can also aid employees with inventory management. As they move around the store they scan the shelves and send up-to-date inventory information to staff.

Softbank have developed a 'humanoid' robot called **Pepper**. Pepper is 120 cm tall and has a touch screen on his chest. He can perceive his environment and is able to sense a person in close proximity, enter into a conversation, give directions and answer questions. Pepper can also play music and take selfies with passers-by. During a trial in a technology store in Palo Alto there was a 70 per cent increase in foot traffic during the week Pepper was introduced. During a second trial in a Santa Monica store there was a 13 per cent increase in revenue.

As the *Harvard Business Review* (HBR) has reported, robots can also deliver convenience by ensuring that shelves are stocked with the right products at the right time.[5]

Auchan, the large European grocery retailer, has launched autonomous shelf-monitoring technology, which uses robots in its supermarkets and hypermarkets. As the robots move around the stores, they capture photos of every shelf and aisle, which are then digitized and converted into metrics and insights about out-of-stock merchandise and pricing. This data is very valuable in retail, as it can anticipate consumer demand.

HBR suggests that we:

consider a hypothetical scenario of a retail robot scanning grocery store aisles and detecting that supplies of sugar-free peanut butter are diminishing at twice the rate of regular peanut butter. That real-time discovery then triggers an automated order for more sugar-free peanut butter to be sent to a specific store. By detecting sudden and unexpected shifts in inventory, the robot would be able to respond quickly without human intervention.

According to ABI Research, Walmart in the United States deployed 350 robotic systems for inventory management across its stores in 2019 alone. ABI Research predicts that by 2025 more than 150,000 mobile robots will be deployed in bricks-and-mortar retail establishments.[6]
According to *Forbes*, a new breed of robots is

coming equipped with machine vision algorithms able to capture and analyse images and video and respond accordingly. New technology is enabling them to analyse and interpret unclean areas and clean by themselves, understand when customers enter the store and greet them, and take photos of new cartons, analysing items in the box and moving them to the right shelves.[7]

Forbes goes on to explain that

At Walmart, scanner robots are able to pinpoint locations where items are out-of-stock, send images to associates who use handheld devices, and also transmit that information to the fast unloader robots that are prioritizing which items get unloaded off trucks. The theory is that when working in conjunction, robots make store associates more productive. And Giant Food Stores and Stop & Shop have deployed a pillar-shaped robot named Marty who travels the aisles looking for spills and runs price checks. The plan is for robots to take over the mundane tasks and leave human employees open to doing more high-value jobs, like customer service. For example, instead of spending time finding items on store shelves, employees could interact with customers to teach them about new products and, ideally, boost sales.

Chatbots of convenience

Chatbots are another form of robotics that contribute significantly to delivering hyper-convenience. We have seen them proliferate on websites and mobile apps, and they have become very popular recently, largely due to advancements in machine learning and natural language processing (NLP). Some customer support live chat services almost seem life-like.

Chatbots are basically artificial intelligence (AI) applications that mimic written or spoken human speech to simulate a conversation or interaction with a real person. The technology is NLP, the same technology used for voice recognition systems by virtual assistants such as Siri, Google Now and Microsoft's Cortana. They process text using a process known as 'parsing', and some chatbots are remarkably authentic, to the point where it can be difficult to determine whether the customer is interacting with a bot or a human being.

Chatbots are becoming increasingly important for retail customer service and support, which now directly impacts loyalty and is just as important as brand name, price and quality. Customers expect quicker, more personalized and convenient service and customer support. Convenience is a must for impatient consumers who are in search for rapid answers. They demand support 24/7, at the specific time of their choosing and through the device or channel they choose.

To respond to this demand for real-time response, retailers can deploy chat solutions, and chatbots are becoming an essential way of scaling up customer service and convenience. According to Capgemini, 73 per cent of consumers have interacted with companies via AI and 69 per cent were satisfied with those interactions.[8]

Although human support is often supplemented by chatbots, as David Kerrigan in his book *When Humans Stop Shopping* points out, it is possible to book a hotel room, retrieve your financial information, pay bills, get a medical diagnosis via chatbots, with no human interaction.[9]

Being able to access 24-hour service is a big part of convenience. According to the 2018 'Chatbots Report', when users were asked what they would use chatbots for, 37 per cent said to get quick answer in an emergency; 35 per cent to resolve a complaint; 35 per cent to get detailed answers or explanations; 34 per cent to find a human customer service assistant; 29 per cent to pay a bill; and 27 per cent to buy a basic item.[10] But 43 per cent preferred to deal with a human being, and 30 per cent were worried about a chatbot making a mistake.

The report findings illustrate that there is a demand for simple, convenient service for which consumers are increasingly turning to chatbots. Additionally and importantly, the report also shows that when it comes to instant response, 77 per cent expected this from online chat, 75 per cent from chatbots, 73 per cent from face-to-face contact, 64 per cent from telephone, 55 per cent from apps, 40 per cent from social media, 34 per cent from websites, and 27 per cent from emails. If your business is planning to embrace chatbots, you need to realize that consumer expectations are high. Consumers prefer chatbots over apps for 24-hour service, and for getting quick answers to both simple and complex questions.

In order for businesses to overcome the limitations of chatbots they should give consumers the option of being able to send an email or schedule a call if that's how they prefer to communicate. However, when dealing with a complex technical issue in particular consumers prefer to speak on the phone. Therefore, while chatbots have a lot to offer in terms of delivering convenience, when it comes to customer experience they often can't replace the human touch.[11]

Ambient retail

Ambient retail combines a range of digital technologies such as location tracking, image recognition, sentiment analysis and customer data, with the sharing of data between apps on customers' mobile devices. The uptake of 5G has allowed this to come into the mainstream, though of course there will be continued concerns about customer data and retailers will need to comply with the UK and European GDPR regulations.

The smartphone camera will be the gateway to convenience for consumers. As Ben Evans said, 'We're going from computers with cameras that take photos, to computers with eyes that can see.'[12] And as David Kerrigan noted in *When Humans Stop Shopping,* the smartphone camera is no longer just about taking great photos; it's now a smart device for recognizing objects either in real life or in a photograph, for recognizing and translating text.[13] These and many other capabilities deliver hyper-convenience in categories that have highly visual items.

In a similar vein Amazon's **StyleSnap** allows users to upload a photo to Amazon who will then identify the item and offer it for sale. StyleSnap can present recommendations for similar items on Amazon that match the uploaded photo. Similarly, Amazon has partnered with Snapchat to offer a new way to search for products on Amazon within the Snapchat app. The user simply points the Snapchat camera at a physical product and when the item is recognized a link for that product will appear on the screen with the option to purchase it from Amazon. Amazon also has the **Echo Show** smart speaker, which can identify images of household items held in front of its camera. The user can ask Echo Show to order another of the same item, using a built-in barcode scanning feature.

Pinterest is also in on the act with its 'Lens' feature. **Lens** is an online/offline visual search tool that can identify objects captured from Pins or by a smartphone and suggest related products. Pinterest Lens searches from photos to create shoppable Pins with products, pricing information and a direct link to checkout. Pinterest says that Lens can recognize more than 2.5 billion objects across home and fashion Pins, including tattoos, nails, sunglasses, cats, wedding dresses, plants, quilts, brownies, natural hairstyles, home decor, art, food and more.[14]

David Kerrigan refers to this phenomenon as 'camera commerce'. He suggests that as consumers purchase directly from the results of image search, this type of search will partly replace text search and as a result we will see the growth of camera commerce. This will deliver further hyper-convenience in retail.

FUTURE-READY NOTE

Get ready for 'ambient shopping' where image recognition and search will impact shopping and the physical store experience.

Image recognition

A large part of ambient retail is image recognition. Product images are processed, analysed and defined. A popular application of image recognition is augmented reality (AR), where an image is recognized and digital information and/or imagery is overlaid on the image to either give further information or richer content to the customer, all of which adds to convenience for the customer.

As the photo data banks of Apple and Google improve and become capable of recognizing most products and environments, consumers will increasingly shop through image recognition apps on their mobile phones. The product could be displayed in a shop, on a poster or just being carried by a member of the public.

This form of hyper-convenient *point and buy* shopping will become commonplace, allowing customers to buy spontaneously and seren-dipitously, often by-passing conventional product search.

However, image recognition technology will also drive visual product search. When the customer is able to simply take a photo of, say, a rucksack someone is carrying and then see that item (plus other similar ones) on retailers' mobile websites or on their social media, that will represent convenient, frictionless shopping that will fast become part of everyday life.

Image recognition can also make buying custom-fit clothes more convenient. A good example of this is the Japanese online fashion retailer **Zozotown**. The service starts when a bodysuit is sent to the customer's home. Using a mobile app with image recognition technology the customer takes measurements in 3D using the dots on the suite as markers on the body. This information gives Zozotown accurate dimensions in order to produce a made-to-measure garment. As well as providing a convenient, personalized service and product, it also has the added benefit of reducing returns rates from online clothing sales.[15]

The Adidas **BodyKinectizer** is a body scanner based on Microsoft Kinect which enables customers to order the correct size of garment while dressing their virtual body, whether the customer is in a shop or at home. The image recognition technology scans the customer's shape and size and then projects a series of garments over the customer's image to demonstrate how the garments will look on them.[16]

As the highly respected Retail Innovation website shows us, there are many brands utilizing different forms of image recognition technology to deliver convenience.[17] Some of the most impressive are Findbox, Mitsukoshi and AS Colour.

Findbox uses image recognition technology to identify products carried by customers in order to suggest either where they can find the same in the store or suggest a suitable matching product that is available in the store. To operate the Findbox in-store, the customer places the thing they want, e.g. a replacement saw blade, on a tray, where a camera scans the product from all angles. These images are used to build up a 3D mesh, which Findbox analyses to look for colours, text, logos, icons and shapes that it uses to search an online database for a match. Findbox also has an app which enables shoppers to take a picture on their smartphone, and the online Findbox database then finds the shop in which it's available.[18]

Another interesting application of image recognition is **Intel's** 'emotion sensing' technology. A camera analyses the viewer's face to see if the product or advert they are looking at is appealing to them. The system can analyse and define emotional response, mood and sentiment.[19]

The **Mitsukoshi** department store in Japan employs a humanoid robot at its information desk in the store. The robot understands and speaks Japanese and is also capable of sign language. As a humanoid robot it has human-like facial expressions. This is another example of robots being used in-store to work as customer assistants.[20]

Convenience can also be delivered at the shop window. New Zealand clothing retailer AS Colour has launched its **Colourmatic** virtual window stylist that helps customers before they enter the store. Consumers can stand in front of the shop window which can then analyse and rate their outfit and advise whether or not the colour combinations look right. It then gives advice on colours and actual pieces they could buy.[21]

Automated retail

Automated retail or vending is key to convenience and such offers can be located exactly where customer are. **L'Oréal,** the global beauty and cosmetics brand, located a series of its Intelligent Colour Experience interactive vending machines in the New York subway. The system features a full-length digital mirror and a vending machine full of beauty products. The vending machine uses cameras and sensors to help suggest products to passing customers. The machine shows customers a digital animation of their silhouette and the colours they are wearing, and asks if they want cosmetics that 'match' or 'clash'. It then presents them with 'a look' and gives suggestions on cosmetics which can be purchased using the vending machine. Customers can opt to email the look to themselves. The vending machine also features a screen with posts and photos from beauty bloggers.[22]

Personalization and speed

Brands can also deliver convenience through more personalized products and services. A good example of this is the digital menu found in quick-service restaurants (QSR). According to Premier Mounts, a firm producing digital signs for restaurants, the average rise in annual sales attributed to digital menu boards at QSRs is 3–5 per cent. As David Kerrigan points out in his book *When Humans Stop Shopping,* it is reported that 'McDonald's spent over $300 million to acquire the AI company Dynamic Yield to introduce its digital drive through menu displays.'[23] This allows **McDonald's** to offer a different menu to each customer, factoring in considerations like the weather (more cold drinks on the menu in hot weather) and speed of delivery from the kitchen. These and other personalized services help deliver hyper-convenience.

Through its subsidiary in South Korea, **Tesco** introduced a digital grocery store in the form of a digital wall in a metro station. The wall showcased digital images of a wide range of grocery products.

Customers scan a QR code of the products they wish to buy, pay for them via a mobile device and then collect their goods from a collection point.

Derek Kerrigan goes on to point out that 'Best Buy in the US have rolled out miniature "e-ink" displays with pricing and product information replacing traditional printed shelf-edge communications.' Dynamic pricing makes life easier for the retailer as they will not incur the normal operational costs for updating prices. As a consequence the customer could benefit as the retailer will be less hesitant to reduce prices due to the reduced cost of doing so. Digital dynamic pricing allows a physical retailer to treat the store more like a website in the way prices can change instantly and also as a response to customer behaviour.

Digital shelf-edges will continue to develop beyond dynamic pricing. They will be used to communicate product information, promotions, reviews, social media content and ideas for the customer with video content. Increasingly, shelf-edge technology will be able to recognize customer age, gender, mood, level of attention, etc, and offer specific products or information relevant to that customer at any given time. This form of personalization again represents great hyper-convenience.

Derek Kerrigan also describes the approach that the **Amazon Fresh** store takes on this, whereby

> the prices presented to a customer can depend on the customer's purchase history, search behaviour and other aspects of the customer's engagement with Amazon. Customers can benefit as they can be offered preferential pricing, particularly if they are a Prime subscriber and of course this also provides Amazon with detailed data and insight on the customer, including information on which items the customer picks up, which they put back on the shelf and which they put in their bag. The Amazon Fresh systems allow customers to place items directly into their bags.

Kerrigan goes on to describe how the Microsoft/Kruger **Guided Shopping** solution uses dynamic displays to show customers around the store item by item, based on their shopping list. The customer begins by inputting the shopping list into the app; this could also be part of their shopping profile. The customer launches the app as they enter the store. As the customer walks around the store a screen next to each product indicates that the customer may be interested in purchasing the item. If the customer decides that they would like to purchase the item, they proceed to scan it and the app informs the customer of the aisle and location.

Self-ordering digital kiosks in restaurants is another illustration of hyper-convenience. They can offer dynamic menu control, promotions and easy upselling and cross-selling. Some of the more sophisticated kiosks can detect a customer's mood and their reaction to a specific offer.

Convenience can also be a matter of perception. David Kerrigan mentions the phenomenon known as 'wait warping'. This is about shifting the perception of time. One way of doing this is to distract the customer with something interesting. It is thought that when customers are allowed to scan their own goods as opposed to waiting in a queue, they perceive this as taking less time than waiting for a faster staff member to scan the items. A very well-known way of reducing the perceived waiting time is to communicate the amount of waiting time that has lapsed. These and other similar strategies make the customer feel in control and are seen as more convenient.

Most of the convenience technology that I have explored is based on scanning codes and using apps. In future we will see increasing use of biometric technologies. One example is facial recognition. In China customers can use Alipay's **Smile to Pay** facial recognition technology to authenticate payments. In the UK **Fingopay** has introduced a system based on scanning a shopper's unique fingerprint, as indeed have Apple with the fingerprint recognition feature on their latest mobile devices.

Amazon has woken the world up to autonomous till-less shops. This is the epitome of ambient, frictionless, hyper-convenient retail. Referred to as the 'just walk out' frictionless store, and with an average size of 2,500 sq ft, the **Amazon Fresh** (Amazon Go in the

United States) store is accessed by scanning the Amazon Prime smart-phone app when entering the store. After simply filling a bag with a choice of own-brand and third-party items, the customer walks out of the store and is automatically billed at the exit. Customers can also collect and return goods bought online.

Interestingly, the technology behind the Amazon Fresh store is not facial recognition. It involves the use of cameras and depth-sensors. The big opportunity for Amazon is not so much about building a vast chain of Amazon Fresh stores (although they may do this), but lies more in the opportunity to sell its 'just walk out' technology to other retailers. In doing that, it begs the question, how much of the customer data will Amazon be able to access? There could be potential ethical issues that this technology presents which limit brands from gaining insight at a personal level.

The Amazon Fresh store is just one manifestation of the hyper-convenience of ambient retail. I agree with David Kerrigan that we will see payments being more seamless, allowing shoppers to spend less time physically processing payments.

Of course, as well as automatic payments being more convenient they will also have the impact of customers spending more readily by being 'tap happy'. This is another ethical question that will grow into a concern for society.

Delivering convenience

As part of our shopping experience, fulfilment is a very important component of convenience. Retailers should consider developing a comprehensive ecosystem of fulfilment beyond click-and-collect lockers, in-store collection or delivery to home. Fulfilment can include a broad range of options, from simple collect lockers to a full concierge hospitality experience with additional services.

A good example of a new type of fulfilment experience is at **Auckland Airport** in New Zealand. Here passengers can order the normal assortment found in airports such as fragrance, cosmetics, confectionery, alcohol, toys, etc, online before they get to the airport or at the airport on departure, and then collect them on arrival back at the airport. On purchase, a receipt is issued with a QR code. When passengers arrive to collect the goods, they are greeted by the ACE robot (Automated Collection Experience) which sits in an enclosed and secure room with 60 bins stacked to ceiling height against three walls. The bins are in three sizes to accommodate a wide range of goods. From behind a glass screen the passengers scan the QR code which triggers the robotic arm to reach out to one of the many drawers and place it in front of an opening in the glass screen, whereupon the passenger takes the purchase. The process takes 22 seconds. This is a great example of a simple, convenient fulfilment service offer that also lends the airport experience an element of drama.

Another form of hyper-convenient fulfilment is a service that allows customers' shopping to be delivered into their car boot when they are not present. As cars become more connected to the internet we are able to control them remotely using a smartphone. We can lock and unlock them, start the engine, turn the lights on, control the alarm, access cameras and run diagnostics. Volvo's **Roam Delivery** goes one step further. Their 'On Call' telematics app enables delivery companies to deliver goods to a customer's car, wherever they might be. This Volvo delivery service gives delivery companies access to the car's location, and it allows them to remotely unlock the car, drop off the delivery and then lock the car again. This will be a very welcome service as many people experience delivery problems with online shopping, mostly caused by not being at home at the time of delivery.

In a similar vein, Amazon is collaborating with the car manufacturer Audi and international delivery company DHL to develop a car-boot delivery service. The system works by the delivery driver using Audi's **Connect** communication system to track the location of a customer's parked Audi. The system generates a unique 'one-off' authorization code for each delivery, and the customer can designate a delivery time slot. On arrival, the delivery driver is able to open the vehicle using the digital device and leave the shopping in the boot. Once the car is closed, the code automatically expires.

Jaguar Land Rover's subsidiary 'In-Motion' and retailer John Lewis have also collaborated on a similar car-boot delivery service. The two businesses have set up a venture called **To Boot** to deliver this service. In order for the customer to access the service, a 'smart box' is placed in the customer's car which makes the car a delivery destination for shopping. During a delivery run, the courier receives a GPS location of the car along with the registration number and a one-time code that permits the driver to access the car boot. The customer is sent real-time updates to their mobile device, including order confirmation, photos showing successful delivery and finally the secure locking of their car.

For any car-boot delivery service it is critical that the system is able to conduct frequent location checks on the car while the delivery van is on its way, in order to inform the driver whether the customer moves the car. The car being moved does not present a problem as it will be geo-located for the delivery driver. It may be that the price and time of delivery will fluctuate if the car is moved. To Boot is planning to offer the service to customers of any make of car in the future, as long as it was manufactured after 2002. The system can also be used for any delivery service.

Click-and-collect needn't be just functional, it can also be a great experience. The Ikea city centre **Order and Collect Points** offer the same range and inspiration as a standard 'big box' Ikea store, the difference being that customers order online, either remotely or from terminals actually in the store, and then collet them immediately from the store. There is also a small range of products on display in the store that can be taken away. Or if it's more convenient, goods can be delivered.

Click-and-collect can even be considered a luxury experience. The **Westfield** shopping centre in London developed a 'concierge-type' click-and-collect lounge in partnership with Collect+ where customers can pick up online orders. The Collect+ lounge is a luxury click-and-collect experience with a premium lounge area. It has fitting rooms that allow customers to try on their purchases before taking them home. There is a dedicated car parking area for the collect lounge with one-hour free parking.

In developing this facility, it has allowed Westfield to offer customers the ability to purchase items online from retailers and have them delivered to the Collect+ lounge. The brands on offer include high-street stores as well as e-tailers that are not stocked at the Westfield shopping centres.

The Collect+ service is part of Westfield's wider concierge service which includes a hands-free service (where shopping can be taken to the customer's car), valet parking and home delivery. An added benefit of the Collect+ lounge is the privacy it can give to luxury-focused consumers who require discretion when purchasing.

High streets and convenience

One of the key factors in driving people back into our high streets will be convenience.

As major brands abandon our high streets we are seeing more vacant units and boarded-up shop fronts. Famous brands, many of which have been around for generations, are being replaced by charity shops, vape stores, pawn-brokers and betting shops. The government (partly through the High Streets Task Force), local authorities and bid teams across the UK are focused on reversing the decline.

Before we can begin to analyse how the four pillars of 'future readiness' can address this decline it's important to understand the causes behind the decline of the UK's high streets. According to analysis from IntechnologySmartCities there are five key causes: online shopping, rising business rates, declining wages, parking problems, and over-expansion and out-of-town malls.[24]

Online shopping

According to Statista.com between 2012 and 2020 the value of online retail sales in the UK increased from around £33 billion to £100 billion, albeit the 2020 numbers were impacted by the Covid-19 pandemic.[25] The Office for National Statistics (ONS) reports that internet sales as a percentage of total retail sales (ratio per cent) increased from 9.1 per cent in May 2012 to 26.7 per cent in August 2020.[26] And according to Retail Insight Network and GlobalData more than half of UK consumers are now shopping online, and UK online spend is forecast to increase by 29.6 per cent between 2019 and 2024.[27]

Andy Barr, co-founder of product price tracker company Alertr, sums it up well:

> As more retailers turn online for their shopping, more and more shops are leaving the high street. Not only can people no longer be bothered to trek into town for their latest buys, it's just so much easier these days to pop online and order what you like with the freedom of having next-day delivery. You can order absolutely everything, from your latest wardrobe additions right down to your food shopping and even your medication if you really wish to... many retailers even have a buy now, pay later scheme, allowing more people to try on and send stuff back without the hassle of paying for it and waiting for the money to re-enter your account. Even with sites like ourselves, you can track the prices of your favourite most-wanted items and get them at the desired price you want, when they drop, which you are unable to do with shops that are on the high street, meaning if you choose to shop in-store you could potentially miss out on some of the best deals.

Barr adds:

> Stores on the high street need to do more to attract shoppers in; creating a unique shopping experience. But that's easier said than done when rents are increasing, footfall is reducing and the appeal of shopping from the comfort of your own home is high.[28]

James Bentley, UK Strategy Director of internet marketing company Awin, says:

> Even the older generation are choosing to branch out to online shopping because it is easier, and thanks to same-day delivery, in some cases quicker, than visiting the high street... the fact that more people are shopping online doesn't automatically mean that the

high street should suffer. However, there are examples of companies creating bricks-and-mortar stores from online-only shops, and increased use of features, such as click-and-collect can encourage higher footfall.[29]

It is thought that as many as 500,000 SMEs across the UK have insufficient online presence or access. When anything can be found in just a few clicks, a lack of online presence can spell the death of small retail businesses, and as a consequence, the death of the high street.

Rising business rates

Increasing business rates have contributed to the struggles of high-street stores.

According to the British Retail Consortium, retail contributes £8 billion in business rates annually; a quarter of the UK's total.[30] An over-dependence on input taxes harms retailers, which are people- and property-intensive businesses, and such taxes have grown disproportionately compared to other taxes such as corporation tax. For every £1 retailers pay in corporation tax, they pay £2.30 in business rates.

My understanding is that BRC is suggesting the government review business rates on the following principles:

- A tax burden that is sustainable (at least 20 per cent lower than the current level) and floats as any other tax.

- Valuations of property that more closely reflect current values – meaning more frequent revaluations and an end to downwards phasing of transitional relief.

- A system that works for users – the Valuation Office Agency needs investment to get valuations right first time and to process appeals more quickly.

However, some have argued that business rates have been used as an excuse by struggling retail businesses to hold their landlords to ransom in order to stay open.[31]

Declining real wages

Since 2008 the UK government austerity measures and stagnant wages have meant that shoppers have less money to spend on the non-essentials, and cost-cutting measures have made people more careful about where they spend. According to the *Financial Times*, the UK has had the weakest wage growth of all G7 countries since the 2009 financial crisis.[32]

Parking problems

A lack of affordable, convenient parking has resulted in many shoppers choosing not to visit their local high street. And where adequate parking is provided it is often prohibitively expensive. Council park and ride schemes are not as convenient and often pricey.

Over-expansion and out-of-town malls

Ironically, in a drive to open more stores to increase convenience for shoppers, the large chains have suffered from the consequences of over-expansion. The hope that multiple stores in one location would bring continued growth has not materialized due to the over-saturation of particular brands in one area. And so numerous brands have decided to close less suitably located branches, many of which have been in local high streets.

However, brands also expanded to out-of-town shopping malls, retail parks and designer outlets, which became destinations with a wide range of retail and food offers along with abundant free parking. And in these locations rents and rates tended to be cheaper.

INDUSTRY EXPERT
Nick Brackenbury

I met Nick Brackenbury, the co-founder and CEO of NearSt, when we shared a platform on a webinar in the middle of the pandemic lockdown. The core idea of NearSt really resonated as it spoke very clearly to the key consumer demand for convenience. Here Nick explains what the benefits are to the shopper, the retailer, the asset owner and our high streets.

As has already been expressed, consumers' lives are becoming increasingly busy and complex, and so convenience and simplicity is one of the most powerful drivers of engagement with brands and shopping. Our local shops are best placed to deliver such convenience. However, we can now help local shops deliver even more convenience by making their inventory visible to customers as part of their online search, and so give them certainty that they will find what they are looking for before they visit the shop. Getting people back into local shops is a vital part of regenerating our local streets, boosting our local economies and galvanizing our communities.

In 2020 the world changed, and we saw sudden dramatic shifts in consumer habits. E-commerce sales surged by 40 per cent, while at the same time shoppers suddenly rediscovered the value of their local shops.

None of this is likely news to you, as a reader of this book.

As the founder of a retail technology company whose sole purpose is to get people back into local shops, the question I'm always asked is, 'How many of these new local shopping behaviours will actually stick?'

I argue that these behaviours aren't new at all, and rather that, just as the pandemic has accelerated online shopping behaviours that already existed, it has also accelerated behaviours and technology associated with shopping locally, online.

If we look at the past half-decade, Google has a parade of stats showing that people are trying to find things locally, online, more and more. In 2016 they noted that 28 per cent of searches for something nearby result in an in-store purchase. In 2017 they revealed that nearly one-third of all Google searches related to location. In 2018 they said that 'near me' mobile searches containing 'where can I buy' or 'to buy' had grown by over 500 per cent in the previous two years. Then in 2020 they revealed that searches for 'who has ... in stock' had grown 8,000 per cent year-on-year during the pandemic. A massive jump, but part of a half-decade long trend.[33,34,35,36]

At NearSt our technology powers local product search for thousands of UK retailers on Google, enabling shoppers to find who has what in stock, without ever leaving Google. Each month we capture over 3 billion data points related to local product availability and search.

In the March 2020 lockdown these types of 'local availability' searches by shoppers spiked to seven times their February 2020 average, and then in the second November/December lockdown they spiked again to eight times their pre-pandemic volume.

Here's the interesting thing though: both times as lockdowns have eased, the volume of daily searches has reduced, but never dipped below three to four times its pre-pandemic volume. At the time of writing in July 2021, we have seen six consistent months where daily local product searches have remained at three to four times their pre-pandemic levels. A sustained quadrupling of people each day going online, to look for products offline in physical stores nearby them.

What's happened? Two things. Firstly, this is part of a long-term trend. Consumers have been getting used to the fact that both their mobile devices and the web as a whole can provide them anything they want, and why should retail be any different? The problem before was that in-store inventory simply wasn't visible on the major search, social and shopping platforms they used.

In the pandemic that started to change, and this is the second big shift that took place. Suddenly many, many more retailers realized they had to start showing their stock online to help get shoppers who were looking for it locally into their stores. Not just on their websites, but on the search engines and social networks where their customers spend their time.

Consumers started looking for local availability more, and retailers started showing it. Two positively reinforcing trends, which both spiked together. While the need to make sure your local convenience store definitely has toilet paper subsided after each lockdown, the consumer habits and retail innovation needed to serve them remained.

Looking ahead, this provides a genuinely exciting opportunity for both physical retailers and consumers. Consumers will start to look for, and expect to find, physical store inventory in more and more places online. In Google, Facebook, Instagram, Snapchat, Pinterest and more. It will start to become as common as things like opening hours being online today. Where consumers go, retailers will follow, spending less time thinking exclusively about how to optimize online e-commerce experiences but also how to build and optimize brilliant physical retailer journeys, online.

I genuinely believe that as this flywheel continues to accelerate, we'll get to a point where many online shopping journeys will be faster and more convenient when the end purchase is made in a physical store. It's a future of retail I am thoroughly excited about.

So, we have seen that in times of complex, fast-paced lives and a rapidly changing environment, peoples' key expectation is convenience. Without convenience and simplicity, the three remaining future-ready pillars become difficult to realize.

Notes

1   Qudini Retail Choreography. Queues for service in retail stores cost the UK economy £3.4 billion, 2017, www.qudini.com/queues-service-retail-stores-cost-uk-economy-3-4-billion/ (archived at https://perma.cc/S3QD-JP49)

2   F Briggs. Shoppers are put off by queues more than seven people deep, Box Technologies and Intel research shows, Retail Times, 2015, www.retailtimes.co.uk/shoppers-put-off-queues-seven-people-deep-box-technologies-intel-research-shows/ (archived at https://perma.cc/H5FG-J2YZ)

3   A Crouch. Too much choice [blog] Andy Crouch, 2017, www.amcrou.ch/too-much-choice (archived at https://perma.cc/6TYC-7GEX)

4   A Birkett. The paradox of choice: Do more options really tank conversions?, CXL, 2020, cxl.com/blog/does-offering-more-choices-actually-tank-conversions/ (archived at https://perma.cc/4LSR-8E66)

5   B Forgan. What robots can do for retail, *Harvard Business Review*, 2020, hbr.org/2020/10/what-robots-can-do-for-retail (archived at https://perma.cc/4MY2-MVMP)

6   AbiResearch.com. Mobile robotic systems: Market update, 2019, www.abiresearch.com/market-research/product/1034058-mobile-robotic-systems-market-update/ (archived at https://perma.cc/H682-2RUL)

7   G Petro. Robots take retail, *Forbes*, 2020, www.forbes.com/sites/gregpetro/2020/01/10/robots-take-retail/ (archived at https://perma.cc/DR4G-G957)

8   R Humphreys. Consumers prefer human-like AI, finds Capgemini, Technology Record, 2018, www.technologyrecord.com/Article/consumers-prefer-human-like-ai-finds-capgemini-71660 (archived at https://perma.cc/PAD4-GQCZ)

9   D Kerrigan (2020) *When humans stop shopping: Consumers, technology and the future of retail*, self-published

10 E Devaney. The Chatbots Report (2018): Reshaping online experiences, Drift, 2018, www.drift.com/blog/Chatbots-report/ (archived at https://perma.cc/V74V-WV2H)

11 Drift. The ultimate guide to chatbots, Drift, www.drift.com/learn/chatbot/ (archived at https://perma.cc/6PWW-9JEG)

12 B Evans. Imaging, snapchat and mobile, Benedict Evans [blog] 2016, www.ben-evans.com/benedictevans/2016/8/15/imaging-snapchat-and-mobile (archived at https://perma.cc/9KJL-J8AZ)

13 D Kerrigan (2020) *When humans stop shopping: Consumers, technology and the future of retail*, self-published

14 K Wiggers. Pinterest's Lens can now recognize 2.5 billion home and fashion objects, VentureBeat, 2019, venturebeat.com/2019/09/17/pinterests-lens-can-now-recognize-2-5-billion-home-and-fashion-objects/ (archived at https://perma.cc/XL32-T5GB)

15 Retail Innovation. Zozotown's body measuring suit and app, 2020, retail-innovation.com/index.php/zozo-body-measuring-body-suit (archived at https://perma.cc/8XRH-3K6E)

16 Retail Innovation. Adidas body scanner lets you try clothes on virtually, 2015, retail-innovation.com/index.php/adidas-body-scanner-lets-you-try-clothes-on-virtually (archived at https://perma.cc/DFF5-LHU2)

17 Retail Innovation. Image Recognition, 2015, www.retail-innovation.com/image-recognition (archived at https://perma.cc/B4SK-TP3U)

18 Retail Innovation. 3D scanner that helps shoppers find an item, 2015, www.retail-innovation.com/index.php/3d-scanner-that-helps-shoppers-find-an-item (archived at https://perma.cc/JR4J-KSJS)

19 Retail Innovation. Intel's emotion sensing cameras, 2014, www.retail-innovation.com/index.php/intels-emotion-sensing-cameras (archived at https://perma.cc/3BPE-RUFG)

20 Retail Innovation. New lifelike humanoid robot starts working in stores, 2015, www.retail-innovation.com/new-lifelike-humanoid-robot-starts-working-in-stores (archived at https://perma.cc/YXG2-KZAA)

21 Retail Innovation. Shop window advises you on your outfit, 2014, www.retail-innovation.com/shop-window-advises-you-on-your-outfit (archived at https://perma.cc/8AC2-UMRA)

22 Retail Innovation. L'Oreal create one of the worlds most advanced vending machines, 2013, www.retail-innovation.com/loreal-create-one-of-the-worlds-most-advanced-vending-machines (archived at https://perma.cc/9Q3T-Y8EM)

23 D Kerrigan (2020) *When humans stop shopping: Consumers, technology and the future of retail*, self-published

24 IntechnologySmartCities. 5 reasons behind the decline of the UK high street, IntechnologyWiFi, www.intechnologysmartcities.com/blog/5-reasons-behind-the-decline-of-the-uk-high-street/ (archived at https://perma.cc/73KX-ZDHC)

25 Statista. Value of online retail sales in the United Kingdom 2012 to 2020, Statista, 2020, www.statista.com/statistics/315506/online-retail-sales-in-the-united-kingdom/ (archived at https://perma.cc/GVN6-MMPK)

26 Office for National Statistics. Internet sales as a percentage of total retail sales (ratio) (%), 2021, www.ons.gov.uk/businessindustryandtrade/retailindustry/timeseries/j4mc/drsi (archived at https://perma.cc/K2TQ-VDTJ)

27 D Williams. UK online shopping spend to grow 30% by 2024, Retail Insight Network, 2020, www.retail-insight-network.com/features/uk-online-shopping-growth/ (archived at https://perma.cc/R59F-PNXV)

28 D Williams. UK online shopping spend to grow 30% by 2024, Retail Insight Network, 2020, www.retail-insight-network.com/features/uk-online-shopping-growth/ (archived at https://perma.cc/R59F-PNXV)

29 D Williams. UK online shopping spend to grow 30% by 2024, Retail Insight Network, 2020, www.retail-insight-network.com/features/uk-online-shopping-growth/ (archived at https://perma.cc/R59F-PNXV)

30 BRC. Business Rates, brc.org.uk/priorities/business-rates/ (archived at https://perma.cc/BBL2-W5GT)

31 BRC. Business Rates, brc.org.uk/priorities/business-rates/ (archived at https://perma.cc/BBL2-W5GT)

32 *Financial Times*. UK wage growth weakest in G7 since financial crisis, 2018, www.ft.com/content/c4437c9e-7ec4-11e8-bc55-50daf11b720d (archived at https://perma.cc/YU3Z-BLMC)

33 Hubspot.com. The Ultimate List of Marketing Statistics for 2021, 2021, www.hubspot.com/marketing-statistics (archived at https://perma.cc/GQ65-YZKB)

34 L Gevelber. Micro-moments now: Why 'near-me' intent is a 'near-you' opportunity, Thinkwithgoogle.com, 2017, www.thinkwithgoogle.com/consumer-insights/local-search-mobile-search-micro-moments/ (archived at https://perma.cc/UC7F-5XQ6)

35 L Gevelber. How 'near me' helps us find what we need, not just where to go, Thinkwithgoogle.com, 2018, www.thinkwithgoogle.com/consumer-insights/near-me-searches/ (archived at https://perma.cc/7VU2-KSZC)

36 D Trovato, N Taniguchi and K Rich. 5 consumer truths to get your marketing ready for 2021, Thinkwithgoogle.com, 2021, www.thinkwithgoogle.com/consumer-insights/consumer-trends/2021-marketing-plan/ (archived at https://perma.cc/ZX7R-WB5J)

05

Reconnecting to community

As smaller, independent, local brands become more popular, larger brands will increasingly position themselves to cater for more local audiences which in turn will spell the gradual end to cookie-cutter retail.

My use of the word 'community' does not only refer to local geographic communities or demographic communities, but also to 'communities of interest'. As mentioned earlier in the book, consumers like to be part of communities with brands at the centre, and these communities of interest are becoming an important part of peoples' lives and greatly influence their purchase decisions, and their relationship with brands, and with each other.

As consumer spending is focused less on products and more on experiences, brands and retailers must shift their focus from product commodities to experiences and communities, where brands sit at the centre of interest-based communities with their stories and experiences driving engagement and loyalty.

Brand tribes

As Mark Gobe said in his book *Emotional Branding*:

> In the stores of tomorrow, buying will be outmoded as a sterile activity, and in its place will stand the 'art of shopping', which is less about purchasing, and more about experiencing the brand.[1]

I would add that consumers of tomorrow will want to experience the brand while being part of a community and feeling a sense of belonging to a 'brand tribe'.

Brands need to forge deeper emotional connections with their audience, shifting from transaction, merely buying and selling products, to *interaction*, where engaging the audience with experiences that relate to the product or to the essence, point of view and values of the brand become a critical part of forging loyalty.

A second important shift is from interaction to *intimacy*. This is where a brand gets to a level where it really understands its audience. This is an understanding beyond purchase behaviour and how an audience engages with the brand. Intimacy is about focusing on the role a brand plays in the life of its audience. It is about the brand having a purpose that aligns with the values of its audience. That is true community that creates emotional connection and fosters a sense of belonging. In a retail setting this is mirrored by a shift from 'point-of-sale' where products are merely displayed with some communication of their benefits, to 'point-of-connection' where customers are encouraged to engage more deeply with the brand with compelling stories, learning, trialling and personalized service.

Consumers' lives are becoming busier, more complex and sometimes suffocating. This is partly caused by the explosion of media, digitization, information and a proliferation of messaging from brands. In response, consumers will become more selective and discerning as to which brands they allow into their lives. With mobile devices they can of course engage with many brands, but conversely the mobile device gives them the ability to shut brands out if they wish to. We will see that consumers will allow brands into their lives only when they add true value. Those brands that only sell commoditized stuff will be given short shrift, or will be judged by the simple criteria of price and convenience.

'Buy brands' and 'join brands'

The commoditization of products along with the growth of online marketplaces such as Amazon, automatic product replenishment, subscription-based buying and voice commerce such as Alexa have meant that consumers' purchasing has become less conscious and more automated. So when consumers decide to truly engage with a brand it will be deeper and more meaningful. They won't just buy brands, they'll join them!

> **FUTURE-READY NOTE**
>
> In future consumers won't just buy brands. They will join them.

So how do we distinguish between a 'buy brand' and a 'join brand'? What is the difference in the behaviour, strategy and approach of a buy brand in comparison to the join brand?

Well, there are many differences, and they are fundamental and far-reaching. Here are some of the key differences.

Consumers buy what a buy brand sells, whereas consumers buy into what a join brand believes. Buy brands reside in the minds of the consumer, whereas join brands are part of the lives of a consumer. Buy brands invest in pre-purchase promotion, join brands invest in post-purchase advocacy. Buy brands engagement with their customers is driven by sales, whereas join brands engagement with their customers is all focused on memorable rituals.

Buy brands' priority is on product sampling and trialling, whereas join brands prioritize learning and community. Buy brands focus on what the brand says to consumers, join brands focus on what consumers say to each other. Buy brands spend most of their time and budget on the content of advertising whereas join brands encourage user-generated content and sharing. For buy brands the customer experience is foremost about transaction, whereas for a join brand transaction is a by-product of a compelling experience.

Buy brands engage with customers merely as buyers whereas join brands engage with customers as users, the focus being on the role the brand plays in its customers' lives as opposed to just the transaction process. Buy brands focus on the experience before the transaction, that is, while the customer is researching and browsing. Join brands, however, focus on the experience after the transaction, that is, quick and convenient delivery, great service and the sharing of the experience with others.

The most significant difference between buy brands and join brands is that buy brands have customers whereas, and very significantly, join brands have members, fans and advocates.

All the above traits of join brands are those that foster community, participation in a common interest, a shared set of values, a shared purpose beyond the brand's sphere of products or services, and a true sense of belonging. This is what will define brand loyalty in the future. Brand loyalty will no longer be driven by price, deals, discounts and points. These have become commodities. When consumers own a plethora of loyalty cards they cease to reflect loyalty. As wallets and purses overflow with loyalty cards they become commoditized and lose their meaning in relation to loyalty.

We are seeing traditional loyalty cards being replaced by digital loyalty platforms. These are more engaging and offer a comprehensive set of services and facilities such as personalized chatbots, information on the retailer, information on stock and increasingly an ability to scan QR codes to gain further information on specific products.

These digital apps can magnify the store experience and are an important platform for merging the physical and digital experience. We will increasingly see these apps offer the ability to order and purchase products and also link directly to the social media platforms of brands.

FUTURE-READY NOTE

Digital apps have the opportunity to magnify the physical store experience.

Nike have been at the forefront of the development of such apps. The Nike app is an extension of Nike.com. It offers the same product range, plus exclusive Nike Member Rewards, including member-only early access to products, unique personalized experiences, insider guidance from Nike experts and personalized invitations to events in store.

The Nike app allows the customer to tailor the store experience based on their preferences, likes and previous research. They can get product recommendations and fast and secure checkout. An additional benefit is free shipping and 30-day returns. The app also enriches the customer experience with in-depth stories to training tips and style advice.

Fashion United has referred to **H&M** and how the brand is transforming its business and customer experience with digital apps.[2] Recently they launched a new app that is targeted at their male customers and tailored to their needs and behaviours when shopping.

Named 'Sorted by H&M' it is a personalized styling and shopping platform for men offering guidance and inspiration. It is described as being 'a seamless shopping experience which responds to the personalized shopping behaviour of the specific customer'.

The app blends human stylists with artificial intelligence (AI), giving tips and suggestions from H&M's menswear range. Like all AI-powered platforms it becomes more accurate and personalized, and hence valued, the more its customers engage with it.

The set-up is described as follows:

Customers are asked to share personal information such as hair colour, eye colour, clothing size, as well as any specific physical features such as a wide neck, broad shoulders or long arms and legs. These features normally make it difficult to find the perfect cut. The app will then use that initial information to provide a range of tips and dressing suggestions.

The experience also includes a personal stylist, whereby the customer can engage with both a chatbot and a human to ask questions such as colour matches, materials for specific seasons or suggestions for what to wear on specific occasions such as parties, interviews, weddings, etc. The app can personalize the shopping experience with suggestions for specific 'looks' that are specific to each individual customer, based on their needs, ideas, requests and preferences.

Such personalized apps can really drive loyalty through a very personalized experience that becomes more accurate and relevant the more the customer uses it. So it becomes more 'sticky'.

Loyalty platforms like these will eventually make customers feel like part of a brand community, feel like a fan, a member. In fact, brands are using such platforms to introduce subscription services. And those brands that offer privileged access to events and experiences in store to customers use the app are indeed creating brand communities with shared interests and values in which customers feel a sense of belonging. That is true sustainable loyalty from a join brand that trumps a buy brand every time.

Urban Outfitters is a good example of a brand that has introduced a subscription service with the aim of building a community of followers and sustained loyalty. Customers pay a monthly subscription fee to access the service which allows them to borrow items to wear for a month before swapping them. Many customers are motivated by the sustainability of clothes being reused.

Gaming

These digital platforms will become more immersive with the introduction of augmented reality (AR) and virtual reality (VR) technology. To become more immersive, they will also adopt the philosophy and engagement of digital gaming. The customer experience will be gamified to add an extra layer of intrigue, discovery and 'stickiness'. Again, these are very important ingredients of fostering loyalty and community. Gaming is increasingly becoming a social experience and with a brand at its centre it can create a community that shares common interests.

The founder of the TFT events, Matthew Bagwell, divides gamification into four segments, called the Four Ms:[3]

- The first is *mystery*. At its core, gamification must be fun and should encourage deeper exploration, with a little bit of the unknown. It's the mystery that keeps the interest of the customer.
- The second is *mastery*. The gamified experience must have challenges by which the customer feels they have achieved an element of mastery, and those challenges should build in layers with increasing difficulty.
- *Membership* is the third M of gamification. This is what gives the loyalty platform the element of community, whereby the experience is social and encourages collaboration.
- And finally, the gamified experience must culminate in a reward, or *meaning*. If the gamified experience is challenging enough then the reward at the end will have real meaning and the customer will be encouraged to share the reward and therefore advocate the brand and engage with the community.

FUTURE-READY NOTE

Base gamification strategies on the Four Ms: mystery, mastery, membership and meaning.

As Stefan Olander, VP Digital Sports at Nike, said in the seminal book *Velocity*, 'Gaming has a lot to teach us about how to make meaningful connections.'[4]

Subscriptions

According to research firm GlobalData, it seems that the growth in the fashion rental market is fuelled by the sustainability agenda.[5] The research states that £140 million worth of used clothing is sent to landfill every year, and that the UK clothing rental market is predicted to be worth £2.3 billion by 2029.

We are now seeing only the first sign of the explosion to come in the fashion rental market. These will include consignment- and subscription-based offers and peer-to-peer services.

The shift to rental may also be a key part of the solution to fashion's sustainability problem. **Rent the Runway**, for example, is one of the pioneers of the fashion rental market and offers women an opportunity to borrow designer clothes for a monthly subscription. (I will be exploring the rental market in other sectors in the following chapters.)

The subscription economy is now pervading almost all categories, and it is beginning to form an important part of our daily shopping habits.

Subscriptions are not new, but what is new is the wide range of large and small companies making it a central part of their business strategy. For these companies, offering subscriptions makes sense as it brings in predictable and regular revenue, it can build stronger customer relations and greater brand loyalty. Subscription services also give brands access to very valuable data on its customers' habits and lifestyles, and can be harvested from ongoing relationships with customers. This encourages brands to see customers for their 'lifetime value' and not just value from transaction to transaction. The key challenge for businesses is setting a subscription price that is attractive enough to tempt customers to sign up while also providing strong returns for the brand.

Pret a Manger launched its 'YourPret Barista' subscription service at a cost of £20 per month which buys the customer five drinks a day, seven days a week, including coffee, tea and smoothies. The customer must allow at least 30 minutes between each drink order. According to *The Guardian*, Pret had been expecting 2,000 or at a push 3,000 people to sign up on the first day. By 3 pm, the scheme had already topped 15,000 subscribers.[6]

At a cost of £20 per month, customers would need to buy at least two £2.75 lattes a week in order for the subscription to pay for itself. This seems like a very modest number of drinks a customer needs to buy in order to justify the cost of the subscription. It begs the question: have Pret a Manger underpriced the subscription?

However, I assume that they have assessed the value of long-term customer loyalty and the building of a Pret community.

Many 'digital-first' retail brands have based their business models on subscription, and as we can see from Pret a Manger, and other businesses such as traditional cheese shop, **Neal's Yard Dairy**, 'physical-first' brands are getting in on the act.

There are many examples of newer brands developing subscription models. The **London Sock Exchange** will deliver to your door a range of socks in a convenient postbox-sized package. Customers can opt for either a quarterly or an annual subscription. Customers are encouraged to refill the box with any old, unwanted socks, and send them back using a prepaid return postage label. The Sock Exchange then recycles the box and the socks.

In 2014, at the age of 26, Freddie Garland launched his business **Freddie's Flowers** from his parents' garden in London, having previously worked for the veg box delivery firm Abel & Cole. Freddie saw how its subscription model for grocery boxes could be transferred to flowers. From 2014 to 2020 Freddie's Flowers built a subscription customer base of 110,000 with a turnover of £30.3 million. For a £25 weekly subscription customers receive one bouquet of fresh flowers delivered to their door each week, complete with flower arranging tips.

The cycling subscription brand **Rapha** is another very good example of this. For a modest £70 annual subscription members of the Rapha Cycling Club (RCC) see many benefits: receiving notice of events and seasonal sales before non-members; reduced express shipping costs for goods ordered online; rider insurance to help in the event of a crash or serious mechanical failure. Members also have access to the RCC mobile app which helps members find rides and connect with other members. Finally, members get half-price coffee at Rapha Club Houses in cities around the world.

We will see car brands develop subscription services as part of a wider mobility service. **Volvo** has 'Care by Volvo' in the UK. You might think this is the same as leasing a car. However, there is a difference. The most significant one is the flexibility it offers customers.

'Care by Volvo' allows customers to change their car or cancel the agreement with three months' notice.

There are many motivating factors for people opting for subscription services. Convenience and simplicity is an obvious one. In developing subscription services brands strive to create a sense of community with additional benefits beyond regularly delivered product. Brands may offer tuition and also incentives to find other subscribers. They may also choose to open physical sites to meet their customers which again builds on the idea of community.

But the most influential driver of the subscription economy is the little dopamine rush that customers receive when a delivery pops through their door.

According to research by Barclaycard the UK is a 'nation of super subscribers'.[7] The research revealed:

- The subscription economy in the UK in July 2020 had increased by 39.4 per cent year-on-year.

- 65 per cent of UK homes are currently signed up to some form of subscription service, with an average of seven contracts per household.

- Men are willing to pay more with an average spend of £57 each month compared to women who are parting with a more restrained £35.

- 53 per cent of respondents said that 'exclusive content' was the main reason for committing to a subscription service.

- 'Convenience' matches exclusivity at 53 per cent.

- The discovery of new brands or products is also popular with 51 per cent specifying it as a reason for signing up.

- 44 per cent said that they bought a subscription service as a gift for friends and family members.

- Unsurprisingly, streaming content was the most popular form of subscription service; food and drink subscriptions came second on the list; beauty, grooming, health and fitness are third, fourth, fifth and sixth respectively.

The three S's of subscription

Barclaycard identified the three S's that the most popular subscriptions possess: security, savings and surprise.

The Barclaycard report explains that *security* gives subscribers the comfort factor of knowing they will never run out of the goods they have subscribed to. This could apply to anything used regularly, from shampoo to protein powder to printer ink. There might be a financial saving too, but the main appeal is convenience.

Savings is clear and understandable. Customers want to feel that they are getting a good deal for their investment and their loyalty to a service. This is the case even with the most premium exercise brand **Peloton**, which can cost up to £2,295 for an exercise bike or treadmill, plus £39 per month subscription. But a key message from Peloton is to compare existing fitness costs and travel time with their home-based set-up. And the brand presents a five-year plan informing the potential subscriber how soon the equipment will 'pay for itself' and the number of precious travelling hours they will save.

The third S, *surprise*, is the most potent in motivating customers to subscribe. This is mostly targeted at customers who are more adventurous and experimental, and who like the dopamine rush of a monthly surprise arriving at their door. A good example of this is the subscription service **Books + Beer** which delivers a couple of craft ales and a new work of crime or nonfiction.

As well as the obvious streaming and telecom services, food and recipe delivery services, magazines, music, cosmetics and contact lenses, the *Evening Standard* has identified more unusual subscriptions including stationery, cat litter, Japanese snack boxes and newspapers focusing on only the good news in the world.[8]

Other examples that the *Evening Standard* identified include: **The Papergang,** a subscription service that sends out colourful papercraft to its subscribers every month. Every box of patterned washi tape, notepads and notebooks, sticky notes and plenty more is themed and includes exclusive stationery and desk accessories designed in collaboration with the chosen Artist of the Month. For every four boxes

Papergang sell, they plant one tree, so in a loose sense they can hint at a circular business model.

Rare Birds Book Club is a book subscription service that hosts an online forum where subscribers can share their thoughts with other readers in the RBBC community, so it's a chance to connect with like-minded individuals.

The Post House sends a fresh edit of home décor every three months. The subscription includes illustrated instruction cards to help subscribers restyle their homes, including during big events like Christmas and Halloween. Recommended products are sourced from artisan producers and businesses specific to the area that the subscriber lives in. The Post House has picked up on the growth in localism and demand for supporting local businesses.

The **Smol** subscription service sends concentrated cleaning fluid for clothes or dishes through the post. Another example is the **Craft Whisky Club** where for £29.99 per month subscribers receive one bottle of rare malt whisky every two months. Each bi-monthly box includes a full-size bottle, as well as snacks to pair with it and information on tasting notes, the distillery and how the whisky is made and matured.

Subscription services have also responded to the increasing popularity of gin, particularly craft gin. **The Craft Gin** delivers its monthly selection of a bottle of gin from small-batch distilleries, plus mixers and a selection of snacks and treats. The monthly cost of the subscription is £40.

Coffee has been a popular subscription category. A good example is the **Old Spike Roastery** which has developed a subscription business with social value at its core. Around 65 per cent of all Old Spike Roastery's profits finance its social mission. One initiative is an eight-week training course that takes people off the streets and turns them into qualified baristas. For £6.95 per week subscribers can get their regular hit of coffee and also feel good about doing good.

Now we are getting very niche. For people obsessed with brownies, they can subscribe to **Gower Cottage Original Brownies**. Run by home baker Kate from the Welsh countryside, the brownies are delivered by post every month for three months. Every first order comes with a jar of Gower Cottage Original Brownie Butter.

Oddbox has capitalized on the fact that more than a third of the fruit and veg grown on Britain's farms is discarded before it leaves the fields because they are oddly shaped. Oddbox takes the oddly shaped carrots, potatoes, onions, apples and pears deemed too ugly for the supermarket aisles, and from that has created a subscription service with weekly, fortnightly or monthly deliveries at a cost from £10.99 per box. Oddbox estimates that it saves enough produce to fill 78 double-decker buses while also saving 1,479,823 kg in CO_2e. All packaging is 100 per cent recyclable or degradable.

Pasta Evangelists deliver regular recipe kits that include fresh pasta, garnishes and sauces in insulated letterbox-sized packages. Subscribers pick dishes from the online menu, then set their preferred delivery frequency.

Another food service is **Sous Chef Monthly Tasting**, which delivers a box of adventurous seasonal foods and store-cupboard staples, such as lemon-infused tagliatelle and tonka beans. As part of the subscription, each month the customer receives a 'secret weapon', a key ingredient that the brand recommends you use time and again.

For a subscription fee of £3.99 every three months, **The Happy Newspaper** delivers a 32-page newspaper that celebrates everyday heroes, random acts of kindness and positive news from all around the world. The Happy Newspaper was conceived as an antithesis to regular, mostly depressing news content.

For £31.95 per month **Cattitude** will deliver a box of delights and fun stuff for your pet. It's an assortment of cat-related treats such as a catnip pillow, organic cat food and toys. The delivery also includes gifts for owners too, and each box has a mix of up to eight products.

With **Who Gives a Crap**, you can subscribe to receive a regular delivery of toilet paper. It was established by the founders as a reaction to learning that 2 billion people don't have access to a toilet and that around 289,000 children under five die every year from diarrhoeal diseases caused by poor water and sanitation.

Who Gives a Crap donates 50 per cent of its profits to help build toilets and improve sanitation in the developing world. So participation is the new consumption. Community is the new consumption. Learning is the new consumption. Access is the new consumption. Sharing is the new consumption.

FUTURE-READY NOTE

Participation is the new consumption.

And in this new world where community is everything, successful brands will be those that go beyond selling stuff, to creating experiences that foster communities that have shared values and shared purpose and that are driven by the values and purpose of the brand.

As brands rethink their physical stores to respond to this new paradigm they will need to shift from being just channels of distribution to places that create compelling experiences. They will need to create environments and experiences that stage stories; that host community gatherings; that facilitate learning and sharing; that entertain, that immerse customers in culture. All in an environment and experience that is driven by warm and personalized hospitality. I will cover the physical store experience in more detail in Chapter 6.

FUTURE-READY NOTE

Physical retail is shifting from channels of distribution to moments of experience.

In the broader sphere of our town centres, reconnecting to community is essential to regenerate our high streets. Over recent years many have lost their connection with and have become irrelevant to local communities, with tired shops and many vacant spaces. They have lacked offers and experiences beyond retail with a scarcity of community services and amenities.

In order to reconnect to local communities high streets must introduce a broader range of offers and experiences. Create more open and green spaces where people can meet. Wider pavements and pedestrianization can encourage street 'spill-outs', with programmed markets and events to tempt people back. Non-retail spaces such as residential, healthcare, childcare and makerspaces would introduce new audiences and a new reason to visit and stay.

Most critically, high-street regeneration must be driven by a clear definition of its ambition and proposition that respond to the complexion of its communities. From this, strategies can be defined and the mix of offers and experiences determined to deliver a differentiated experience and a unique sense of place.

The key to 'reconnection' is a deep understanding of the wants, needs and desires of local communities and potential visitors to a high street, constantly tracking the sentiment of these audiences and responding to the insight by delivering offers and experiences that resonate and respond to peoples' needs, interests and passions.

Notes

1   M Gobe (2002) *Emotional Branding: The new paradigm for connecting brands to people*, Allworth Press, USA
2   D Wightman-Stone. H&M launches styling and shopping app for men, FashionUnited, 2021, fashionunited.uk/news/fashion/h-m-launches-styling-and-shopping-app-for-men/2021031754500 (archived at https://perma.cc/G4A7-LVW6)
3   K Brown. The 4 M's of Gamification (retold for Team Building), Linkedin.com. 2015, www.linkedin.com/pulse/4-ms-gamification-retold-team-building-kathy-brown/ (archived at https://perma.cc/NCR9-JB83)
4   A Ahmed and S Olander (2012) *Velocity: The seven new laws for a world gone digital*, Vermilion, London
5   A Santi. The power of the fashion rental revolution. Raconteur, 2020, www.raconteur.net/retail/fashion-rental-revolution/ (archived at https://perma.cc/486E-VZKE)
6   T Lewis. From coffee to cars: How Britain became a nation of subscribers, *The Guardian*, 2021, www.theguardian.com/lifeandstyle/2021/may/09/from-coffee-to-cars-how-britain-became-a-nation-of-subscribers (archived at https://perma.cc/9VKX-CFAF)

7 Barclaycard. Generation subscription: The UK is now a nation of 'super subscribers', 2022, home.barclaycard/insights/2020/09/The-UK-is-now-a-nation-of-super-subscribers/ (archived at https://perma.cc/DU8J-ZUWW)

8 A Shah. Best subscription boxes: the food, homeware, books and beauty subscription boxes with UK delivery, *Evening Standard*, 2022, www.standard.co.uk/shopping/esbest/home-garden/best-subscription-boxes-a4236041.html (archived at https://perma.cc/5US3-KNRR)

06

Remaking place

In this chapter, I will be looking at places. When I use the word 'place', I refer not only to the physical space but also to the experience of place, that experience being both physical and digital. And 'place' in a retail context does not only refer to shops, but to any experience that a brand develops to engage its audience and tell its stories. It is an established fact that we are 'over-retailed'. In the past decade an unprecedented number of shops and shopping centres have closed, mostly due to the growth of online shopping, and this phenomenon will continue. The evidence is undeniable:

- According to UBS and data from The International Council of Shopping Centres, at the end of 2020 there were 115,000 shopping centres in the United States (112,000 in 2010 and 90,000 in 2000). This amounts to 59 sq ft of shopping-centre space per US household.[1] UBS estimates that around 80,000 physical stores (9 per cent of the total) in the United States will shut by 2026. This number is based on the assumption that e-commerce sales rise from 18 per cent to 27 per cent of total retail sales. According to Coresight Research 9,832 stores closed in the United States in 2019 and 8,741 in 2020.[2]

- UBS also anticipates that most closures will be in the fashion and accessories sector with an estimated 21,000 closures from this sector by 2026, many of which are located in shopping centres.

- According to the Local Data Company and PwC, 11,120 UK chain operator outlets closed between January and October 2020. This represented twice as many as in 2019. This of course is partly due to the Covid-19 pandemic; however, I believe that only accelerated the inevitable.[3]

- The research firm Euromonitor estimated that the compound annual growth rate of physical retail in various categories will be as follows:
  - convenience stores 3.8 per cent
  - discounters 3.7 per cent
  - vending 1.8 per cent
  - health and beauty 1.7 per cent
  - home and garden 1.5 per cent
  - supermarkets 1.4 per cent
  - electronics and appliances 0.7 per cent
  - hypermarkets 0.6 per cent
  - mixed retailers 0.5 per cent
  - leisure and personal 0.1 per cent

The retailers' response

According to Real Capital Analytics, US retail assets accounted for 42 per cent of US total distressed assets since 2007.[4] As a response to the dire situation many large 'big box' retailers (such as department stores) and shopping centres currently find themselves in, many owners and investors are now repurposing their assets.

A good example of this is **John Lewis and Partners** in the UK, who have 32 John Lewis department stores and 330 Waitrose grocery stores. The group is planning to enter the BTR (build to rent) housing sector and aims to build 10,000 homes at 20 of its retail sites. Building homes above or beside Waitrose supermarkets makes perfect sense as it can create communities of customers in close proximity to the stores. The plan is also to furnish the homes with John Lewis furniture and accessories. I am certain that the intention is that they become part of their customers' lives and so build future loyalty as those customers move onto the next rented apartment or indeed buy their own home.

John Lewis has also been granted planning permission to convert floors three to eight of its iconic Oxford Street store into office space for rent. The changes would leave the retail space covering the basement, ground, first and second floors. The added benefit of creating office space above the store is that it would bring a new customer base to the store, who will be there on a regular basis and not just when they want to shop. I am sure this will be a growing trend among 'big box' retailers as they come to terms with the fact they will need less retail space in future.

We are also seeing shopping centres drastically reduce their reliance on transactional retail and introduce new uses such as offices and co-working, housing, wellness, education, hotels and generally more community amenities such as job centres, elderly care centres, healthcare clinics, makerspaces and other uses that would never have been imagined to be part of a shopping centre only a few years ago.

In comparison, in the United States Amazon has been buying struggling shopping malls to convert them into distribution centres. Globally, many large REITs (real-estate investment trusts) have been converting retail real estate into residential and office developments. One of the main catalysts for repurposing is the decline of MSUs (main space users) such as department stores and large 'leisure boxes'. It is estimated that there are approximately 1,000 severely struggling shopping centres in the United States, and of those fewer than 50 have been sold over the past few years. These 1,000 or so centres will inevitably have increasing vacancy rates, making them unviable in the future but attractive for investors who have the vision and capital to repurpose them.

Repurposing

Commercial real-estate information provider CoStar suggests that, of the 1.1 billion sq ft of excess retail space in the United States, shopping centres account for 90 million sq ft. In the UK Savills estimates that 40 per cent of retail space is surplus and 'ripe' for repurposing.[5]

The repurposing boom has mainly been fuelled by plummeting valuations of shopping centres due to falling rents and a lack of investment. Traditionally, shopping centres have been valued on three key criteria: tenant lease duration, rent and covenant. However, these criteria have been disrupted as brands demand shorter leases and negotiate more favourable rent terms. Additionally, consumers are turning away from large international or national chains who have the best covenant, with their cookie-cutter approach to stores being less attractive to consumers who are increasingly turning to independent or direct-to-consumer brands. This in turn has encouraged the larger chain operators to localize their offers with stores that are more relevant to the local community and their customers.

So, as shopping centres are drastically reduced in price they are becoming more attractive to investors. In some instances, shopping centres in Europe are selling at 10 times less than their valuation only a year or two previously. So, if an asset was worth £50 million, it can now be acquired for £5 million, which will inevitably attract many potential buyers. However, these types of investors are not intending to retain the assets as exclusively retail. The only way they will be able to increase valuation and earn a good return on exit is to redevelop and repurpose the asset.

The retail hierarchy

Figure 6.1 illustrates a reimagined 'Maslow Hierarchy' depicting the history of shopping centres. In the early days, retail was all about *trading*. Shopkeepers stacked their shelves with goods and sold them (hopefully) at a margin. Shopping centres leased concrete boxes with glass fronts from which retailers traded goods. This was followed by the era of more sophisticated and nuanced *retailing*, where we began to understand the psychology of the consumer and employed techniques that drove footfall, dwell and engagement. Famously, fast-moving consumer goods firm Procter & Gamble referred to these engagement points as 'moments of truth': the first moment of truth being in-store when the consumer was engaged with the product, and the second when they took it home to use it.

Shopping centres began to understand customer journeys and missions. They segmented their centres into districts, paying attention to the adjacencies of different categories of store. The space planning of shopping centres became very sophisticated with the accumulation of data that led to a deep understanding of customer flows, vertical and horizontal circulation, sight lines, key entrances, 'step stoning' customers through 'nodes' and key portals while creating a change of pace in moving from one district to the next, in order to keep the customers engaged and encouraging them to stay and return.

The next step in the hierarchy was when retail places played a part in peoples' wider *lifestyle*. Brands saw stores as an important part of developing a lifestyle associated with their brand. Shopping centres started to introduce leisure and entertainment offers. We saw the proliferation of cinemas, bowling alleys, events, ice rinks and even ski slopes, all of which of course sat neatly next to the shops and restaurants. Shopping centres became key destinations for leisure and entertainment and the night-time economy.

FIGURE 6.1 'Maslow hierarchy' for retail

More recently in the hierarchy, brands and retailers have begun to see their stores as places for *community*. Places where their fans and other consumers who are interested in the lifestyle that the brand represents would gather to participate in experiences that relate to the brand.

Similarly, shopping centres began to see themselves as part of a local and wider community and realized the centres themselves needed to be more connected, more open and have offers beyond retail and entertainment, including community amenities and services such as childcare, health and wellness, co-working, adult education, exhibition spaces, etc. They set out to attract the local community not just for shopping but for regular visits as an important part of their daily lives. The idea here was to shift from a 'shopping rhythm' to a 'community rhythm': to increase the frequency of unpredictable shopping visits to daily visits for community services and amenities.

> **FUTURE-READY NOTE**
>
> Shift from a 'shopping rhythm' to a 'community rhythm'.

The next step in the hierarchy is the era of retail as *media*: in a future-ready world, retail will no longer be about real estate but about content, of which real estate will be a by-product.

> **FUTURE-READY NOTE**
>
> Retail will no longer be about real estate. It will be about content.

As transactional retail gradually migrates online, retailers and brands will increasingly use their stores to recruit customers and drive them to their e-commerce and social media platforms for further engagement and transaction.

> **FUTURE-READY NOTE**
>
> The physical store will be less about transaction and fulfilment and more about recruitment and retention.

In this world of retail as media, shopping centres and our local shopping streets will have an opportunity to host brands and create experiences that activate public spaces to create compelling content that visitors are eager to share. Instead of thinking of shopping centres and local shopping streets as a series of in-line concrete boxes with glass fronts, we must introduce 'stage sets' for regular programmed events, markets, performances, etc, to be curated over a calendar year to drive attention, surprise, discovery and engagement while galvanizing both local demographic communities and communities of interest.

FUTURE-READY NOTE

Shift from demographic segmentation to interest segmentation.

These activated spaces can be the glue that connects zones, districts and neighbourhoods encouraging consumers to explore. In the case of shopping centres, such activations can also connect the inside to the outside, allowing the centre to integrate with the local community while blending with shops, street markets and events taking place in its surrounding streets. In doing so, this can integrate with the urban grain and streetscape, making it more permeable, inclusive and connected. Employing this approach would attract more local independent brands and operators which will help shopping centres break the shackles of cookie-cutter brands and experiences.

FUTURE-READY NOTE

Shopping centres must be permeable and blend with the urban streetscape, making them more activated, inclusive and connected.

The experience economy

Over the past several decades, in developed economies we have seen the growth of what has been termed the 'experience economy' – where people seek not just to buy and consume 'stuff', but are turning their attention to buying and participating in 'experiences'.

Some have suggested that we are rapidly reaching the point of 'peak stuff', and in mature economies we no longer need more 'stuff'. While he was Head of Sustainability at IKEA, Steve Howard said, 'If we look on a global basis, in the West we have probably hit peak stuff. We talk about peak oil. I'd say we've hit peak red meat, peak sugar, peak stuff... peak home furnishings.'[6]

The business publication *Management Today* identified that the products we buy have got considerably cheaper over the decades. It identified a piece of research by Cambridge University that found:

> as clothing prices have come down in the UK, the number of garments bought has soared four-fold. The study found that the average British woman buys half her bodyweight – 28 kg (62 lb) – in clothing every year. However, the average British family spends about 45 per cent less on clothes today than 40 years ago... *Which?* magazine's best buy Hoover Automatic 3221h washing machine cost £88 in 1969, a sum equivalent to £1,249 today. A typical 22-inch colour television set would have cost about £300 then (£4,261 today). A TV cost more than a month's work for an average earner in 1969, but costs less than two days' work today. The costs have gone down and the number to choose from way up.[7]

I spoke about the 'choice paradox' in Chapter 4 and how too much choice can impact a consumer's ability to make a choice. As we reach 'peak stuff', we have more choice than ever before.

Management Today also identified an interesting stance from Benjamin Scheibehenne, a research scientist at the University of Basel in Switzerland, who said that it might be too simple to conclude that too many choices are bad, just as it is wrong to assume that more choices are always better. He goes on to say that it depends on what information we're being given to assist us in making those choices, the type of expertise we have to rely on – from ourselves and our own knowledge or outside authority – and how much importance we ascribe to each choice.[8]

Mr Scheibehenne goes on to point out that

It's critical to separate the concept of choice overload from information overload… how much are people affected by the number of choices and how much from the lack of information or any prior understanding of the options?

Now that consumers are buying more goods online, algorithms are making more choices for us. Digital platforms have vast amounts of information and insight on each individual consumer to enable them to direct your clicks. *Management Today* quoted Eric Schmidt, the chairman of Alphabet, Google's parent company: 'We know where you are. We know where you've been. We can more or less know what you're thinking about.' And *Management Today* went on to suggest that Eric Schmidt may as well have said: 'We know how to choose for you.'[9]

It is also interesting to note that for the first time in history we have three generations simultaneously downsizing, getting rid of stuff and simplifying their lives. Baby Boomers are downsizing as their children leave home and with so much wealth tied up in their homes, they are using the cash as their pension. As they move to smaller homes, they need less stuff. Gen X and Gen Y (Millennials) have grown up during a time of mass urbanization. According to the UN, 55 per cent of the earth's population now live in cities. This has increased from 37 per cent in 1959, and it is predicted to grow to 68 per cent by 2050. Due to the impact of Covid-19 we will also see the increase in suburban populations along with the resultant increasing urbanization of suburbia.[10] So, they tend to live in smaller dwellings and also have less space for stuff. Additionally, they have responded to 'peak stuff' with their preference for buying experiences and digital subscription-based services such as music and movies over physical goods.

With urban living comes a new approach to mobility. Younger generations drive less and so buy fewer cars. According to *Auto Express* the proportion of those aged 17 to 20 holding a driving licence has fallen by almost 40 per cent in recent years, dropping from 48 per cent in the early 1990s to 29 per cent in 2014. Licence rates for those aged between 20 and 29 dropped from 75 to 63 per cent over the same period. Car usage is also significantly down, with those aged between 17 and 29 taking 36 per cent fewer trips in cars in the period 2010–2014 compared to the late 1990s:[11,12]

> If Millennials and Gen Z can avoid having to drive a car, they will happily and eagerly find a means around doing so.
> Baby Boomers grew up believing that getting a driver's licence was a rite of passage… There has been a shift in the cultural norms and attitudes towards cars and the act of driving.

Forbes goes on the explain that 'The later generations are less inclined to make a large investment in buying a car. Ride-hailing apps have obviously driven this. The latest drivers are more down-to-earth and see driving as perfunctory.'[13]

Forbes elaborates on the idea of choosing not to own a car with the concept of FOMO (fear of missing out). And that FOMO is triggered because of the rapid renewal of car models.

The car dealership experience seems stuck in the dark ages and maybe that is why later generations are turning their backs on car buying. However, there are 'digital first' brands emerging that can offer a frictionless car buying experience that appeals to later generations. Later generations are also hesitating to buy cars for reasons of sustainability, the stresses of traffic and most importantly, as the car has become more of a commodity item, it has lost its status appeal.

Although later generations are not buying cars as much as previous generations, they are embracing car sharing and are using brands such as Zip Cars to do so, and we will see this market grow rapidly.

If an increasing number of people are buying less stuff, it seems that more of us are edging closer to the peak of Maslow's hierarchy of needs, where what matters most is not the esteem needs of prestige, status symbols and accomplishments, demonstrated by what you own, but by 'self-actualization' with self-fulfilment needs such as creative activities, learning experiences, travel, social interactions, mindfulness, ecology, etc. Or maybe these are the new status symbols?

However, we still have too many people at the lower end of Maslow's hierarchy of needs, particularly if you consider access to the internet as a basic need at the base of Maslow's hierarchy pyramid.

The being economy

So how is this approach and thinking beginning to impact the places we visit, the places where we hang out, socialize, shop, learn and work? We are seeing an evolution from the 'experience economy' to the 'being economy', where consumers demand places just 'to be'. Places whose function is not pre-determined or deliberately prescribed. I describe these as 'on-demand' places whose function is determined by its audience. In fact 'on-demand' places are distinguished not by function but by etiquette.

FUTURE-READY NOTE

We are seeing a shift from the 'experience economy' to the 'being economy'.

The Highline in New York and Hastings Pier in the UK are two interesting examples of places that have been designed with no specific pre-determined activation in mind, whose function is determined by its audience. **Hastings Pier** is known as the 'People's Pier'. Designed by dRMM Architects, the pier won the 2017 Stirling Prize for Architecture. The local community were very involved in the development of the design. What makes it unique is that the space is not populated with permanent attractions.

The Chair of Hastings Pier Charity, Maria Ludkin, describes the pier as a 'symbol of regeneration', and said:

> Hastings Pier has invited curious visitors, stimulated conversations, and engaged and welcomed all who use and support us. Accessible and sustainable, it frames a spectacular seascape and offers unlimited variations for relaxation, contemplation and play.

Alex de Rijke, Founding Director of dRMM Architects said that the Hastings Pier project, 'was ignited by the community, shaped by the community and now enjoyed by the community'.[14]

The sociologist Ray Oldenburg coined the term 'Third Place' which he described as public places where people can gather and interact. In contrast to first places (home) and second places (work), Ray Oldenburg's third places are 'being places' – places that do not demand a specific activity or behaviour but informal places where people can just 'be'.

In his books *The Great Good Places* and *Celebrating the Third Place* Ray Oldenburg writes about the importance of informal public gathering places. Oldenburg demonstrates how and why these places are essential to community and public life, arguing that bars, coffee shops, stores, public plazas, terraces and other 'third places' are central to local democracy and community vitality.

He goes on to explain that third places:

> allow people to put aside their concerns and simply enjoy the
> company and conversation around them. Third places host the regular,
> voluntary, informal and happily anticipated gatherings of individuals
> beyond the realms of home and work.

Oldenburg explains that beer gardens, main streets, pubs, cafés, coffee houses, post offices and other third places are the heart of a community's social vitality. Providing the foundation for a functioning democracy, these spaces promote social equity by levelling the status of guests, providing a setting for grassroots politics, creating habits of public association and offering psychological support to individuals and communities.[15]

The main cause of the closure of shops over many years has been the growth of online shopping. To bring life back to our high streets shopping centres and retail parks, the notion and role of the physical shop has to be rethought. We have to reimagine the experience that is to be delivered to audiences visiting stores. According to Local Data Company (LDC), more than 17,500 chain stores closed during 2020, and they estimate that another 18,000 shops could close down for good in 2021. This has decimated our high streets, shopping centres and retail parks across the UK.[16]

The Fourth Place

I refer to the new notion of the physical space (store), a new type of experience, as the 'Fourth Place'. This new type of experience will need to respond to audiences' new relationship with time, with place, with other people and with consumption. These audiences are also increasingly commitment-phobes, and are promiscuous when it comes to their relationships with brands and retailers. Generally, they are less committed to relationships, to work and to big institutions and big brands.

Their new relationship with *time* is reflected in the fact that their work is more flexible, leisure time and work time are increasingly becoming blurred, and they are used to shopping 24/7. Being constantly connected globally they can be engaged across all time zones simultaneously, so time becomes less critical.

Their new relationship with *place* is reflected in the fact that the places they work, live and play are also blurring. With the proliferation of smart home and connected media, the home has become not only a place to live, but a place to shop, a place to work and, with the explosion of online fitness and streaming entertainment services, it has become a gym, a cinema and music venue. So the breaking down of the rigid delineation of what happens in different places has led to a new relationship between our audience and place.

Our audiences' new relationship with *other people* is reflected in the growth of peer-to-peer services and engagement. We can see with the growth of platforms such as eBay, Etsy and Vinted among others how peer-to-peer commerce has grown. The growth of the sharing economy has also recalibrated the relationships that our audiences have with each other. They use digital platforms to share products and services, and with the platform 'Next Door' they can do this at a very local level in their communities.

The new relationship with *consumption* has taken hold through the thirst for knowledge, learning and buying experiences and not just products. E-commerce in combination with rapid fulfilment means that our audiences can buy what they want, when they want, how they want. And 15-minute delivery will be commonplace very soon.

So, with the disruption in retail combined with our audiences' new relationship with time, place, other people and consumption we must rethink and reimagine the future of the store. And in doing this we need to define the fourth place. The fourth place should not be seen purely as physical space. In future, retail will not be about real estate, it will be about content and therefore the fourth place must think and behave like a media platform – a platform for experience, learning, collaboration, participation, making and conviviality, both physical and virtual.

The future for physical retail spaces

I can see that retail physical spaces will polarize into three typologies: transaction and fulfilment, community and recruitment.

Of course, there will always be a place for traditional shops where people buy stuff and so the first typology is based on *transaction and fulfilment*. In future an increasing number of these spaces will be autonomous, automated shopping experiences, similar to those of Amazon Fresh and Wheely's Moby Mart from Shanghai, which is a roaming, automated store that lets you get in and out without the usual checkout experience. For the transaction and fulfilment retail typology the revenue model would be a traditional lease or turnover rent. If the space was used for fulfilment the revenue model could be based on the number of items fulfilled from online shopping or indeed the value of the transactions. Revenue could also be based on the impact that the physical space has on downstream online sales uplift. Another measure of revenue could be purely the size of the space.

The second typology is the *community* space where brands create experiences that bring together their fans and other audiences who have a shared interest or passion. Lulu Lemon, Sweaty Betty and Rapha are three good examples of brands who have created places for their brand communities where their fans gather to participate in interests, activities and passions they share. The revenue model of the community typology could be based on football, on dwell time (the amount of time that people spend in the space), a subscription model or, if there is an element of transaction, part of the revenue could be on a turnover basis.

A good example of a community space is **Burberry's Maker House,** where Burberry teamed up with specialist craft retailer The New Craftsman to showcase the work of designers and craftspeople in an old warehouse. The space featured a series of stations and spaces inspired by that season's Burberry collection. Each space was occupied by a maker who demonstrated various crafts and techniques. In one of the spaces was the Precision Workshop where saddlers, embroiderers and bookbinders demonstrated their craft process, while the Sensory Lab included designers who experimented with colour and scent.[17]

A good example of a smaller brand developing a community space is **Look Mum No Hands,** the London-based café, wine bar and bicycle accessories shop and bike workshop. LMNH puts on regular screenings of major cycle races including the Tour de France. These events attract many enthusiasts as well as other customers wanting to soak up the atmosphere and they position LMNH as a key place to meet if you are a keen cyclist.

I refer to the third typology as the *recruitment* space. Here brands and retailers use the space to create experiences that are designed to recruit customers, and then encourage them to engage downstream with online e-commerce sites or social media platforms. The main purpose of this typology of space is to drive media impressions that will have a halo effect on the brand. The revenue model of the recruitment typology would be based on the data that demonstrates the space's ability to drive media impressions and its impact on sales via mobile devices.

Another way of measuring value and therefore revenue is to capture the data that measures sentiment, peoples' feelings and opinions about their experience. A great example of a recruitment space was when the sneaker brand **Converse** opened its 'One Star Hotel' in London for a period of two days.[18] During the two-day period it attracted 5,345 visitors with an average dwell time of 40 minutes. More impressively, over the two days the experience drove 1.7 million live-stream views and 40,000 new Instagram followers. The sales achieved during the two days was a modest $50,000. The data showed that during the two days the Converse experience was responsible for a total of 226 million media impressions. So the revenue model for the recruitment typology would be based on capturing the data that demonstrates the value of the space to a brand, i.e. its ability to drive media impressions.

SWELCH: the blended space

In order to prepare for the future and ensure sustainable success, our shopping centres and high streets will have to kick the addiction to transactional retail. And as a matter of urgency, create 'blended' places, bringing together the workplace, healthcare, education, residential, makerspaces and community amenities, and blending these with retail, food and beverage (F&B), leisure and entertainment to animate the public realm and blur the lines between tenanted space and public space.

Brands, shopping centres and high streets must see their places not only as channels of distribution but as moments of experience, employing a data-driven curatorial approach that animates the public realm while blending retail, F&B, entertainment, learning, culture, co-working, hospitality, wellness and makerspaces. I call this SWELCH: places that bring together shopping, working, entertainment, learning, culture and hospitality.

FUTURE-READY NOTE

Retail must shift from 'channels of distribution' to 'moments of experience'.

SWELCH represents the shift that I refer to, from a 'shopping rhythm' to a 'community rhythm', delivering permeable, blended places that connect to community and the streetscape. Places that bring back that sense of excitement and surprise, while activating our public realm.

We must arrest the rapid homogenization of shopping centres and high streets that have delivered cookie-cutter brands and clone high streets, and leave behind outmoded hermetically sealed shopping centres that turn their back on community, and high streets that have been disconnected from their communities through increasing irrelevance.

Serendipity is the most powerful consumer emotion. It drives interest, intrigue, curiosity, surprise and, as a result, footfall, engagement, dwell and sharing. Our vision for shopping centres and high streets must be to create *serendipity machines*.

FUTURE-READY NOTE

To draw in the crowds and keep them coming back, places must be *serendipity machines*.

We can build compelling places that are serendipity machines by focusing on the following attributes:

- Places that people want to visit, hang out in and re-visit.
- Places that are alive and deliver continuous 'newness'.
- Places that stop people in their tracks and tempt them to find out more.
- Places that are not just full of shops with merchandise, but experiences that people remember as mementos of their visit.

FUTURE-READY NOTE

Shift from merchandise to mementos.

- Places that have a change of pace and mood that people find convenient for everyday needs while also coming across things they never expected.

- Places that get the heart racing with events and spectacle.

- Places where people feel a sense of belonging and are imbued with a truly authentic and unique 'spirit of place'.

- Places that turn their back on the old approach of clone cookie-cutter shops.

- Places that communities enjoy so much that they are eager to tell friends and family and also their whole social network through social media.

- Places that are not obsessed with and courted by big brands but ones that embrace smaller independent brands and businesses and blend them with bigger national and international brands, and create the conditions and strategies for helping the smaller independents thrive and grow.

- Places that kick the addiction to transactional retail and think not of 'point-of-sale' but 'point-of-connection', which foster deeper, more sustainable emotional connections with their audiences.

FUTURE-READY NOTE

Shift from 'point-of-sale' to 'point-of-connection'.

- Places that communicate with their audiences not through one-way monologue but through two-way dialogue: communication, conversations and initiatives that involve and galvanize the community, and encourage participation, contribution of ideas and co-creation in order to help shape the future of place.

- Places that employ social media not as a broadcast channel but as a dialogue channel, to encourage and incentivize participation, sharing of ideas and the coming together of communities of interest.

FUTURE-READY NOTE

Social media is not a broadcast channel. It's a dialogue channel.

So, if we are to create places (whether they are shopping centres or high streets) that are relevant and commercially, socially and culturally sustainable, which bring the crowds back and deliver the most important set of future-ready mantras, they must:

- speak like a magazine
- change like a gallery
- build loyalty like a club
- share like an app
- seed like an incubator
- connect like a community
- engage like a show

If we can deliver such future-ready places the metrics of success must adapt accordingly. The new metrics of success will no longer be based on direct commercial 'productivity' of transactional retail space. The new key performance indicators (KPIs) are no longer solely sales per square metre. We must develop ways of measuring new value such as engagement per sq m, surprise per sq m, delight, smiles, clicks, shares, dwell, sentiment, engagement, participation, footfall attention and experience per sq m. And how do these new metrics fit into wider social, environmental and cultural value? I will cover this in Chapter 8.

FUTURE-READY NOTE

The metrics of success have changed for stores. Shift from sales per sq m to experience per sq m.

In future the physical store will no longer be the end point of the customer journey; it will be the beginning. As physical stores become more experiential, customers will start their engagement by participating in an experience such as an event or a class which in turn may prompt them to explore further, leading to either purchase in-store via their mobile device or purchase online at some point in the future.

With the proliferation of click-and-collect we will increasingly see retailers differentiate their offer with bespoke and experiential 'concierge-collect' experiences. These will be a critical part of the store experience. They could be the social and convivial heart of the store, anchored with F&B in a lounge-type setting and offering personalization of goods, demonstrations and partner brand activations. This type of offer gives retailers and brands the opportunity to make the shift from selling merchandise to delivering an experience which transforms the merchandise into a memento of the experience. However, when retailers and brands create experience mementos it is critical they are designed and delivered to be 'on-brand' and in every respect are synonymous with the brand's values and purpose.

Retail design and rituals

Store design transcends interior design and architecture, and is driven more by social anthropology and ethnography than architecture. Retail design must be based on an understanding of audience journeys and missions of which interior design and architecture are by-products.

FUTURE-READY NOTE

Retail design is no longer driven by interior design. It is increasingly driven by psychology, ethnography and anthropology.

In retail design I like to refer to the design of audience journeys and experiences as the 'software' and the physical architecture as the 'hardware'. In designing the 'software', the human experience and service proposition, we are in fact designing a series of brand 'rituals', which when designed effectively can deliver the essence of the brand. Rituals are the embodiments of a brand's DNA, what it stands for, its personality, how it behaves, its tone of voice. And of course at the heart of the ritual is the person delivering it. So as physical retail becomes less about buying stuff and more about experiencing the brand, the interaction with the people who represent the brand becomes more critical, whether they are physically present or virtual.

In order to guide retailers and brands on the development of rituals as part of their store experience, a good starting point is represented by the following six pillars of ritualized experience.

FUTURE-READY NOTE

Retailers must shift from commoditized 'service' to customized 'on-brand' rituals.

Arrest

The first is *arrest*. As a customer passes the store or checks their mobile device, how do we stop them in their tracks, encouraging them to cross the threshold? Can we create the most arresting window display which is both physically arresting but also digitally interactive? Once the customer decides to enter the store can we gain their attention? Is it just another gondola with a '50 per cent off!' sign, or can we create a striking installation that changes on a regular basis, delivering constant surprise?

The Korean eyewear brand **Gentle Monster** demonstrates how best to create interest and surprise with its store full of installations that on the face of it have nothing to do with eyewear but are designed to display the products. Each of the brand's stores incorporates a creative, experiential 'story' that blends retail with art. In particular its store features installations that reference the traditional agriculture of pre-industrial Korea. Quiet and Zen-like, the store contrasts with the buzz of downtown Los Angeles. On entering the store you are greeted by furry bird-like objects that 'come to life' as customers pass by, enticing them inside.

Entertain

As the customer moves further into the store we must deliver the second pillar, *entertain*. This will keep the customer interested and encourage them to find out more. To deliver compelling entertainment that keeps the customer interested, stores need to rethink standard visual merchandising and deliver that moment of anticipation and excitement with 'visceral merchandising'. Merchandising that is more akin to an interactive installation than just products on shelves. Merchandising that immerses customers in stories and captivates and surprises them with an ever-changing experience which merges the physical and the digital while expressing the brand, and creating an unforgettable ritual that customers are eager to share.

The latest **Lush Cosmetics** store is a great example of the retailer who has moved beyond selling products on shelves and has created a series of great experiences through its stores, each of which is based around its products. From the foaming bath at the front of the store with two associates enticing customers to enter and wash and soften their hands, customers move through a series of different experiences such as the haircare or facial area, each of which keep them entertained, encouraging them to stay longer and explore further.

Learn

The third pillar is *learn*. Once the customer is encouraged to stay can we create an experience or put on a show that teaches them something about the product, service or brand? This could range from group lectures such as the Samsung Experience Store in New York, or less formal workshops such as classes in the Apple store. The education piece could also be digital, via screens or via the retailer's app on a mobile device.

A survey by Westfield revealed that one-third of people are interested in attending a lifestyle class at their favourite store. Many brands are now offering classes as part of their store experience. You can learn about coffee beans and how to make the perfect espresso as part of the Nespresso Connoisseurs Club. You can learn all about health wellness and fitness in a Sweaty Betty store or attend events and take yoga classes in the Lulu Lemon store.

IKEA formed the **IKEA Dining Club** as a response to research that revealed that we no longer feel empowered or skilled to cook. The Dining Club has been set up to not only educate but also to entertain, and takes the form of a DIY restaurant where customers can join with their friends to cook dinner under the expert guidance of a professional chef. The space includes a fully functioning demo kitchen, a virtual reality kitchen and a lecture theatre for events.

Context

The fourth pillar is *context*. Here it is important to demonstrate the role that the product or service plays in the life of the customer, for example, attaching cocktail cards to a bottle of vodka which can inspire the customer.

Another example is the Danish homewares brand **Hay** that developed a concept called Hay House to demonstrate the context of their products in a customer's life, in this case, their home life. Hay House is located in Copenhagen on the second and third floors of an apartment building and is a home store that has been designed to look and feel like a proper home. The apartment allows customers to live with the products, to see and feel them rather than just seeing them in a conventional store, online or in a catalogue. It gives customers ideas on how to lay out each room, how they can circulate around and interact with each product. In developing the apartment Hay House has suggested specific rituals that relate to the brand in the context of a real home.

The 'context' pillar of ritualization could also include gifting. Brands can create a differentiated offer through the development of personalized gifting – from premium Fortnum & Mason hamper gifts to the Amazon gifting offer whereby shoppers can request their purchase to be gift wrapped with a personal message.

Bookblock is an online brand that offers curated gift boxes delivered to the customer. The range includes customizable gifts for specific occasions such as notebooks for Valentine's Day, Mother's Day, birthdays, housewarming, wedding day, etc.

Personalization

Personalization is increasingly becoming a key demand from consumers, and so this represents the fifth pillar of ritualization. Delivering exclusive or personalized experiences can take many forms. It can involve a personalized service proposition or indeed a personalized product. This could range from a simple personalized label on a whisky bottle to being able to personalize the specification on a car purchase.

BMW's brand Mini is a pioneer in this area of product personalization including the related digital services and innovative production processes. As a car brand, Mini has a uniquely extensive and diverse range of special equipment and original accessories which already allow customers opportunities to personalize their Mini. However, **Mini Yours Customized** has taken this to a new level to include creative interaction between the manufacturer and the customer, offering the customer an opportunity to select between different options and integrating them actively in the design process while retaining the typical Mini language of design.

The Mini Yours Customized service offers customers the opportunity to choose from a range of upgrade products, allowing them to transform their own vehicle into a unique, personally styled, customized special, defined by their own style and creativity. Mini customers can specify or design different colours, patterns, surface finishes and icons, and even integrate their own texts and their signature into the design.

First, customers select, design and order the upgrade parts available in the product range of Mini Yours Customized using the Mini Online Shop. The customer is guided through each stage as they create their personalized Mini, helped by a list of themed design ideas. For example, the designs could include icons, colours, patterns, motifs and lettering from themes such as travel, active leisure or the history of the Mini brand to express the personality, individual interests and lifestyle of the customer. Interior trim can also be personalized and integrated in the dashboard on the passenger side where it replaces the standard factory trim. Customers can also share their own designs with other users through social media as part of the Mini community.

Once the customer has confirmed the order the individualized products will then be manufactured using 3D printing and laser lettering production processes. The parts are designed to be integrated into the vehicle and the customer can do this more than once so the car can be further customized throughout the customer's ownership. And if the vehicle is sold the personalized components can be exchanged.

Configuration is carried out in an online shop dedicated to Mini Yours Customized products. The 'customizer' is the centrepiece of the web shop. The customer's designs are transferred in digital form to the Mini production facility, based in Germany, and the data is used for the manufacture of the unique products. A digitally controlled 3D printer will receive instructions during the course of the design and configuration, in order to produce components in precisely the form designed by the customer.

Mini's digitized 3D printing process has been tailored to the production of individual products in large numbers for the Mini Yours Customized offer. The 3D printers used are professional production facilities providing high-grade plastic components which conform to the same high standards of form, functionality and safety as the components supplied from the factory in the original Mini range of accessories.

The personalized ritual can also be delivered through the process of buying, even with vending. **Unilever** produced the world's first smile-activated vending machine, branded as Share Happy, which dispenses ice creams only when the customer smiles at the vending machine. The thinking goes that ice cream makes most people happy and so a smile can be associated with the buying of ice cream, which seems to be universal.

As a brand ritual you cannot really get any more personalized that an individual smile. Unilever's idea of a smile-activated vending machine sits very well with the firm's mission: 'encouraging people everywhere to share moments of happiness'. The vending machine uses 'smile recognition' technology. When consumers approach the vending machine, their image appears on a monitor, but in the context of a playful virtual reality world. A message then prompts them to give their biggest grin which is measured by a 'smile-o-meter'. After giving their permission, their photo is taken and uploaded to Facebook. Once this is complete, they are invited to choose a Wall's ice cream from a touchscreen menu. The facial recognition technology can also determine the person's age, gender and emotion, which of course represents valuable data for Unilever. This highly personalized 'ritual' makes the buying of a normal ice cream unique, infinitely shareable and completely 'on-brand' for Unilever. Since its launch the vending machine has been rolled out globally, proving the universality of smiling being associated with buying ice cream.

Eyewear brand **Tom Davies** has positioned the brand around ritualized personalization, a service offer built on the principles of fit, form and function, and based on a four-step branded ritual. Step One starts with a bespoke eye test which also sets out to understand the customer's ocular health and lifestyle. Step Two involves the selection of the frame type, colour, material and design whereby the customer is advised on the perfect frame shape that suits the natural features of the face, fitting perfectly to their nose, head shape and ears. Step Three involves taking detailed dimensions of the face to enable a custom fit of the frame in accordance with the features, shape and size of the customer's face. The fourth step is the placing of the order for the handcrafted glasses.

Simplicity

The sixth and final pillar of brand ritualization is *simplicity*. As consumers lead increasingly complex lives and are more time poor than ever before, we must create store experiences that are as intuitive and pain-free as possible. In order to make the store experience easy we need to create ritualized experiences that are frictionless and service propositions that are not over-complicated, while ensuring the experience is still 'on-brand'.

One of my favourite ritualized experiences is the fantastic **Foot Locker** 'Audio Tour'. This allows customers to learn about the products within the store in their own time with no distractions with a very simple click on the Foot Locker app. Similar to many museums and art galleries, where you see visitors with headphones listening to audio commentary that gives them information about the exhibits, Foot Locker introduced this idea to its stores. The mobile Audio Tour 'ritual' gives Foot Locker customers an opportunity to access more detailed information about a pair of shoes they are interested in. The Audio Tours feature commentary from famous sports stars, as well as footwear designers and renowned sneaker experts, sharing anecdotes and insights about the shoes with consumers. The Audio Tour ritual shifts Foot Locker from a product brand to a 'story brand', a very deliberate repositioning of the brand.

We have seen a growth in visitor numbers to museums and art galleries. More people attend talks and lectures, evidenced by the growth of brands such as TED and Intelligence Squared. As podcasts and live-streaming become ever more popular, consumers are used to consuming stories and culture from brands, and with its Audio Tours, Foot Locker has tapped into this zeitgeist. In order for Foot Locker customers to access the Audio Tours they must connect their headphones to their mobile device on entering the store, and then visit the brand's mobile website. When they are close to the display of the shoes they are interested in, they can then enter a unique product code displayed next to the selected shoes. This then allows the customer to listen to the information about the shoes as well as commentary and stories.

As consumers increasingly shop online, rituals such as the Foot Locker's Audio Tours become an important part of making the store experience unique and compelling. And combined with the ability to touch, feel and try merchandise, the store experience can compete with the online experience, particularly if it is as easy and convenient as the online experience. Consumers are increasingly sharing their brand experiences, particularly online. The great benefit of the Foot

Locker Audio Tours is that they equip customers with the stories and anecdotes that they can then share, which in turn gives them a kind of status in their social group.

Digital payments are another way of making the store experience easy. Digital payments have proliferated, particularly as customers are more reluctant to use paper money as a consequence of Covid-19, and we are seeing leaps of innovation in this space. Near field communication (NFC) and quick response (QR) codes have proliferated at the expense of cash and PIN-based credit cards. However, the new facial recognition payment systems have encountered challenges from reluctant consumers, and demonstrating how hard it is to separate people from their mobile devices.

The Ant Group, China's financial technology (fintech) giant, embarked on an ambitious effort to install facial recognition devices at retailers that would allow people to make payments by smiling at a screen without having to use their phones. Ant's Alipay invested substantially to promote usage of the machines via merchant subsidies and shopper rebates. Alipay's competitors WeChat and Tencent also invested in the space. The payment technology has largely failed to gain popularity mainly due to cumbersome sign-up processes and concerns about how facial images and data would be used. Many Alipay users are happy to make payments by scanning QR codes with their phones, preferring that to using credit cards or cash. While the facial scans weren't meant to replace QR codes, Ant hoped they would incentivize people to transact more often at restaurants, convenience stores and supermarkets.

It seems that consumers find paying with their phones convenient enough. Covid-19 led to an increase in mask-wearing, which has also hampered wider adoption of the facial recognition technology.

FUTURE-READY NOTE

We must move beyond customer service as a series of pre-determined steps to more organic, human-centric experience rituals that reflect a brand's essence.

Beyond the shop

Creative spaces

Brands are increasingly engaging with consumers beyond the bounds of retail and the shop.

Looking again at the BMW-owned car brand Mini, they have also embraced another new type of experience for its customers and fans beyond the confines of the typical car dealership or online platform, in order to reflect the essence of the Mini brand which has been built on a fun, urban lifestyle, mobility and the efficient use of space. 'Mini Living' has been exploring how the creative use of space through innovative design can support the needs of people living in busy cities.

Mini Living has created a micro-house where customers can share three core experiences. The first is *relax*, where Mini Living has created the space as a refuge from the stresses of everyday urban life, and an escape with meditation soundtracks and one-to-one mindfulness sessions with a yoga teacher. The second experience is termed *create*. Here the space is all about igniting creativity around photography and design, where customers are inspired by professional photographers and a brand collaboration with *Wallpaper* magazine. The third and final part of the experience is *connect*, where an installation celebrates the idea of socializing and catching up with friends. This involves an immersive dining experience with the idea of fostering new connections and relationships.

The purpose of the Mini Living initiative was to create a series of experiences and environments that reflect and reinforce the core values and DNA of the Mini brand, with experiences that are not necessarily tied to the purchase of the car. In fact Mini developed these experiences to reflect and endorse the lifestyle of their customers and typically the things that are important in their lives. In doing so, Mini as a brand demonstrated the role it can play in peoples' lives beyond the purchase of the product.

Product brands are also 'stretching' their experience beyond the store and into the hospitality sector. One such brand is the Spanish footwear brand **Camper**, which created the Casa Camper hotel brand, bringing the Camper spirit and values to the hotel world, and combining the two core brand values of functionality with friendliness. Another brand that developed a hotel offer is **Muji**. In the Ginza district of Tokyo, Muji has a combined hotel and store called Atelier Muji Ginza. It consists of five specific experiences: two galleries for exhibitions, a café, a library showcasing books on design and art, and a lounge for events and workshops.

Shopping centres

Shopping centres are also moving beyond the physical store. Alibaba's **Tmall** in China hosts fashion shows which are streamed live online and showcase around 100,000 listed brands in order to attract international audiences. The live-stream experience has been positioned as 'see now, buy now'. The live-streamed fashion shows enable millions of consumers to click on items on show and purchase immediately, and included appearances by well-known celebrities and influencers. The interaction between brands, celebrities and the consumer drives the growth of the shows, and enables ordinary consumers to access a catwalk show.

Tmall has described this as 'shortening the fashion consumption chain', whereby consumers can gain access to products before they hit the shops, but critically through the medium of entertainment (a fashion show). A typical show could last up to eight hours. And the brands that are showcased can range from the luxury brand Burberry to more mainstream brands such as Ted Baker and Zara.

A CBN report found that 80 per cent of mainland China's online fashion consumption has been through the Tmall platform, where brands are increasingly launching new product lines between 15 and 30 days ahead of offline release. According to Tmall, the platform is now home to 80 per cent 'Tier 1' brands such as New Balance, Calvin Klein, Topshop and Topman.[19] The report also indicates that during the 2020 11:11 Global Shopping Festival, approximately 300 million Alibaba Taobao users watched live streams during a period of 11 days. So live-streaming is set to become a serious competitor to shopping malls unless they embrace it as part of their offer.[20]

According to *Vogue Business*, live-streaming has become increasingly popular (specifically in China) as consumers crave immersive experiences and personalized recommendations. According to Deloitte, the live-streaming market reached $4.4 billion in 2018, growing 37 per cent on the previous year and attracting a total of 456 million viewers. However, luxury brands must question whether it is possible to maintain a high level of quality in such a huge open marketplace. Ultimately, this concern may be the primary reason why more luxury brands have yet to jump at the chance to sign on to Tmall's growing platform. *Vogue Business* goes on the explain that through live-streaming, influencers can engage tens of millions of potential consumers per day. A good example of this is the influencer Kim Kardashian who sold 150,000 units of her KKW perfumes during a live-streaming session on Alibaba's Tmall, which attracted over 13 million viewers in China.

Amazon has also got in on the act with the launch of **Amazon Live**. Here live-streaming video shows have hosts presenting specific products available for sale on the platform. The online brand Wayfair also puts on live-streaming events which they call the 'Way Day sales event'.

As well as live-streaming, shopping malls are also embracing the idea of live physical spectacle and art. SKP in Beijing created a new shopping space called **SKP-S**, which takes the form of event-driven retail combined with an art exhibition. It takes up the mall in its entirety and all the brands participate, including luxury brands such as Louis Vuitton, Gucci, Cartier, Valentino and Fendi, all combining fashion and art. The first brand visitors encounter is the eyewear brand Gentle Monster. It's 'Future Farm' installation has robotic sheep moving and breathing alongside metal flowers that open and close to simulate photosynthesis that power the mechanical sheep. The 'Digital-Analog Future' theme showcases an imagined life for humans on Mars. The experience contains thematic installations and works of art, such as a 3D carving machine, Human Habitation on Mars, Mars Rover, Space Capsule, Robots and Human Conversation, Fossils of Human Civilization, Sculptures, a penguin Mirror Installation. SKP describe this as 'Not only a mall, but also a collective party of all the brands' and 'Not only a mall, but also a large collection of global limited-edition products.'

SKP have managed to pull off a difficult task in convincing all the brand stores to develop unique store designs that are very different from those in other shopping malls. Each brand has a theme that constantly changes and is delivered through the curated programming of the store. Gucci, in addition to its standard offering, has opened a furniture store and a beauty experience boutique. The brand Golden Goose opened its Golden Goose Lab, offering services such as polishing, lettering and gold inlay. Gentle Monster's store incorporates a theme of 'an imagination of new humankind travelling through a wormhole between Mars and Earth'. Meanwhile, it has also brought the brand's first artistic dessert store, NUDAKE, to the mall. The SKP-S experience includes co-branded collections, limited-edition products and products not yet on the market, while the retailers set out to deliver their most unique and personalized products and experiences.

The Cartier store also had an exhibition with a cheetah theme where two products that had not been launched anywhere else in the world were displayed. There is also a 'SKP Select' store selling sneakers exclusive to SKP-S and which cannot be found in any mainstream brand store.[21]

The **K11** mall in China was a pioneer in mixing art and commerce in retail. First launched in Hong Kong, the K11 project has sites in Shanghai, Wuhai, Shenyang and Guangzhou, with more to come. The 'art mall' concept is rooted in displaying local emerging artists from the collection of the K11 Art Foundation and allowing the public to appreciate artworks during their shopping journey. That has led to a curation approach that connects artworks and mall merchandise. Dickson Sezto, the founder of the Shanghai TX Huaihai mall refers to the curation of art and retail as 'curetail' which is based on brands using the combination of art and culture to help with more compelling storytelling. The key for brands and retailers is the localization of curation strategies.

A good example of this phenomenon was the Claude Monet solo exhibition in the K11 mall in Shanghai. The exhibition drove high footfall levels. During the period of the exhibition sales increased by 20 per cent – interestingly most of the sales uplift came from art-related gifts and merchandise.

Immersive experiences

Those shopping malls who want to remain future-ready are adopting curatorial strategies that engage customers. The SKP-S centre introduced its theatrical shopping experience by showcasing a digital future that tells brand stories in the language of young consumers, enticing them to spend more time in stores where the curated centre can be used to rejuvenate brands and enrich their storytelling. Although the young Gen Z consumers are engrossed in their mobile devices and social media they are still very interested in physical stores and the social interaction they enable

According to the 2020 Generation Z Fashion Consumer Insight Report by Hylink Digital Solutions and Weibo, 'shopping tops all other offline social activities'. Activities like shopping in stores, visiting immersive art exhibitions and participating in 'Instagrammable' experiences are what drive Gen Z engagement. Some 33 per cent go to an offline store to test out a product and 42 per cent go to the offline store because of an intriguing event or exhibition.[22]

A good example of this new type of immersive experience that is forming a critical part of the future-ready shopping experience is the 'Wild Cinema' project in Shanghai **TX Huaihai.** Launched alongside the Shanghai-based contemporary art fair ART 021, the project features public artworks and installations from established local artists as well as international artists such as Anish Kapoor and Amalia Pica. According to TX Huaihai the experience drew over 11,000 visitors on its opening weekend. As well as engaging with the art and posting selfies, visitors also shopped the curated retail offers which included streetwear shops and many local independent fashion brands.

So, Beijing's SKP-S mixture of luxury and Shanghai's TX Huaihai futurism and youth culture spectacle both show the way forward in creating real cultural spectacle being delivered as part of a retail experience, which in turn develops unique curated experiences and offers that work in synergy with the programmed installations.

Generational responses

In both these cases Gen Z was more engaged and responded more meaningfully than Millennials. There is often a lazy tendency to refer to Millennials and Gen Zers as having similar behaviours. But in reality they have very different needs and characteristics. Of course, both groups are similar in that they lead highly digitally based lives, each having very distinctive expectations, needs, routines, habits and priorities. However, marketers will discover significant distinctions within each generation.

How they engage with luxury brands illustrates a very telling difference between the two groups. Gen Zers have made brands such as 'Supreme' very popular. For them luxury is about access, about being in the know and responding to the rarefied 'here today gone tomorrow' product 'drops' which represents new luxury for them.

Brands such as **Supreme** and cosmetics brand **Fenty** understand how to be part of the culture of their fans beyond just selling them stuff. Building a culture-driven community around the brand is a sure way of developing true loyalty where the customer does not just *buy* the brand but *joins* the brand and turns to those brands that play an important role in their day-to-day lives beyond the usual monologued communications.

In China Gen Zers are unique when compared to other countries. Chinese Gen Zers are the product of the single-child policy, growing up in households without siblings and enjoying the full attention and love of four 'parents', i.e. their real parents as well as grandparents. They have also been a part of China's highly accelerated and unique economic growth which has presented them with opportunities the likes of which have never been seen before in China. This has meant they have been raised in an environment that is unique; they have had a unique upbringing and lifestyle fuelled by a different approach to parenting and a more carefree lifestyle which has given them different values and beliefs from previous generations. They generally have an optimistic outlook and are very self-confident.

According to OC&C Strategy Consultants, 41 per cent of Chinese Gen Z respondents are optimistic about the future compared with only 26 per cent globally. 'This is a generation that has never known worry, so they spend more and save less,' says Adam Xu, a partner at OC&C. Adam Xu goes on to say that this generation is 'willing to take on debt in order to fund their purchases, and this partially explains why Generation Z is more likely to buy luxury brands than Millennials'. Although Gen Zers are very engaged with brands, they can also be promiscuous, and it can take time to build their trust. Therefore, brands must be transparent, honest and have true integrity.[23]

Circular commerce

Gen Zers like to engage with 'circular commerce' brands. These are brands that start off as a social network, generally established by influencers or celebrities. A circular commerce brand is built with the influencer or celebrity starting off by building an audience into a social network and trusted community where opinions, lifestyles and thoughts are shared openly.

The influencer or celebrity can then introduce a product line that is relevant to the community, and which has been developed from the insight gained from all the interactions with them. This data and insight is absolutely crucial in ensuring that the product and brand which evolves is developed and co-created with the community, so it is totally relevant to their needs, desires and lifestyles.

The products are then launched through the social media site, whereby it then becomes a 'social commerce' site. Once the products are launched and the network of followers purchase them and share their experiences with their networks, very valuable data and insight can be captured which will then inform the ongoing development of the product range.

The central tenet of circular commerce brands is that the products they produce and market are directly and continuously informed and co-created by their community, whereby their reviews, thoughts and opinions in sharing their experiences with the rest of their network is fed back into the development of the product range. Hence creating a circular commerce ecosystem to sell the product to the community via the social network.

Circular commerce brands have moved beyond being business-to-consumer (B2C) brands; they are developing into consumer-to-business (C2B) brands, whereby the consumer community is firstly established and the brand grows out of that. A great example of a circular commerce brand is the Fenty line of cosmetics and beauty products launched by the celebrity Rihanna.

OC&C Strategy Consultants found that that 25 per cent of Gen Z consumers say 'It is important to have a unique view on style and creativity.' Consequently, they suggest that retailers focus on personalized services and customized experiences and products. Bespoke experiences, made-to-order designs and limited-edition collections will attract the Gen Z consumer. This insight reveals the main reason why I think that 'circular commerce' brands will become commonplace and continue to flourish.[24]

FUTURE-READY NOTE

Pioneering brands are being created as consumer-to-business (C2B) brands.

Department stores

We are witnessing the death of department stores as we know them. As Doug Stephens memorably recounted in his book *Re-Engineering Retail*, 'The future of retail is the death of wholesale'.[25] The explosion of direct-to-consumer (D2C) brands are fuelling the demise of the department store. In order for department stores to survive they must shift from being a distribution channel for brands to becoming a host of the brand experience and brand storytellers.

Department stores must shift from being spaces with shelves, rails and tills to places designed to facilitate brand activations, stage sets where department stores can curate and host stories and events. Doug Stephens continues in his book *Re-Engineering Retail:*[26]

> Retailers will no longer be able to compete against marketplaces or their own brand partners' direct selling. At the same time brands will no longer be willing to depend on retailers to adequately uphold their brand perception, customer experience, expectations, price integrity and goals for market penetration. The result will be a bifurcation in the market that will lead to a completely new economic model between brands and retailers.

Although direct-to-consumer brands will continue to grow, customers will also still expect to be able to find stores that showcase multiple brands. Doug Stephens goes on to address the rise of the multi-brand store with the following words:

> This will give rise to an entirely new breed of experiential retailer that goes extremely deep within a category of goods and creates extraordinary experiences for consumers across a range of brands and products. Part media outlet, part sales agent, part design firm, experiential retailers will use their physical shopping spaces to perfect the consumer experience across a category or categories of products. They will define and design the ideal experiential journey and they will employ expert product ambassadors and technology to deliver something truly unique, remarkable and memorable. So memorable, in fact, that it leaves a lasting experiential imprint on the shopper.

As old, irrelevant department stores die we will see the emergence of a new breed of multi-brand, experientially driven department stores across the world. Doug Stevens described this brilliantly as

> ... rows of shelving will give way to brilliantly creative spatial designs and artful merchandising, allowing space for media and total interaction with products. Social media will be infused into the experience, offering at-the-shelf reviews, ratings and product comparisons... retailers that can design and execute these outstanding customer experiences will not be satisfied to eke out a meagre margin; instead, they will charge brands an upfront fee, or rate card, based on the volume of positive exposure

they bring to the brand and the products they represent in-store. And brands will willingly pay to have their products represented and their unique stories told in these remarkable physical retail media spaces of the future.

As the old department stores such as JC Penney and Neiman Marcus in the United States, Debenhams and House of Fraser in the UK all disappear, and as examples such as Globus and Jelmoli in Switzerland, John Lewis in the UK and Sears, Lord & Taylor and Macy's all face existential challenges, we are seeing a new breed of multi-brand store emerge. According to *Forbes*:

> From 2009 to 2019, US department store sales fell 26.7 per cent, from $186.6 billion to $135 billion, in a retail market that grew 49.2 per cent, excluding gas stations, automobiles and auto parts. And through the first five months of 2020, department stores are off another 21 per cent, while retail is down only 1.7 per cent.[27]

Back in 2011 JC Penney CEO Ron Johnson was very perceptive when he observed: 'Over the past 30 years, the department store has become a less relevant part of the retail infrastructure, largely because of decisions the stores have made... they didn't think about the future so much as try to protect the past.' He went on to explain that the problem with department stores was their 'lack of imagination – about the products they carry, their store environments, the way they engage customers, how they embrace the digital future. There's nothing wrong with the capability. There's a problem with the execution.'

One multi-brand store that is bucking this trend is Texas brand **Neighborhood Goods**. This is a department store with a difference and one that points the way to the future. *Forbes* goes on to describe Neighborhood Goods as a store that

> is based on fostering deep connections within its local community and being a place where brands can shine in an ever-changing rotation, so guests have something new to discover in each shopping trip. And each store is anchored by a locally-tailored restaurant and event space.

Neighborhood Goods also operates a very different business model to traditional department stores. Its business model does not deploy capital to buy large amounts of inventory for the store. Neighborhood Goods co-founder and CEO Matt Alexander explains in an interview to *Forbes* that 'Some brands pay us a fixed fee to be in the room and they make 100 per cent of what they sell. Others pay a lesser fixed fee and we take a percentage of sales, which is the more common route.'

He goes on to explain that

> Each [Neighborhood Goods] retail store has a story, and then all the products featured there have their own story, so that is where the role of curation comes in. We deploy a huge amount of technology to capture traffic demographics and behaviour so that we can understand how to best optimize and modify what is going on in the space.
>
> Because of its control of granular consumer data and with staff focused on retailing and consumer engagement experiences, not inventory management and control, Neighborhood Goods is an attractive home for digitally-native brands looking to cross over into physical retail...
>
> Physical retail can be a remarkable important channel for them (D2C brands) to efficiently and profitably acquire customers. Our role is to be a platform where these brands can find success and opportunity... We work to make sure that each brand is relevant and the right mix for each city or area. Our job is to establish a loyal, long-term relationship with the customers, as well as the brands we partner with... So we take care to tell those brand stories with true passion to make it a memorable experience for the customers.

Alexander concludes by pointing out that 'Traditional department stores, by virtue of their business model, have to be quite transactional.' Then he finally adds, 'Yes, we want to sell products. We engage with the customers by building close relationships in a very different and less transactional way.'

Other brands that represent the reinvention of the department store include Showfields in NYC and Goodhood in London. **Showfields** in particular is a very special type of retail experience. It puts theatre and spectacle front and centre of the customer experience.

Any brand that it partners must deliver a unique experience, not just a cookie-cutter roll-out of its normal high-street store. Showfields also attracts many D2C brands that are seeking physical space to tell their stories and showcase their products. Their aim is not so much to sell goods as to recruit and retain customers. On the same site, Showfields has also opened a free co-working space called The Loft and its adjacent rooftop garden, which it rents out for event space.

Showfields describes its store as 'the most interesting store in the world'. Co-founder and Chief Revenue Officer Katie Hunt explains to *Business Insider* that 'Retail is not dead, it just needs to evolve.' Hunt goes on to explain that

> Showfields sets itself apart by serving as a platform for lesser known e-commerce brands that might not have the resources to move into physical retail. The goal is to demonstrate the power of taking an online company offline, to both brands and shoppers.

Although the German retailer **Globetrotter** is not strictly a department store, as a multi-category outdoor adventure store it offers many lessons that legacy department stores can learn about customer experience and store design. Globetrotter was founded by Klaus Denart and Peter Lechhart in 1979. It is the largest independent outdoor retailer in Europe. To support its 12 store locations in Germany it publishes a quarterly magazine called *Globetrotter*, which has a circulation of 400,000.

In the store, every outdoor adventure is catered for and supported by very knowledgeable and passionate associates. Mountaineers can use the pressure chamber to test whether altitude has an effect on them. There is also a diving and canoeing pool. A cold chamber with a temperature that can drop to minus 28°C allows customers to test clothing and other equipment designed for the harshest environments. At Globetrotter customers can book appointments with personal sales consultants who are all well trained and well travelled. The stores also have a travel agency and a doctor's office for travellers, in which customers can get medical travel advice and vaccinations for travel.

Another specialist store that points the way forward for large format retail is the specialist toy store **Camp**. Although Camp is a toy store, its focus is not really on selling toys. The sale of toys is a by-product of a series of other-worldly experiences. Only around 20 per cent of the store is taken up by merchandise; the remaining 80 per cent is a stage set for curating and performing theatrical performances and events that both children and their parents can enjoy. The experiences are themed on a quarterly basis and more often than not are sponsored by brands.

As well as the conventional revenue from selling toys, Camp has a series of additional revenue streams. It sells clothing and gifts, and has a food and beverage offer. It also derives revenue from selling tickets for the themed events it puts on and from brands who agree to sponsor the events. Another unique aspect of the Camp store is the team of associates. At Camp you won't find normal sales associates; most of the staff are trained actors and performers and they play a critical role in writing, directing, stage managing and all the other aspects of putting on a show.

Although Camp sells many household-name toy brands and well-known toys, they are not front and centre. It is the store events and performances that bring the crowds in. They come to experience the performances and the events, and, very much like a museum or art gallery, they then purchase the products that are related to the event, which of course are also sponsored by the toy brands.

What Neighborhood Goods, Showfields, Globetrotter and Camp have in common is that they all see their store experiences not only as transactional, but as moments of experience where transaction is a by-product of the experience.

The power of voice

With greatly increased bandwidth and speed, 5G and 6G will usher in a new era of technology driven retail experience. Image recognition, predictive analytics, AI and voice will all become commonplace in retail.

Increasingly accurate predictive analytics can predict what consumers need without them having to place an order for the products. This is particularly prevalent in everyday goods that are regularly replenished such as washing powder, shampoo and many other grocery categories.

We will see a significant proportion of search migrate to voice platforms. As consumers search and then order products via voice platforms such as Amazon's Alexa and Google's Duplex, the voice platform becomes the gatekeeper to the brand, the conduit through which the engagement between the consumer and the brand is controlled. This has ushered in the era of 'V-commerce'. And critically the data that is generated through V-commerce and the customer engagement and preferences belongs to the voice platform.

And of course, as those preferences become predictable, then automatic replenishment is the natural next step. The challenge for brands will be how to interrupt the automatic replenishment process if they want to sell a new variation of the product or a completely new one. The answer of course is to buy voice media space in order to engage the consumer via the same voice platform.

According to the Brand Minds website and the Google 2019 Voice Search report, V-commerce is the next stage of e-commerce, designed to include voice shopping. It minimizes friction, elevates ease and convenience to a new level in which there will be no going back. Why waste time by standing in line to order your custom coffee when you could tell Alexa to have it ready for in-store pick-up?[28]

According to the same report and website:

- eMarketer stated that by the end of 2021 the number of US voice assistant users will reach 122.7 million, representing 42.2 per cent of US internet users and 36.6 per cent of the US population.[29]

- Google reports that
  - 62 per cent of those who regularly use a voice-activated speaker say they are likely to buy something through their voice-activated speaker in the next month[30]

- of those who regularly use a voice-activated speaker 4 per cent say they order products they need like groceries, household items, etc, at least once a week

- of parents who own voice-activated speakers 72 per cent said they are likely to use them to buy something in the next month, compared to 51 per cent of non-parents

- 66 per cent of owners use voice-activated speakers weekly, while 70 per cent believe that the digital assistants will not only help them shop but understand their preferences and make routine purchases on their behalf within five years

There is no doubt that V-commerce will fundamentally redefine shopping and the store experience. It will make shopping easier, quicker and more convenient. It will also allow brands and retailers to develop even more personalized experiences and build relevance and more sustainable loyalty. The opportunity for retailers in embracing digital assistants is not just as a means of selling more products but as a way to ensure customers can access a trusted source of information and service, and in doing this they have the opportunity to develop deeper emotional connections with their customers.

Brands are increasingly developing 'voice skills' to engage customers via voice platforms. 'Skills' in this context are like apps for V-commerce. Amazon has developed over 100,000 skills for the **Alexa** device. Two of my favourites are 'Alexa Guard' and 'Send a Hug'. Alexa Guard turns smart speakers into security devices. They detect sounds such as glass breaking or a smoke alarm going off. The Alexa app will then notify the user when it hears anything suspicious, which is particularly beneficial if the user is out of the house. The 'Send a Hug' skill lets the user's friends and family know that they are thinking of them by sending a digital 'hug' via Alexa. With the voice command of 'Alexa, send a hug', a virtual hug will be delivered to any of the user's Alexa contacts.

Brands are also developing skills for voice platforms that can be used by customers either in their homes or via a smart speaker located in the store. For example, customers of Starbucks can use an Alexa skill to reorder their usual cup of coffee from one of the last 10 stores they've ordered from. **Domino's Pizza** has developed a skill whereby customers can build a new pizza order from scratch or place a repeat order or check an order's status.

Levi's the denim brand allows shoppers to use voice platforms to get help on return policy, how to use gift cards, searching for a pair of jeans or finding their nearest store. They can also track orders and get information on the latest promotions. With this Alexa skill, users get answers to common questions about the jeans manufacturer's services.

The Scotch whisky brand **Johnnie Walker** has developed Alexa skills to allow customers to choose the right whisky by guiding them through a series of questions about flavour preference and price. However, if they simply want to buy a bottle of Johnnie Walker whisky, they say 'buy a bottle' and Alexa will help them find the nearest store or delivery option. However, if the customer chooses the 'Try a Guided Tasting' voice option, Alexa will conduct a personalized tasting session based on which Johnnie Walker label they select (e.g. Red, Black, Gold, Blue, etc). The session will guide them through a process of sniffing the whisky aromas followed by tastings through sipping the whisky. As they progress through the process, Alexa will give helpful tips and ways to serve.

INDUSTRY EXPERT
Elisa Cecilli

I worked with Elisa Cecilli for several years as a colleague, and we completed many exciting projects together. Elisa has unique antennae that can detect key consumer and cultural trends and unearth relevant insights to show the way forward for brands and places. In this piece she explores future priorities for consumers and retail.

The healing power of retail in our post-Covid lives

2020 and 2021 revealed an unbearable truth: when everything that makes us human is abruptly taken from us, the only thing we are left with is the internet. Locked in our flats and houses with most of the places we love closed until further notice, we cherished every single interaction that happened in real life. Our walks to the local supermarkets became glimpses of freedom and screens of all sizes became our windows on the world.

Forced to redesign our lives and social norms around new restrictions and collective fears, we started challenging the notions of all the physical environments we inhabit. Why would we still need offices when work can happen at any time, anywhere and with no need for formal clothes? And why should we still go to a shop when everything can be conveniently delivered when and where we need it?

The next decade of research and development of new urban models, regeneration strategies and retail business models will offer us a fresh perspective to redefine the role of the city itself in a remote-working and online shopping world. Paris Mayor Anne Hidalgo announced the French capital will become the world's first 15-minute city, while a self-organized group of 500,000 Berlin inhabitants committed to create the world's largest car-free zone in a city. In the meantime, through smaller-scale initiatives, forward-thinking brands, retailers and estate developers are paving the way to a new modus operandi that helps us imagine the shop of the future.

The shop of the future is about people

Recent estate developments and co-housing initiatives promise to shape a new generation of neighbourhoods where the local community comes first, and houses and buildings cater for residents' needs and empowers people to do things communally instead of alone. Founded in 2021, US-based residential housing company **Mily** aims at targeting city-dwelling young families by providing family-oriented design features, kid-friendly spaces and on-site childcare solutions, and provides residents a sense of belonging to a community of like-minded parents who can support each other. In the UK, award-winning Cambridge-based co-housing community **Marmalade Lane** asks all residents to have a stake in the common parts and contribute to the management of the community. As well as 42 private homes, Marmalade Lane offers access to the Common House: a place for residents of all ages to socialize, host guests and eat together. It includes a large kitchen, lounge with wood-burning stove, laundry facilities, children's play room, a small gym, a workshop that provides a place for hobbies and a small internal shop. The ambition of the project is to create a safe community where neighbours know they can trust and will support each other.

As an already well-established pre-global lockdown trend, brands and retailers are tapping into people's interests and values to create community hubs. Recent years taught us that communities need much more than that: they need safe places where they can get together with others to find support when dealing with their daily struggles, and bigger societal and environmental changes that are pushing them to redesign their lives. All of this, while having a laugh. Hint: Run your shop as you would run a street party.

The shop of the future is part of collective rituals

In 2020 the pandemic fuelled rapid acceleration of online buying, which following a 25.7 per cent surge in 2020, rose to $4.213 trillion.[31] A study by eMarketer expects retail e-commerce sales worldwide to climb a further 16.8 per cent in 2021, to $4.921 trillion.[32] Even the most sceptical consumers have been persuaded by the convenience of doorstep deliveries and the opportunities to hunt for better prices. In this landscape, there is something missing though: the little pleasures about going out for shopping, which are all about human interactions. Before the mass adoption of the internet and the ubiquity of smartphones, going out shopping was a satisfying ritual. Something we did to catch up with friends and family, get personalized recommendations from people we trust, and experience the satisfaction of discovering something new. E-commerce doesn't offer any of this as it removes the rituals of shopping from the equation. It's not about interactions. It's about products.

Online brands are becoming increasingly aware of this and are experimenting with new ways of replicating the dynamics behind human interactions that happen in real life. During the pandemic Netflix launched Netflix Party (now renamed as **Teleparty**), a browser extension for watching TV remotely with friends and family members. It synchronizes video playback and adds group chat to Netflix, Disney, Hulu and HBO with the ambition of bringing back the joy of sharing the same room with a special someone and watching a favourite TV series together.

Indian online matchmaking and matrimonial platform Shaadi partnered with Leo Burnett India to launch the **Weddings from Home** initiative that aims to help people get married during the pandemic. In order to recreate one of the most meaningful moments of such an important in-person event, they delivered the wedding menu to guests' homes so that they could all feel part of the same ritual and enjoy the banquet together instead of simply watching the ceremony via Zoom.

Serendipitous discoveries, opportunities for real, human conversations and the excitement to go out with the people you love are all already embedded in the essence of a physical shop. Retailers need to re-establish their role in the local community as places of joy: the joy of exchanging, learning from others and taking part in ritual collectives, and most importantly the joy of feeling human. Hint: Run your shop as you would run a family dinner.

The shop of the future belongs to the community

The warning of the proverb 'What goes around comes around' has never been more relevant. Over recent years consumers have been increasingly aware that governments are not committed enough to meet the Paris Agreement's basic standards. The National Oceanic and Atmospheric Administration announced that July 2021 was the hottest month since record-keeping began 142 years ago.[33] According to a recent report by the United Nations, if countries want to limit warming to any level that is manageable, they have to just cut back the greenhouse gas emissions very deeply and immediately.[34] Global advertising company Wunderman Thompson found out that 85 per cent of people are prepared to rethink the way they live and spend to tackle climate change, and demand that global and small companies adopt a different approach to the production of goods and services.[35] To tackle this unprecedented challenge, brands and retailers have to adapt, adopt a 360-degree strategy that rethinks the way their goods are produced, sold and discarded, and ultimately work closely with local communities to create virtuous cycles of sustainable consumption.

In 2019 French preowned luxury clothes marketplace **Vestiaire Collective** launched a 'Circularity in Fashion' consumer guide to make it easy for consumers to understand how the circular economy works by identifying seven key requirements for a fashion brand to claim to be circular: on-demand and custom-made; green and clean; high quality and timeless design; fair and ethical; repair, redesign and upcycle; rent, lease and swap; second-hand and vintage.[36] Launched in New York by second-hand fashion platform thredUP and denim brand Madewell, **A Circular Store** offers a full wardrobe of preloved clothing and features mending stations, repair services and upcycling workshops. Through QR codes shoppers access information on how to best care for their products: from washing instructions to how to properly recycle the item at its end-of-life. Swedish fashion giant H&M acquired a majority stake in second-hand platform **Sellpy** that helps customers embrace more sustainable shopping habits by sending their worn clothes to Sellpy for free in a special bag. When a garment is sold, the customer receives a percentage of the proceeds, with a minimum of 40 per cent. Items that do not find a buyer are recycled or donated to charity.

These are very small initiatives that show how retailers can enable consumers to adopt a more sustainable way of living. Over the next decade companies are going to be held accountable for their impact on local communities, and 'not harming the planet' will no longer be enough. There's a need to rethink the way they do business by assuming their responsibility: from the very early stage of product development, through the design of the distribution chains, to how waste and unsold products are reused. Brands and retailers have to own their role in enhancing new, sustainable shopping habits and creating a better future for the generations to come. Hint: Run your shop as you would run a council.

Digital in the physical place

I refer to the digital domain in the physical space as the 'parallel experience', the overlaying of digital information on the real world. Recent research from Barclays showed that consumers are more likely to visit experiences featuring virtual reality (57 per cent) and augmented reality (52 per cent). According to *Forbes*, the global market for VR and AR in retail will reach $1.6 billion by 2025.[37]

When we overlay digital content on the physical world, the world around us becomes our web and the mobile device our cursor. As Sánchez-Crespo from Novarama observed, 'By making the real world a playground for the virtual world, we can make the real world much more interesting.' Retailers have the opportunity to magnify the customer experience using augmented reality (AR). They can overlay a depth of digital information that would be very cumbersome to create physically and also confusing to the customer.

Overlaying digital information on a real-world product or environment can enrich the customer experience, whether through richer product information or interaction, the ability to personalize a product or via deeper and more immersive brand storytelling. It can be very timely and convenient as the information can be personalized to respond to a specific customer and their location. More specifically the customer's location can be used with AR to help the customer navigate the store. Daniel Beauchamp, head of VR at Shopify said,

'When we think about AR shopping, it's not just about seeing what something looks like in your space and seeing the size of it. It's also about seeing the materials and the details of that product.'

Virtual reality can transport customers into a deeply immersive experience and allow retailers to deliver an 'other-worldly' experience. Retailers can also use VR to research scenarios, experiences and environments without the big investment required to create the same thing physically. VR can be used to create virtual tours of stores or shopping centres. This can be delivered *in situ* or at the location of the customer's choosing. Customers can view and get information on any product as though they are in the store.

Virtual reality can also be used to train associates. During training they can be immersed into a very realistic environment where they could be taken through service rituals where mistakes can be made in a virtual world to limit the risk of making them in the real world with real customers. With the latest VR technology, training can take place in simulated real-life situations. Although VR and AR can be used in many sectors of retail, the home, fashion and beauty sectors have been the pioneers.

HOME, FASHION AND BEAUTY

When customers are shopping for their home they can use AR to visualize a piece of furniture or a specific paint colour in the context of a room in their home. This will give them an accurate idea of the design but also the size and proportions. The furniture retailer **Made.com** has gone one step further. It has created a shoppable interactive virtual reality experience to showcase its range of products. Customers can view the products in the showroom while wearing a VR headset. However, the showroom takes the form of a virtual apartment and allows customers to move around the apartment and click on items that they like and wish to explore further. They also have the option of accessing further information on each product and also about the designer's approach and their inspirations. Whether it is accessed via a laptop or VR headset, Made.com's virtual showroom has given the brand access to customers throughout the globe.

In the beauty category AR plays a big part in helping customers try on cosmetics and other products before they commit to buy. Unlike trying real products, AR gives the customer so much more choice and convenience. And although the retailer would prefer a customer to be trying products in store, with AR technology there is no reason why the customer cannot do this from their home.

Following in the footsteps of their book and grocery stores, Amazon now have their eyes set on the beauty sector. **Amazon Salon** is a new type of beauty salon. Configured over two floors in London's Spitalfields, Amazon Salon uses AR technology to deliver hair consultations. Customers are also able to see how different hair colours would look as they are overlaid on their real hair on the AR tablet screen. Just as in any normal hair salon the Amazon seller has a range of beauty products for sale. The difference here is that a customer can point at a product which would then appear on a tablet screen that is fixed to the shelving and will give vast amounts of information about the product the customer selected. The screen can display the range of sizes in that product and also show brand videos. If the customer likes the product they merely scan the QR code on the shelf which takes them to the Amazon website where they can purchase and get delivery direct to their home. As well as the AR product experience, Amazon Salon offers the normal range of hairdressing services for both adults and children.

In the fashion sector augmented and virtual reality have really taken hold – from virtual catwalk shows and videos depicting the designers explaining the inspirations to AR smart mirrors in changing rooms. A good example of the latest use of the technology is **Machine-A**, a concept fashion store that uses augmented reality to create a life-like store environment. The brand has created a series of QR codes planted in different locations, e.g. embedded in fly posters and billboards throughout London. After a customer scans one of the QR codes, a digital representation of the store appears on their screen, and allows them to explore the latest collections. They can also access personal messages from specific designers who also explain their influences and inspirations in creating the collections.

According to Deloitte's *Augmented Shopping* report, by the end of 2021, 100 million consumers are expected to shop using AR either online or in-store.[38] The report goes on to describe what happened when a national furniture chain launched their first AR app that allowed customers to see how a piece of furniture would fit in their home and then place orders without having to visit a physical store. Customers collectively used the AR experience 1,000 times per day on average, achieving conversion rates between 65 and 69 per cent within the app. Reportedly, as a result the company saw a double-digit increase in online sales. The Deloitte report further notes that beauty brand L'Oréal's AR make-up experiences have doubled website engagement time and tripled conversion rates, and goes on to suggest that Sephora's Virtual Artist app saw 200 million shades tried on during more than 8.5 million visits to the AR feature.

The universal uptake of 5G connectivity and the more convenient access to QR codes will make the technology a key part of everyday life. Again according to the Deloitte report, 71 per cent of people stated that they would shop more often as a result of AR tools. Augmented reality has the ability to immerse customers much deeper into a brand, its products and the lifestyle it represents, and can provide deeper engagement and personalization halo.

The key for retailers is to ensure that a customer can progress from an AR experience directly to the brand's e-commerce website where they can purchase products. AR is also valuable in helping retailers capture data on customer preferences which can be fed back to allow them to create even more relevant and compelling AR experiences.

The beauty, fashion and footwear category is making use of AR technology to bring the process of trying on clothes and shoes into customers' homes. This provides the customer with a vast amount of choice – and of course they don't have to go through the laborious task of changing into different clothes in conventional, cramped changing rooms.

In future AR and VR will become even more commonplace. With the continued development of AR headsets the experience will be even more realistic, and will play a crucial role in changing the experience of place.

GAMIFICATION

Gamification is another development that is rapidly changing the physical experience and the essence of place. Brands and retailers can use gamification to immerse customers and engage them on a whole new level. This can lead to increased loyalty and sales. Gamification is a way of encouraging customers to engage in competition and strive for completion and reward; this is a response to our natural instincts to win. The goal of gamification is to turn customers into players by providing gamified experiences that they are willing to participate in, be competitive and enjoy. As well as engaging customers, gamification can drastically increase dwell time and customer retention. It allows retailers and brands to gather data and through positive experiences can provide rewards that improve loyalty and brand sentiment.

It is thought that the average advert viewing time can be as low as 1.5 seconds, and only 20 per cent of ads are viewed for more than two seconds. Conventional in-store advertising tries to interrupt customers when they are busy or have least time to spare. However, gamified experiences can grab their attention with invitations to participate in play.

Gamification can also present challenges if not done correctly. It can feel superficial if not aligned with the brand. If the rewards are insufficient it can make customers feel that they have been interrupted for no reason. And of course if the games are not well received it could have a detrimental effect on the customers perception of the brand. Ksabaka, who produce gaming experiences for brands and retailers, developed a gamification experience for the chocolate brand **Milka**. Shoppers were invited to join hands and interlock fingers to create a Milka chocolate bar which was referred to as a 'special moment of tenderness'. Consumers were then encouraged to take a photo of their interlocking hands to share it on social media channels. They then had a chance to win a visit to the home of Milka, the Swiss Alps.

Another example from Ksabaka was their work with **Barilla**, the Italian pasta brand. In this case the aim of the gamification initiative was to bring the brand to life in an interactive, fun and engaging way, to demonstrate the versatility of Barilla pasta and to encourage in-store sales. Shoppers were encouraged to explore different types of pasta and sauces. Using a revolving wheel they could design their own recipe based on their pasta/sauce preference. The recipe could then be sent to the consumer's mobile device via SMS. If customers went on to purchase a Barilla product within the store they were entered into a draw to win spa vouchers.

INDUSTRY EXPERT
Narain Jashanmal

I have known Narain Jashanmal for many years as a dear friend and a client. Below he explores the convergence of physical and digital experiences in-store. Narain is eminently qualified in this arena as he has been a retailer and wholesaler and has worked closely with many retailers and brands.

More than any other technological advance of the past 30 years, smartphones, coupled with ubiquitous connectivity, have changed how, when and where people shop and what they buy. A recent analysis by Gartner forecasts that by 2022 the installed base of smartphones will be close to 4.5 billion units, over three times larger than desktop and laptop computers at their combined peak.[39]

Smartphones are always-on location-aware pocket computers with cameras. They place a digital layer on the physical world, which brought some of the behaviour that people had learnt on desktop computing. Much of what happened next was new and at a scale never seen before, which required new ways of organizing and presenting information. For businesses, this offered as many challenges as it did opportunities. It gave people new ways to discover and explore the world and connect with each other and businesses.

The organizing mechanism of the desktop internet was Search, which had a profound impact on marketing and advertising. The process by which brands communicated about themselves and their products to consumers was upended.

The same was true of how and where people discovered those brands and products. Before Search, mass-market advertising was broadcast-driven: companies paid agencies to book one-way media on television, radio, billboards and newspapers to reach millions of people with the same message and build national, even global, brands.[40] There was a symbiotic relationship between advertisers and media – the name 'soap opera' was coined because soap manufacturers were their initial sponsors. Department stores dominated first at regional, then at national level, in no small part due to their use of newspapers to communicate product availability and prices to people. Previously, haggling was the norm.

People had limited means to communicate with businesses and no way beyond word-of-mouth to seek out information about a business's reputation, a brand's quality or a product's price. In countries with a royal family, a warrant from the king or queen offered a seal of approval, but this was by definition for a limited number of producers.[41]

Search empowered people to make informed buying decisions. It was a crucial part of the foundation that gave rise to e-commerce as well as an ecosystem of price comparison and review services. It exposed metadata that businesses used to share product details with each other, which became the basis for product-detail pages on shopping websites. As shoppers became more demanding and their searches more specific, new functionality such as real-time, postcode-level inventory availability became necessary, which facilitated omnichannel shopping by giving retailers the capability to list the same inventory on- and offline and giving shoppers the ability to shop between and across channels.

A new form of advertising was born with little resemblance to the glossy, lifestyle-driven brand messaging that had preceded it. In the United States, the centre of power of the industry shifted from Madison Avenue to Silicon Valley. Search engine marketing (SEM) matched demand with supply in ways that had not previously been possible. It took the express intent within people's search queries and, through an algorithmically mediated auction, matched it precisely with a finite subset of options from the thousands of available ones. Taking dozens of data points into account: location, time of day, your search and web browsing history, your affinity with other people in the same cohort as you and what advertisers thought made you an exciting prospect for them – all intending to make the advertising as relevant as possible.

While Search remains a vital way of navigating information on smartphones, it is not as dominant as it was on desktop. For one, mobile is more visual. Due to the small screens of smartphones, photos, and increasingly video, supplanted text as the medium of choice. Search itself has evolved with voice and images becoming inputs for queries, enabling applications such as visual search on mobile. This latter point has obvious relevance to shopping as it gives people the ability to take a photo of a product and find out not just what it is, or who made it, but where to buy from and at what price.

As people's time spent online, on phones, shifted from the web to apps, it opened up new capabilities to app developers. Gaining permission to access the contacts on a person's phone to understand and match people with other people they already know is also using that developer's app. This was termed the 'social graph', a digital map reflecting the network of real-world relationships, the strengths of connection between people and their affinity with each other. When the social graph was combined with another permission that developers could ask people for – their location – a new wave of businesses in the local, peer-to-peer and on-demand space was born. In a loose sense, the early players represent a turbo-charged version of classifieds that took advantage of smartphone cameras to make it easy for people to create listings and location awareness to match buyers and sellers based on proximity. Subsequent businesses more radically reinvented their industries by using the scale of smartphones to create highly liquid marketplaces for everything from chauffeur-driven cars to vacation homes to fine-dining delivered to the home in the way that only fast food used to be.

Embedded within almost all of these services is the ability for the parties involved in the transaction to message each other. This mirrors the rise of messaging apps more broadly – messaging apps have long displaced SMS by a substantial margin. Part of the fabric of people's everyday communication, they also play a significant role in shopping. Whether the simple act of sending a friend a picture of something you've discovered to get their opinion on it or connecting with customer service at a business to initiate a product return, messaging has become central to people's online experience and a bridge between the online and offline worlds. The most recent generation of fast-growing social media apps combines multiple previous trends – status updates, messaging and video – into a single new format.[42]

Online video has very little to do with formats that preceded it, such as cinema or television. The vast majority of it is created by amateurs – termed 'user-generated content' (UGC). For the platforms that host and distribute this content, it represents an infinite source of zero marginal cost media that entertains and informs similar groups of people to those who create it. This has given rise to new subcategories of content that blend entertainment and commerce, such as beauty tutorials, product reviews and unboxing videos.

The people, known as creators, who are particularly adept at producing engaging videos become brands unto themselves, in some cases with subscriber bases or followings larger than that of businesses. Many try to use their celebrity to launch their own product lines. People seek them out for their taste, style and opinion as a source of inspiration, validation, or simply discovering what's new and cool.

Another industry that has grown significantly on mobile is gaming, in which entertainment and commerce once again intersect. Many more people play games on smartphones than on consoles or gaming PCs, and games are the predominant revenue driver among mobile apps. The evolution of the distribution model, from physical cartridges and discs to apps delivered wirelessly via app stores, also brought about a new business model: in-app payments. This gives people the ability to subscribe to remove ads, skip to the next level, or novel options such as digital ornamentation and in-game currency. The latter two are interesting because they are effectively a shadow economy: virtual goods paid for with real money, some of which can be traded within games or even arbitraged and sold to other users.

The concept of a Metaverse, a virtual world that reflects and represents the real world but with its own rules and identity, is not a new one – it's been a staple of science fiction for a long time – but rather one that has re-entered the vernacular recently. What has defined these worlds in their current form is that they're siloed experiences, disconnected from each other. There is a growing movement around 'What comes next?'

One defining metaphor for online shopping is the 'infinite shelf' or perhaps one shelf that's infinitely long. This has led some businesses to try out how to reintroduce scarcity – a characteristic of offline shopping – on one or more dimensions. Product drops, live video shopping and limited editions only available for a brief window of time are examples of this. These are all burgeoning online and prompt questions about the future role of physical stores.

Convenience is often cited as an example of an advantage that retail has over e-commerce – that people can visit shops and buy something more quickly and efficiently than they can online. However, on-demand delivery services have been notable beneficiaries of a Covid-19 dividend. In a broad sense, the pandemic accelerated prevailing trends, to the detriment of some and a boon to others. As of now, it is unclear which newly developed behaviours will stick and which will fade.

Given the narrative outlined above, it is safe to bet that smartphones – and whatever comes after them – will continue to reshape how people shop while increasingly blurring the line between the physical world and the digital one.

In this chapter I have explored in depth the various ways retailers and brands can create compelling experiences to engage their customers in-store.

Now I'm going to explore the idea of the place experience on a larger scale in terms of our high streets and town centres.

The wider place experience

For decades now we have seen the growth of what the real-estate industry refers to as 'mixed-use' developments. This is where a development is made up of a series of buildings each with a different use, for example residential, workplace, education, healthcare, hospitality, manufacturing, etc. Mixed-use developments would generally have a mix of retail, food and leisure at the ground level. In planning and designing mixed-use developments many developers do not consider carefully enough the connectivity between each of the buildings and so often we end up with a series of siloed buildings that are disconnected to each other. The connection and synergy to the ground-level commercial offers are also often ill considered.

We must rethink old, siloed, disconnected mixed-use developments that make up much of our town centres and reimagine them using a connected 'blended-use' approach.

Blended-use strategies: hospitality and workplace

For our town centres to be sustainable and to thrive commercially, environmentally, socially and culturally, we must implement blended-use strategies. A blended-use approach identifies the potential 'blending components' within each typical use typology. Use typologies may include hospitality, workplace, health and wellness, education, residential and manufacturing.

For example, the blending component or 'blending agent' within the hospitality use typology could be a hotel lobby that is activated with a range of offers and experiences including food and places to meet and work. In a blended approach the hotel lobby would be permeable, inclusive and connected to the surrounding community. Critically, the hotel offers experiences that would connect to the surrounding streetscape and retail, food, entertainment, leisure and culture in the vicinity, forming a critical component of the public realm activation.

For workplace, the blending agent would be a co-working facility. From a real-estate perspective, co-working should be treated differently to conventional workplace. For too long the real-estate industry has seen co-working as just another form of workplace that can be treated like conventional offices.

However, co-working is different. It is a response to a new, nomadic 'dip-in-dip-out' culture of work which has been driven by digital nomads and is now influencing all working generations. Digital nomads lead an 'always-on' way of life whereby they are constantly connected and see work as one part of their daily routine that involves flipping between work, leisure, wellness, culture and hospitality.

In a post-pandemic world where it is now acceptable and even encouraged to work remotely, the 18-month Covid-19-driven compulsory experiment of working from home has made many realize that work need not be associated with one specific place called an office or studio.

Covid-19 has also accelerated the fragmentation of workplace and is beginning to mirror what has been happening to retail. What I mean by this is that functional, transactional retail is gradually migrating online, and of course this has also been accelerated by Covid-19. And as a result physical stores will be increasingly used for brand culture and the gathering of like-minded people, storytelling, social, participatory experiences, learning and entertainment.

Similarly, functional work is migrating to 'working from home' (WFH) or 'working near home' (WNH), and we are seeing a wide range of alternative places where people will undertake work, the most common of which are co-working facilities. We are also seeing hotels adapting their lobbies to accommodate workers more effectively. Coffee shops are moving beyond 'a table with a power socket' to fully-fledged work facilities blended with a public-facing coffee shop, sometimes referred to as the 'coffice'. With more functional work taking place remotely, the office will become a place for brand culture (of the employer brand), collaboration, idea sharing, learning, social and participatory activities.

I write this at the beginning of the lifting of Covid restrictions in the UK. Many people will not be returning to work in offices or indeed working at home. Some will elect to embrace a more nomadic lifestyle and work 'on the move'.

DIGITAL NOMADS

This idea of a nomadic day-to-day life is spreading well beyond the stereotypical backpacker travelling the world on her or his gap year. Globally, we are seeing the rise of a new and growing group of remote workers who have elected to live their lives travelling while working full-time. Of course, reliable and fast digital connectivity is allowing this phenomenon to take shape. And Covid-19 has not merely accelerated this but has spread it at warp speed, and in the process is blurring leisure travel and the world of work.

Digital nomads who work on the move elect to live various types of lifestyle. Some travel for long periods, during which they cross countries and continents. Others travel for shorter periods on 'work-cations'. These take the form of working sabbaticals lasting up to several months. Some digital nomads travel internationally while others remain in their country of residence or stick to one country, never crossing its border. One thing all digital nomads have in common is a love of travel and new adventures, and they embrace the idea of working anywhere, as long as they can get internet connection.

Airbnb, the short-term accommodation provider, found in a recent survey that stay durations are increasing and that nearly a quarter of its stays were longer than 28 days in the first three months of 2021.[43] It also found that travel is happening to a much wider range of places and accommodation types. Airbnb CEO Brian Chesky said, 'The lines between travel, living and working are blurring... and Airbnb hopes to make it easier for people to move around the world in whatever way they want.'[44]

Where once Airbnb positioned itself as an alternative to traditional, inflexible hotels, it is now evolving into an accommodation platform that offers an alternative to its customers' permanent homes. In this instance Airbnb's customers move between accommodations where they may spend months in each.

Furthermore, as an alternative to Airbnb-type 'accommodation hopping', digital nomads are also electing to live and work from a wide range of places such as beach huts, tree houses, shepherds huts and even converted vans.

Type 'van life' into Instagram and you'll see millions of people following a plethora of sites dedicated to people travelling, living and working from vans converted into mobile micro-homes. These are who choose to embrace a location-independent, technology-enabled lifestyle that allows them to travel and work remotely, anywhere with an internet connection. Some are selling their permanent homes, and free of mortgages, bills and the commitments of owning and running a permanent home, are choosing to buy and convert a van and take to the road. Of course permanently working remotely and on the move does not suit every type of work. Invariably it is tech, creative or remote tele-service type jobs that suit the lifestyle.

A study by MBO Partners showed that the digital-nomad population in the United States increased from 7.3 million to 10.9 million between 2019 and 2020.[45] Since Covid-19 has hit it has become far more acceptable for firms to allow their workers to work remotely and on the move.

Of course remote working isn't for everyone. Many people enjoy the stability, convenience and familiarity of a single place of work. They like the community of colleagues, the predictability and routine. Those who work remotely don't have the same support structures, colleague collaboration, sharing of ideas or the social and cultural life of the workplace.

More broadly speaking, digital nomadism can be inequitable. Many people do not have the choice of nomadic working. This may be due to the type of work they do, or to a lack of opportunity to take the risk of irregular and unpredictable remuneration of 'gig economy' nomadic working. They may have debts and commitments that need a regular income.

If you live in a big metropolitan city, the cost of living is often very high. Rents and the cost of food and energy in cities like London and New York are very prohibitive. Many people in those and similar cities who are not prepared to go totally nomadic are opting to relocate to the outskirts of cities or further afield to find more cost-effective accommodation, but with the consequence of increasing the cost of commuting. An additional motivation for moving outside cities is that Covid-19 has made many people prioritize health and wellness. And so moving to more rural or suburban locations generally gives people more space and a greener environment. And with the opportunity to work from home for part of the week, the cost, time and hassle of commuting is not such an influencing factor.

People who are able and willing to embark on a digital nomadic lifestyle often seem to be privileged or lacking the commitments that would tie many people down. According to the MBO Partners research, Covid-19 has impacted the demographic mix of digital nomads.[46] The percentage of digital nomads represented by baby boomers fell from 27 per cent in 2019 to just 17 per cent in 2020. The Gen X share fell from 25 to 22 per cent in the same period. However, the younger Gen Z and Millennials increased their share from 48 to 62 per cent. This phenomenon was partly due to the fact that the older generation were more susceptible to Covid-19 infection and so were more reluctant to travel.

The MBO Partners research goes on to explain that digital nomads work in a wide variety of fields. IT represents 12 per cent, education 11 per cent, consulting, coaching and research 11 per cent, sales, marketing and PR 9 per cent, and creative services 8 per cent. Looking at these different professions it is obvious that the type of work involved lends itself to remote working, on the condition of course that there is easy and fast internet connectivity available. The research goes on to point out that

- more men pursue digital nomadism than women with a 59:41 split
- 81 per cent of digital nomads report being highly satisfied with their work and lifestyle
- 34 per cent planned to be nomadic for less than one year
- just over 53 per cent report that they plan to continue as digital nomads for at least the next two years.

The research also reveals, very significantly, that 'nearly half of traditional (fixed) workers report that they plan to be nomadic for less than one year. This group believe at some point over the next year they will be asked to return to the office at least part-time.'[47]

There seems to be an element of inequality developing in remote working. And this is another aspect of life that Covid-19 has magnified and accelerated. Most digital nomads are white and mostly from professional backgrounds and from Western societies. Research by the Economic Policy Institute suggests that in the United States one in four white workers are able to work from home, compared to one in five black workers and one in six Hispanic workers. The same piece of research found that one in three workers with a degree were able to work from home during the pandemic, compared to about one in 20 workers with only a secondary school education.[48]

Another piece of research from McKinsey revealed that

In the US workforce... just 22 per cent of employees can work remotely between three and five days a week without affecting productivity...
In contrast, 61 per cent of the workforce in the United States can work no more than a few hours a week remotely or not at all. The remaining 17 per cent of the workforce could work remotely partially, between one and three days per week.[49]

Remote working is obviously less suited to people who work in the services sectors such as hairdressing, social care or in the manual labour areas of work such as manufacturing or logistics. More often than not it is the well-educated, office-based workers that are able to work remotely.

HYBRID, CO-WORKING ENVIRONMENTS

I am in no doubt that the nature of work and the workplace will change for the long term. It seems to me that we will not continue working exclusively remotely or indeed exclusively in a fixed place of work. The future of work is going to be hybrid. Generally, people will increasingly work partly from home or near home and partly in an office. As hybrid work becomes more common, we will see the cost and hassle of daily commuting become less of an issue, and so more people will relocate and work further away from their office if they only need to be there once or twice a week.

For a 'blended-use' approach to developments, co-working is critical as it aligns well with retail and F&B to help activate the public realm, which can give life to our town centres and respond to a new way of working and living.

Co-working environments can take many forms, from the conventional office-type spaces to less conventional spaces that are often appropriated as workplace. These can include small lounges, public terraces, hotel lobbies and coffee shops.

A 'blended-use' approach to shopping centres, high streets and town centres will be critical to ensure 'future readiness'. They will have to kick the addiction to transactional retail and shift from a *shopping rhythm to a community rhythm* and create 'blended' places, bringing together workplace, healthcare, education, residential, makerspaces, community amenities, and blending these with retail, F&B, leisure and entertainment to animate our public realm and blur the lines between tenanted space and public space.

I have explored the 'blending agents' within the hospitality and workplace use typologies. When considering the broader development and urban regeneration context and in reimagining the tired, disconnected and siloed approach of mixed-use, we can also now consider the blending agents of other uses.

Other blended-use strategies

EDUCATION

Let's consider the education component of a future blended approach to developments and urban regeneration. The blending agent of the education component could be a series of facilities that are shared with communities such as sports facilities, adult education facilities, event and performance space. In a blended-use development these components of a school or higher education building would allow community access in the evenings and weekends, making the education building more sustainable socially, culturally and economically. They would also bring life to the public spaces and contribute to the night-time and weekend economy.

A very different and interesting example of an education building forming part of the public realm is the Central St Martins College of Art building in London's Kings Cross. Here you can meander through the streets behind Granary Square and be able to look through windows into the workshops and studios of the art and design students. These windows are located opposite primary retail locations. They bring interest and intrigue to the development and create a unique experience.

RESIDENTIAL

Now let's consider the residential use typology. We are seeing an increasing number of brands either occupy or develop residential space, to allow their customers to live with the brand. Two examples include the Dutch homewares and accessories brand Hay and the UK's John Lewis. **Hay Stay** apartments in Copenhagen are described as an 'urban oasis for travellers and locals alike'. The apartments have a range of private and communal spaces that offer a sense of community. Hay Stay and other such initiatives have the effect of consumers being surrounded by the brand's products – furniture, lighting and accessories –and so can 'live the brand'.

As described earlier in this chapter, **The John Lewis Partnership**, owner of the 42-strong John Lewis department store chain and 330-strong Waitrose grocery chain, is considering developing residential property above and beside some of its stores. The developments would potentially be in the form of build to rent which could allow the brand to furnish the properties using John Lewis home products. Residents may also be able to hire furniture from John Lewis as part of their rent. This type of initiative can reinforce a focus on sustainability but also a recognition of the increasingly nomadic lifestyle of many consumers.

There are many such examples that reflect a trend of brands moving beyond just selling product but creating the circumstances for their customers to live with their products and associate them with their everyday life.

When considering 'blended-use' developments and residential use, we can now see the potential of brands being able to use residential properties to showcase their products and even encourage customers to stay over to experience the products in 'real life' before buying them. So in planning a blended-use development, some elements of the residential parts might act as showrooms for customers to visit and even stay for one night. The location of these in the masterplan could be on the ground floor to align more closely with retail and F&B and help activate the public realm.

So, I have looked at workplace, hospitality, education and residential components of a blended-use development. Now let's turn our attention to healthcare.

HEALTHCARE

An increasing number of healthcare treatments and therapies are moving from the clinical 'back of house' areas of a healthcare building such as a hospital or wellness clinic to becoming more consumer-facing. Treatments such as dermatology, physiotherapy, cosmetic dentistry, beauty-based cosmetic surgery and a wide range of physical and mental health treatments and therapies are all becoming important consumer offers.

So in defining the proposition and strategic masterplan for a blended-use development we must consider these offers and experiences and locate them and strategically align them with retail, food, leisure and entertainment. Once again this will help activate the public realm and create a compelling and unique destination with an authentic spirit of place that is an antidote to the years of cookie-cutter, clone shopping centres and town centres.

MANUFACTURING

Finally, let's consider the role of manufacturing in a blended-use development. Micro-manufacturing in the form of 3D printing, 3D weaving and small-batch craft-based manufacturing are becoming important components of a 'front-of-house' consumer offer.

In fact, these types of offers present us with an opportunity to develop a completely new experience and building typology when considering a blended-use approach.

A new place typology

I describe this as a 'make, work, learn, sell' typology: a building with the four types of use blended and connected. The *make* component could be, for example, a 3D printing facility or a micro-brewery. The *work* component could be an incubator space for small businesses with an integrated co-working facility. This would be linked to an event space and *learning* facility where ideas are shared and where presentations can be given to potential investors and collaborators. This component could also include a stage/lecture theatre with seminar rooms. The *sell* component on the ground level would be a retail offer that sells the products produced in the 3D printing facility or it could be a bar selling the drinks brewed on the premises.

So, we can observe that this new approach, which blends making, working, learning and selling, is where I see the opportunity for a new and unique building typology. This could introduce to any development or town centre a unique experience which is both a business-to-business (B2B) environment but also a business-to-consumer (B2C) offer that animates the public realm and aligns to retail, food and entertainment.

I see a 'make, work, learn, sell' building as a vertically stacked hub building for development or town centre. At the higher levels would be a co-working community that could be a facility for freelancers and an incubator for new start-ups. This would be connected to a leisure, events and learning facility where businesses could share ideas and present to potential investors. It could also provide a place for events, entertainment and also a wellness offer. The lower levels would accommodate a micro-manufacturing facility or makerplace producing goods that would then be sold at the ground level. This could vary from a straightforward coffee roastery connected to a coffee shop on the ground level, or a micro-brewery connected to a bar. The micro-manufacturing facility could be more high-tech with 3D printing or 3D weaving providing products that can be sold in the ground floor retail space or indeed online, making the retail space more of a place for customers to meet and learn and share ideas.

This type of new building would galvanize communities, and create real energy in our town centres by introducing new ideas, new types of experiences and contributing the essential ingredient of activating the public realm.

To ensure our shopping centres and town centres are future-ready we must kick the addiction of retail-driven developments. We must reinvent the outmoded, disconnected approach to mixed-use developments. I passionately believe that we must adopt the principles of a connected, compelling blended-use approach. A blended-use approach to developments can break down the silos of 'mixed-use' to create truly connected communities with new and vibrant public realm activation that respond to a new rhythm of footfall. One that does not rely on the fast decreasing shopping-based footfall.

We must shift from a 'shopping rhythm' to a 'community rhythm' that future blended-use developments can deliver. This will imbue our shopping centres and town centres with regular and sustainable football and an activated public realm with programmes that extend, dwell and create a sense of excitement and anticipation to draw in the curious crowds all year round so they may enjoy experiences that fill the day and illuminate the night. That will lead not only to commercial value but to social and cultural value.

A future-ready blended-use development strategy must bring together a mix of occupiers, both ephemeral and longer term, international, national brands and regional brands, local independents and influencers. It is essential that the strategic masterplan is formulated to bring together these types of occupiers and locates them strategically, so they work in synergy, are connected and make any place an intuitive experience for people. We must not fall into the trap of an outmoded approach that locates big brands in primary space and smaller brands and community amenities 'shoved into' tertiary spaces.

To ensure long-term commercial, social and cultural sustainability it is critical to attract diverse occupiers, and develop diverse lease models to deliver diverse revenue. The commercial development landscape is very fluid and unpredictable. To mitigate the negative effects of this we must design and plan our shopping centres and town centres as blended-use developments that can accommodate this wide range of occupiers. The future of Coima's Porta Nuova development in Milan demonstrates this very well.

A blended-use approach to strategic masterplanning incorporates a wide range of occupiers, blended and connected to create a compelling, community-focused public realm, activating a range of experiences that deliver the most powerful consumer emotion, which is *serendipity*. If a blended-use development is to be successful and truly future-ready it must be a *serendipity machine* that delivers intrigue and surprise, where audiences are encouraged to visit, stay and return where they can find out what's next and what's new.

Here they will meet like-minded people as part of a community that shares, not demographic profiles, but true passions and interests which connect people not only to each other but to the brands that wish to engage them with compelling, relevant experiences, adding value to their everyday lives, their communities, the wider world and our planet.

Notes

1 L Thomas. More retail pain ahead: UBS predicts 80,000 stores will close in the US by 2026, CNBC, 2021, www.cnbc.com/2021/04/05/store-closures-ubs-predicts-80000-stores-will-go-dark-by-2026.html (archived at https://perma.cc/Z4TA-WBDF)

2 L Thomas. More retail pain ahead: UBS predicts 80,000 stores will close in the US by 2026, CNBC, 2021, www.cnbc.com/2021/04/05/store-closures-ubs-predicts-80000-stores-will-go-dark-by-2026.html (archived at https://perma.cc/Z4TA-WBDF)

3 Local Data Company. PwC Press Release: Store closures: twice the rate of last year as net decline now at highest level in five years, www.localdatacompany.com/blog/store-closures-twice-the-rate-of-last-year (archived at https://perma.cc/8J66-MUSM)

4 H Crimmins. Chart: Retail, hotel assets dominate US distress inflows, Real Capital Analytics, Inc, 2020, www.rcanalytics.com/chart-retail-hotel-distress-inflows/ (archived at https://perma.cc/Z4ER-VZJ8)

5 Savills. Retail rightsizing and repurposing becomes crucial as vacancy rates reach 142 million sq ft, www.savills.co.uk/insight-and-opinion/savills-news/310166-0/retail-rightsizing-and-repurposing-becomes-crucial-as-vacancy-rates-reach-142-million-sq-ft (archived at https://perma.cc/MBD9-K6SZ)

6 S Farrell. We've hit peak home furnishings, says Ikea boss, *The Guardian,* 2016, www.theguardian.com/business/2016/jan/18/weve-hit-peak-home-furnishings-says-ikea-boss-consumerism (archived at https://perma.cc/WC9H-UCJH)

7 M Gwyther. Have we reached 'peak stuff'?, *Management Today*, 2017, www.managementtoday.co.uk/reached-peak-stuff/innovation/article/1426034 (archived at https://perma.cc/EQQ3-RXAJ)

8 M Gwyther. Have we reached 'peak stuff'?, *Management Today*, 2017, www.managementtoday.co.uk/reached-peak-stuff/innovation/article/1426034 (archived at https://perma.cc/EQQ3-RXAJ)

9 M Gwyther. Have we reached 'peak stuff'?, *Management Today*, 2017, www.managementtoday.co.uk/reached-peak-stuff/innovation/article/1426034 (archived at https://perma.cc/EQQ3-RXAJ)

10 United Nations. 68% of the world population projected to live in urban areas by 2050, says UN, United Nations Department of Economic and Social Affairs, 2018, https://www.un.org/en/desa/68-world-population-projected-live-urban-areas-2050-says-un (archived at https://perma.cc/LVW6-HB89)

11 H Griffiths. Number of young adults with driving licences falls by 40 per cent, Autoexpress, 2018, www.autoexpress.co.uk/car-news/102466/number-of-young-adults-with-driving-licences-falls-by-40-per-cent (archived at https://perma.cc/YGW2-VGHP)

12 L Eliot. The reasons why millennials aren't as car crazed as baby boomers, and how self-driving cars fit in, *Forbes*, 2019, www.forbes.com/sites/lanceeliot/2019/08/04/the-reasons-why-millennials-arent-as-car-crazed-as-baby-boomers-and-how-self-driving-cars-fit-in/?sh=5e8ace1263fc (archived at https://perma.cc/Q2LB-RGTK)

13 L Eliot. The reasons why millennials aren't as car crazed as baby boomers, and how self-driving cars fit in, *Forbes*, 2019, www.forbes.com/sites/lanceeliot/2019/08/04/the-reasons- why-millennials-arent-as-car-crazed-as-baby-boomers-and-how-self-driving-cars-fit-in/?sh=5e8ace1263fc (archived at https://perma.cc/Q2LB-RGTK)

14 UK Construction Online. Hastings Pier wins RIBA Stirling Prize 2017, 2017, www.ukconstructionmedia.co.uk/news/hastings-pier-wins-riba-stirling-prize-2017/ (archived at https://perma.cc/X47J-WZTU)

15 Project for Public Spaces. Ray Oldenburg, 2008, www.pps.org/article/roldenburg (archived at https://perma.cc/2M99-HJH3)

16 PwC. Over 17,500 chain stores closed in 2020 with the impact of the pandemic yet to be felt, 2021, www.pwc.co.uk/press-room/press-releases/over-17-500-chain-stores-closed-in-2020-with-the-impact-of-the-pandemic-yet-to-be-felt.html (archived at https://perma.cc/5VX6-2TX4)

17 The New Craftsmen. Burberry x TNC: Makers House, 2016, www.thenewcraftsmen.com/services/brand-collaborations/makers-house/ (archived at https://perma.cc/D53F-WX3Q)

18 Dazed. Here's what you missed at Converse's One Star Hotel, 2018, www.dazeddigital.com/fashion/article/39054/1/heres-converses-one-star-hotel-princess-nokia-iamddb-leo-mandella-asap-nast (archived at https://perma.cc/8QQN-XMY2)

19 L Hallanan. Live streaming drives $6 billion USD in sales during the 11.11 global shopping festival, *Forbes*, 2020, www.forbes.com/sites/laurenhallanan/2020/11/16/live-streaming-drives-6-billion-usd-in-sales-during-the-1111-global-shopping-festival/ (archived at https://perma.cc/EB46-SS5A)

20 Vogue Business. China's live streaming boom, 2020, www.voguebusiness.com/consumers/live-streaming-china-shopping-kim-kardashian (archived at https://perma.cc/WN9N-UW8U)

21 W Wu. How mixing art & retail can work in China (and how it can't), Jing Daily, 2020, jingdaily.com/how-mixing-art-retail-can-work-in-china-and-how-it-cant (archived at https://perma.cc/TQ2G-3B5X)

22 Hylink. Generation Z fashion consumption report: Fashion 2020 and Beyond, www.hylinkeurope.com/gb/generation-z-fashion-consumption-report-fashion-2020-and-beyond/ (archived at https://perma.cc/Q6R5-AB8A)

23 Occstrategy.com. Widest geographical study of Gen Z reveals an emerging borderless tribe, occstrategy.com/en/about-occ/news-and-media/article/id/3421/2019/01/widest-geographical-study-of-Gen-Z-reveals-an-emerging-borderless-tribe- (archived at https://perma.cc/8N7A-8HDY)

24 Occstrategy.com. Widest geographical study of Gen Z reveals an emerging borderless tribe, occstrategy.com/en/about-occ/news-and-media/article/id/ 3421/2019/01/widest-geographical-study-of-Gen-Z-reveals-an-emerging-borderless-tribe- (archived at https://perma.cc/M5K6-SB5Y)

25 D Stephens (2017) *Re-engineering retail: The future of selling in a post-digital world*, Figure 1, Vancouver

26 D Stephens (2017) *Re-engineering retail: The future of selling in a post-digital world*, Figure 1, Vancouver

27 P Danziger. Neighborhood Goods proves its new department store model works, as Macy's and JCPenney flounder, *Forbes,* 2020, www.forbes.com/sites/ pamdanziger/2020/07/05/neighborhood-goods-proves-its-new-department-store-model-works-as-macys-and-jcpenney-flounder/?sh=73687cb27976 (archived at https://perma.cc/8MP4-6SGN)

28 L Uță. How voice is changing customer behaviour and the way you do marketing, Brandminds, 2019, brandminds.ro/how-voice-is-changing-customer-behaviour-and-the-way-you-do-marketing (archived at https://perma. cc/NKE6-DZHU)

29 V Petrock. Voice Assistant Use Reaches Critical Mass, 2019, www.emarketer. com/content/voice-assistant-use-reaches-critical-mass (archived at https:// perma.cc/KJR4-SAKJ)

30 Thinkwithgoogle.com. www.thinkwithgoogle.com/consumer-insights/consumer-trends/voice-technology-purchasing (archived at https://perma.cc/7LRF-QADZ)

31 K von Abrams. Global Ecommerce Forecast 2021, Insider Intelligence, 2021, www.emarketer.com/content/global-ecommerce-forecast-2021 (archived at https://perma.cc/2NEV-7U6S)

32 K von Abrams. Global Ecommerce Forecast 2021, Insider Intelligence, 2021, www.emarketer.com/content/global-ecommerce-forecast-2021 (archived at https://perma.cc/2NEV-7U6S)

33 National Oceanic and Atmospheric Administration. It's official: July was Earth's hottest month on record, 2021, www.noaa.gov/news/its-official-july-2021-was-earths-hottest-month-on-record (archived at https://perma.cc/ RY2A-NUDW)

34 United Nations' Intergovernmental Panel on Climate Change (IPCC). Sixth Assessment Report, 2021, www.ipcc.ch/report/ar6/wg1 (archived at https:// perma.cc/YHM8-NE2N)

35 Wunderman Thompson. Regeneration Rising, 2021, www.wundermanthompson. com/insight/regeneration-rising (archived at https://perma.cc/5M65-LV4M)

36 E Alexander. Introducing circular fashion: The shopping concept that could save the planet, Harper's BAZAAR, 2019, www.harpersbazaar.com/uk/fashion/a27189370/circular-fashion-definition (archived at https://perma.cc/H87Y-YWJ5)

37 N Joshi. Retailers have a lot to gain from AR and VR, *Forbes*, 2019, www.forbes.com/sites/cognitiveworld/2019/10/01/retailers-have-a-lot-to-gain-from-ar-and-vr/?sh=42021857a1c9 (archived at https://perma.cc/8W7U-2JVR)

38 A Cook, L Ohri, L Kusumoto, C Reynolds and E Schwertzel. Augmented shopping: The quiet revolution, Deloitte Insights, 2020, www2.deloitte.com/uk/en/insights/topics/emerging-technologies/augmented-shopping-3d-technology-retail.html (archived at https://perma.cc/5DSK-CNFL)

39 L Goasduff. Gartner forecasts global devices installed base to reach 6.2 billion units in 2021, 2021, www.gartner.com/en/newsroom/press-releases/2021-04-01-gartner-forecasts-global-devices-installed-base-to-reach-6-2-billion-units-in-2021#:~:text=The%20number%20of%20devices%20(PCs,in%20use%20than%20in%202020 (archived at https://perma.cc/WF58-6R7H)

40 T Lindeman. Retail stores, newspapers move beyond symbiotic ties, *Pittsburg Post Gazette,* 2005, www.post-gazette.com/business/businessnews/2005/10/09/Retail-stores-newspapers-move-beyond-symbiotic-ties/stories/200510090175 (archived at https://perma.cc/6F2A-7B9K)

41 V Howard. Department store advertising in newspapers, radio, and television, 1920–1960, *Journal of Historical Research in Marketing*, 2010, 2(1), 61–85

42 B Evans. WhatsApp sails past SMS, but where does messaging go next? [blog] Benedict Evans, 2015, www.ben-evans.com/benedictevans/2015/1/11/whatsapp-sails-past-sms-but-where-does-messaging-go-next (archived at https://perma.cc/9ASW-NAGC)

43 AirBnB. Airbnb report on travel & living, 2021, news.airbnb.com/wp-content/uploads/sites/4/2021/05/Airbnb-Report-on-Travel-Living.pdf (archived at https://perma.cc/SQB6-YBHS)

44 BBC News. Pandemic has changed travel forever, says AirBnB boss, 2021, www.bbc.co.uk/news/business-58643720 (archived at https://perma.cc/4M48-G3ND)

45 MBO Partners. Covid-19 and the rise of the digital nomad, 2020, www.mbopartners.com/state-of-independence/2020-digital-nomads-report/ (archived at https://perma.cc/EJ9D-4TQN)

46 MBO Partners. Covid-19 and the rise of the digital nomad, 2020, www.mbopartners.com/state-of-independence/2020-digital-nomads-report/ (archived at https://perma.cc/EJ9D-4TQN)

47 MBO Partners. Covid-19 and the Rise of the Digital Nomad, s29814.pcdn.co/wp-content/uploads/2020/10/MBO-Digital-Nomad-Report-2020-Revised.pdf (archived at https://perma.cc/WLC6-RLU2)

48 E Gould and J Kandra. Only one in five workers are working from home due to Covid: Black and Hispanic workers are less likely to be able to telework, Economic Policy Institute, 2021, www.epi.org/blog/only-one-in-five-workers-are-working-from-home-due-to-covid-black-and-hispanic-workers-are-less-likely-to-be-able-to-telework (archived at https://perma.cc/XDT3-8JP3)

49 McKinsey & Company. What's next for remote work: An analysis of 2,000 tasks, 800 jobs, and nine countries, 2020, www.mckinsey.com/featured-insights/future-of-work/whats-next-for-remote-work-an-analysis-of-2000-tasks-800-jobs-and-nine-countries (archived at https://perma.cc/J5Q9-2WUD)

07

Repositioning value

The fourth pillar of future readiness is 'repositioning value' and what our audience will see as representing true value to them personally, to their community, to the wider world and our planet. And how brands and retailers will deliver value not only through their products and services but in the way they engage with their audiences, foster and galvanize communities, and through their actions in relation to the future of our planet.

Aligning with our audience's rapidly changing behaviours and expectations calls for a repositioning of what we see as 'value'. Audiences will increasingly turn to brands that exist for a bigger purpose, one where environmental, social and governance (ESG) priorities are baked into their whole reason for being.

As we lead increasingly wired, digital lives we crave compensatory human contact and intimate experiences. Our audiences will increasingly value experiences that are convenient, social, enriching, authentic, surprising and scarce, as well as those that represent good value for money. And they will turn to those brands that deliver memorable experiences they can share while also making it easy and worth their time and effort.

FUTURE-READY NOTE

Our audiences are looking for time well spent, as well as time well saved.

They will abandon ubiquity and turn their backs on cookie-cutter experiences or those that are too polished and contrived. Our audience will increasingly value personalization, authenticity, as well as health and wellness.

They will demand experiences and environments that are softer, more human and, in a way, 'imperfect'. And they will turn to brands that offer value-added products and services that are personalized to meet specific needs desires.

Repositioning retail value

Nike has been a pioneer in allowing its customers to personalize their purchases. It initially launched NikeID which it later developed into **Nike By You.** This is a service that allows customers to personalize and design their own Nike merchandise, including footwear and sportswear. Customers can access the service via the Nike website or using terminals in-store. The Nike By You digital interface is very intuitive. The customer can choose which area of the shoe to personalize, changing the colour and fabric. If the customer does not feel confident enough to design the item, they can choose from a range of 'off-the-shelf' customized designs or buy designs other customers have created.

However, our audiences are also becoming more promiscuous in their relationships with brands and will abandon a brand if it does not keep up with rapidly evolving expectations, and changes in what their audience deem as real value.

Over recent years we have seen many retail brands that have lost relevance and that were too slow to change to meet new demands and expectations of value. We saw many go into administration during 2020/21.

Debenhams was established in 1778 and was the oldest retail chain in the UK, but it went into liquidation on 1 December 2020. In January 2021 the online retailer Boohoo acquired the Debenhams brand, and the firm announced that it would be closing all of its stores, though it still has an online store. It seems that Debenhams gradually became less relevant to customers. From 2003 it went through a series of acquisitions by private-equity firms, during whose ownership debts were increased, as well as public ownership.

It may be that ultimately Debenhams did not survive because it could not compete with the convenience, choice and value of the likes of Amazon, or with the experience offered by stores such as Selfridges and the customer service offered by stores such as John Lewis. Also, it may be that the various owners of Debenhams over the years were not able to define and implement a relevant and compelling long-term strategy.

Arcadia, the owner of the high-street brands Burtons, Topshop, Dorothy Perkins, Miss Selfridge, Wallis and Evans, went into administration in November 2020. The group had around 440 stores and employed approximately 12,000 staff. Arcadia was most successful during the five years between 2003 and 2007. However, it then seems to have lost relevance and could not respond to changing consumer habits and expectation. It might be that it did not invest sufficiently in its online offer, or its store experience and it seems that it was not nimble enough in changing its product offer to meet the demands of the 'fast fashion' consumer. The Arcadia brands lost ground to the likes of Primark, Next, Zara, H&M, and more recently online players such as Boohoo and Pretty Little Thing. And Arcadia followed the same pattern as many retailers, in as much as its demise was probably hastened by the Covid-19 pandemic.

Bonmarché, the clothing retailer at the value end of the market, went into administration on 2 December 2020, resulting in the closure of 226 stores and the loss of more than 1,200 jobs. **Jaeger** and **Peacocks** were two retail brands at either end of the market both owned by the EWM Group. Jaeger, with approximately 76 outlets and employing 347 staff, was positioned at the premium end of the fashion market, while Peacocks occupied the value end of the market and had 423 stores and 4,200 staff. All three brands went into administration at a similar time. The probable reason for this was changing customer preferences to which they could not respond quickly enough.

The once booming lingerie brand **Victoria's Secret UK** went into administration in June 2020, affecting 25 stores and 800 staff.

Although the Covid-19 pandemic seemed to have been the thing that tipped the firm over the edge, Victoria's Secret is an example of another brand that did not see how changing consumer expectations and attitudes, and a shift in the wider culture, such as the 'Me Too' movement, seems to have made its brand and offer feel increasingly out of touch. The brand's image was seen as objectifying women by some. And so some felt that the brand slowly became less relevant to modern women.

The emergence of innovative start-ups in the furniture sector such as Casper and Made.com have made more traditional brands such as **Benson Beds** and **Harveys Furniture** seem very old fashioned. Both brands were put into a pre-pack administration at the same time. The Alteri group has invested £25 million into Bensons Beds which has 242 stores and 1,900 staff and is planning to update the offer and the brand's operations. Harveys Furniture is the second largest furniture retailer in the UK, with 105 stores and 1,575 staff. The company continues to trade but is in danger from more agile and innovative competitors.

It's not just retailers who've been having a challenging time. Shopping centres have also found it difficult. **Intu Properties** used to own and manage some of the UK's best-known shopping centres including Lakeside in Essex, Trafford Centre in Manchester, Merry Hill near Birmingham, Nottingham's Victoria Centre and much-loved local centres such as the Glades in Bromley, Kent, which it sold a few years before it went into administration on 26 June 2020.

Part of Intu's problem seems to have been the amount of debt it carried. A shopping centre owner such as Intu going bust has serious consequences that are more far-reaching than a specific retailer going bust. The Intu shopping centres that survive will require funding to ensure they can adapt to the rapidly changing retail landscape and consumer expectations. Again, the Covid-19 pandemic has only been part of the problem. Many of Intu's centres have been in decline for several years.

Many such businesses failed because they did not rethink their value proposition. And by that I don't only mean price and product offering, but value in meeting the needs of its communities and their changing lifestyles, behaviours and priorities.

A firm such as Intu going into administration will have an impact on commercial property valuations, on the confidence and commercial viability of many of its tenants. Additionally, there will be wider impacts such as the value of pension funds, shares, unit trusts and tax revenues. There will also be an impact on local jobs and community cohesion.

These and many other examples emphasize the importance of retail brands keeping 'on the pulse' of what their people see as value, and how value is continually being repositioned.

At the heart of repositioning value in retail is the physical stores' shift from being channels of distribution to delivering moments of experience. And these experiences will need to be *authentic* and *hyper-personalized*. They will need to be programmed, delivering constant newness. They will need to be *curated* and be driven by compelling *storytelling*. They will need to be *co-created* with the brand's audience while responding to deep insights of the human truths of behaviour and expectations.

FUTURE-READY NOTE

Physical retail is shifting from channels of distribution to moments of experience. From a distribution channel to a media channel.

The growth of the sharing economy also demonstrates the repositioning of value. It has partly been driven by a move from 'asset-heavy' to 'asset-light' living, whereby people want to be unburdened by 'stuff'. We generally have too much stuff in our lives and we suffer from too much clutter. And we don't use this stuff most of the time.

FUTURE-READY NOTE

There is a shift from 'asset-heavy' to 'asset-light' living.

The average US home has 300,000 items, and 10 per cent of Americans rent offsite storage. There is 7.3 sq ft of self-storage space for every man, woman and child in the United States. In the UK between 2018 and 2021 the share of people who used self-storage rose from 1.29 per cent to 2.28 per cent. And in 2021, 5.8 per cent of respondents were considering using a self-storage service.[1]

Some 25 per cent of Americans with two-car garages don't have room to park cars inside them. They spend $1.2 trillion annually on non-essential goods which are generally items they do not need! And the US home organization industry is worth $8 billion and has more than doubled in size since the early 2000s, growing at rate of 10 per cent each year.

Over the course of our lifetime, we will spend a total of 153 days searching for misplaced items, and we lose up to nine items every day.[2]

This is just a cursory glance at statistics that demonstrate our excessive consumption and unnecessary accumulation of stuff.

The sharing economy

Millennials (born between 1980 and 1996) and Centennials (born around the turn of the century) like to live more nomadically; they like to be agile and do not commit as readily as previous generations to their places of work or living. This represents significant opportunities for the sharing economy and those brands and businesses that embrace it. In future we will be defined more by what we do than what we own. We are seeing a gradual shift from individual ownership to shared access.

This phenomenon was succinctly expressed by Lynn Jurich, CEO of Sunrun, 'The new status symbol isn't what you own, it's what you're smart enough not to own.' Lynn Jurich referred to this as 'dis-ownership'.[3]

Earthshare.org claims that the average power drill only gets used 6 to 13 minutes in its lifetime. So why would you need to buy a drill if you can have access to it whenever you need? Access often matters more than ownership. So sharing is more convenient because it can provide what you need, when you need it. It is also sustainable as it can reduce the number of products manufactured and so reduce the amount of resources required.

Mark Zuckerberg once stated that 'Every product and service that can be shared will be shared', referring to the opportunities for those businesses who will respond to a growing shift from individual ownership to shared access.

The Green Alliance blog has noted that

> General estimates suggest that every tonne of product that makes it to the UK market requires 10 tonnes of fuel and resources to produce, a figure rising to 100 tonnes if we include water. When it comes to power drills in particular, WRAP says that 91 per cent of a drill's environmental impact occurs in the materials and processing phase, and only two per cent occurs in use.[4]

The sharing economy is currently where social media was 10 years ago, and I am certain that this economic model (and way of living) will continue to grow and disrupt most industries. The number of US citizens participating in the sharing economy is expected to hit 86.5 million by the end of 2021. In 2016 it was 44.8 million. According to research by SpendMeNot.com:

> The sharing economy is set to reach $335 billion by 2025. Companies working in the sharing economies will grow by 2,133 per cent in 12 years. Over 86 million Americans will use the sharing economy by 2021. Crowdfunding will grow by $196.36 billion between 2021 and 2025. Some 28 per cent of users are willing to share their electronics. Sharing homes is the least desired activity in the sharing economy.[5]

The same research report also cited research by PwC which states that

> Companies that use the sharing economy model are forecast to grow their revenues exponentially. The sharing economy had just $15 billion in revenues back in 2013. By 2025, the number is set to skyrocket to $335 billion... this only represents the revenue of sharing economy companies in the following sectors: lending, home sharing, ride sharing, music and video streaming, and online distance work. And that sharing

economy firms grow much faster than the traditional operating companies. Between 2013 and 2025, sharing economy revenue will increase by the mind-boggling 2,133 per cent. By contrast, companies using the traditional operating model will grow their revenue by just 39.6 per cent.

China's State Information Centre says that the Covid-19 pandemic increased China's sharing economy by 2.9 per cent in 2020, and expects the sector to grow by 10–15 per cent in 2021.[6] The current transaction volume of China's sharing economy is over \$522 billion. This makes China the biggest sharing economy in the world. The report goes on to suggest that it is expected to maintain an annual growth pace of 10 per cent in the following five years.

According to the National Centre for Biotechnology Information (NCBI), in 2020 39 per cent of the surveyed US consumers had used one sharing category (typically car sharing and ride sharing), and they had an average age of 43. However, 29 per cent of the consumers surveyed had used three sharing categories (typically mobility, tourism and retail), and this cohort had an average age of 35.[7]

A report by investment management firm Schroders has outlined that between 2013 and 2025, online lending is forecast to expand at a CAGR (compound annual growth rate) of 63 per cent. This covers crowdfunding and peer-to-peer lending. Only 14 per cent of the respondents said they haven't participated in any sharing initiatives.[8]

This shift from individual ownership to shared access presents many advantages and opportunities for creating new value. Shared use also means shared experience where we are progressing from merely sharing to collaborating. This is sometimes referred to as 'collaborative consumption'.

Collaborative consumption

Brands that embrace collaborative consumption and deliver products and services via online digital platforms that match available goods and services with needs will thrive in the new 'access economy'. Once a collaborative consumption community is established they can share knowledge and skills in relation to the products and services that are being shared. Collaborative consumption also has the advantage of convenience, where products and services can be accessed only when they are required and so respond to 'just-in-time' living.

The explosion in the number of single-person households has also fuelled the collaborative consumption economy. Single-person households generally have less space for stuff and so see a great advantage in being able to access products only when they need them.

We are seeing an ever-increasing number of people living alone in the UK – an increase of 4 per cent over the last 10 years. In 2020 the proportion of single-person households ranged from 22.8 per cent in London to 33.6 per cent in Scotland and the North East of England.[9,10]

In 2020 the proportion of single-person households in Europe was 49.1 per cent. Between 2010 and 2020, there was an increase of 20 per cent.[11]

We have also seen a plethora of products and services embrace the collaborative consumption economy.

ENERGY

In the energy sector there are community projects that are challenging established utilities, such as the Oakland Solar Mosaic project in California and the Hardin Hilltop Wind Farm project in Jefferson, Iowa. In both examples, individuals and businesses can purchase electricity generated collaboratively at a local level from these renewable sources.

TRANSPORTATION

Collaborative consumption is also fuelling a revolution in transportation. We have seen the explosion of bike sharing which has become a key component of urban transportation infrastructure in cities around the world. Bicycles are the fastest growing form of transportation in the world.

Car sharing is also becoming more mainstream. Car sharing can be broadly segmented into two different types; traditional schemes operated by companies offering cars for rent on a flexible basis, and peer-to-peer schemes that have owners renting their own car for others, or sharing a ride to an agreed destination.

Two leading examples of car sharing schemes are **ShareNow** and **Zipcar**. They charge a range of one-off annual subscription fees and hourly rates for the use of the car. Prices depend on the level of service and type of car. Subscribers can reserve cars in advance via a website or app, and depending on the scheme, the car may be returned to the same location as the pick-up or anywhere within a designated area. The apps are used to get into the car and for starting it. From the app, you can also find cars close to you and check petrol prices.

ShareNow is a German car sharing firm, formed from the merger of car2go and DriveNow. It is a joint venture of Daimler AG and BMW. At time of writing it had over 4 million members and more than 14,000 cars. Zipcar, which is based in Boston, had 860,000 members across the United States, Austria, Canada, Spain and the UK. Zipcar is now part of Avis Budget Group, one of the world's largest traditional car rental firms.

There are also a number of peer-to-peer car sharing companies, of which Turo is the world's largest. Turo, Getaround and Hiyacar apps work as communications-based system between renter and rentee. Other car sharing schemes include Virtuo, E-Car Club (electric cars only), car2go and RelayRides.

TOOLS AND SKILLS

Tools and products for home use is a growing sector for collaborative consumption. The best schemes are peer-to-peer apps that give neighbours access to a selection of tools for home improvement or construction projects while also facilitating a community of sharers that help and advise each other on projects, skills, tips and techniques. Neighbours can also make money by charging for the tools that are shared. Three examples of such apps include ShareMyToolbox, Sparetoolz and Sharetool.

The sharing economy does not only cover physical products; people are also sharing their time and skills. A good example is **Time Banks** which allows neighbours to barter their time and skills such as car repair, lessons, gardening, etc. The idea is that people can deposit the time they spend in the 'time bank' which can be exchanged later.

One of my favourite sharing-economy firms is the **Library of Things** (LoT). During a really interesting conversation with the Library of Things co-founder and Partnership Director, Rebecca Trevelyan, she explained how the business was set up and its latest development. The LoT's mission is stated as 'To make borrowing better than buying for people and planet.'

Library of Things allows people in communities to hire from a range of products, mainly for the home, which they access and pay for via an app. The wide range of products (e.g. tools, toys, kitchen equipment, etc) can be picked up and dropped off via self-serve kiosks located in convenient locations such as high streets, libraries, cafés, shopping centres, railway stations, etc.

There are three key challenges that LoT aims to respond to: for the planet, for individual people and for communities.

For the planet, the BBC suggests that 'If everyone on the planet consumed as much as the average US citizen, four Earths would be needed to sustain them.'[12] E-waste is the largest waste type in UK landfill, increasing at double the rate of plastic waste. E-waste is defined as the chemicals such as mercury, lead, beryllium, brominated flame retardants and cadmium that are harmful to the environment when electronics are mishandled during disposal. All these chemicals end up in our soil, water and air.

Very interestingly, Nick Jeffries in the report 'Case Studies from a Circular Home' states that[13]

> In 2001, as part of a contemporary art project called Break Down, 37-year-old British artist Michael Landy undertook a detailed audit of all his belongings. The final count ran to 7,227 individual items with an overall weight of 5.75 tonnes. Compared to a typical US household, which contains on average 300,000 items, Michael Landy's possessions seem quite frugal. Many of these items are quite idle – 80 per cent are used less than once a month and in fact some are used for only a few minutes in their whole life. The remaining time they are stored away, gathering dust. From time to time, they might be packed and moved to another location. Storing all of this underutilized household equipment is the reason that 1 in 11 Americans need to rent 'offsite storage', the fastest growing real-estate segment in the past few decades.

The LoT app is a platform that could have the effect of galvanizing communities where they can not only share products but also share skills, knowledge and their experiences in using the products they have shared. They can also organize get-togethers and classes via the app such as repair parties and repurposing events that further decrease waste and emissions and bring people together.

This type of platform may resonate with people who live in small homes and do not have the space to store goods, and of course it saves money, as hiring products only when you need them is a lot cheaper than buying.

LoT was established in 2018 and in the last three years (which has included the Covid-19 pandemic) it has secured five live locations in London, with five more imminent. During that period 5,000 people have borrowed items in the five London locations with 10,000 items being borrowed. They estimate that collectively borrowers have saved £145,000 as a consequence of electing not to buy the products they have shared. This has also spared the planet 88 tonnes of emissions through landfill and purchase prevention, with 40,000 tonnes of waste saved from landfill.

So Library of Things is a great example of a business that could measure its value through a 'triple bottom line' approach: profit, people and planet. This illustrates very well the repositioning of value to include not only financial value but also environmental, social and cultural value.

Peer-to-peer sharing

In the sharing economy globally, we are seeing specific categories of product or service that are most popular for sharing. And of course the sharing economy is not only based on a business-to-consumer model; it also encompasses consumer-to-consumer (peer-to-peer) sharing.

Around 20 per cent of sharing economy converts share online services or lessons. Platforms such as Quupe connects people in local communities to those who own an item they need and are ready to rent them. Apps such as Fon let you share your internet connection at home. Peer-to-peer shared services can include gardening or painting, which can either be paid for or bartered. Some 23 per cent share power tools; 17 per cent of people are happy to share their furniture; while the least popular sharing category is the home itself with about 15 per cent happy to share their home.[14] (Airbnb is not included in this as a large part of Airbnb listings is owned and managed by companies not individuals.)

Sharing a car is one of the most popular examples of the sharing economy, and 21 per cent of people are prepared to share their cars. **Uber** is a pioneer in ride sharing. Its revenues in 2020 amounted to $11.14 billion. Almost 19 million Uber trips are completed each day, and in December 2020, Uber had 93 million monthly active platform consumers.[15]

Many brands are exploring the opportunities in the sharing economy. In the fashion sector some brands have realized that consumers are happy to rent clothes and that there is an opportunity for creating a subscription model to deliver this.

The US-based fashion retailer **Urban Outfitters** has developed clothes renting service called **Nuuly**, which offers its subscribers the opportunity to rent from the brands assortment as well as a selection of partner brands. The assortment includes vintage pieces as well as new clothes. Subscriptions cost $88 per month which allows subscriber six items per month. Apparently, on average, the total new sale price of the six items would total around $800.

B-Corps

Many firms are embracing the idea of the triple bottom line. In fact this principle is now becoming formalized, with an increasing number of firms around the world registering to become B Corporations (B-Corps).

The B-Corp organization is a not-for-profit entity that aims to use business as a force for good. Any for-profit entity that achieves certification as voluntarily meeting higher standards of transparency, accountability and performance is termed a B-Corp, this certification being provided by the B-Lab, a non-profit organization. Currently there are just over 4,000 B-Corp registered companies in 150 industries across 77 countries.

Certified B-Corps are businesses that meet the highest standards of verified social and environmental performance, public transparency and legal accountability to balance profit and purpose. B-Corps aim to redefine the criteria of what success means in business. They are focused on reducing inequality, lowering levels of poverty, contributing to a healthier environment, helping to build more cohesive and inclusive communities, while creating more high-quality jobs with dignity and purpose and building a more inclusive and sustainable economy. B-Corps focus on the triple bottom line of 'profit, people and planet'. Obviously profits and growth are critical components to ensuring the company can have a positive impact for their employees, communities and the environment.

B-Corp certification doesn't just evaluate a product or service; it assesses the overall positive impact of the company. If a business achieves B-Corp certification it is legally required to consider the impact of its decisions on its workers, customers, suppliers, community and the environment.

To achieve certification a company must achieve a minimum score on the third-party validated 'B Impact Assessment'. This assesses a company's impact on its workers, customers, community and environment. The 'B Impact Report' is then made public on the B-Corp website, Bcorporation.net.

Once a company achieves B-Corp certification, it becomes subject to new legal governing documents. These are referred to as its Articles of Association (or Articles of Incorporation) which, along with the Memorandum of Association, form the company's constitution and defines the responsibilities of the directors. For a B-Corp these legal documents require the board of directors to balance profit and its purpose in relation to its people and community and the wider planet.

This combination of third-party validation, public transparency and legal accountability help certified B-Corps build trust and value.

In the words of the B-Corp organization: 'People want to work for, buy from and invest in businesses they believe in. B-Corp Certification is the most powerful way to build credibility, trust and value for your business.'

The growth of B-Corps is a clear indication of the repositioning of value and is a response to what people and consumers increasingly care most about. And I believe they will turn their attention and buying power to B-Corps.

> **FUTURE-READY NOTE**
>
> Repositioning value can be based on a 'triple bottom line' approach of profit, people and planet.

Customer lifetime value

Another critical part of repositioning value is customer lifetime value (or CLV). CLV is a measurement of how valuable a customer is to a brand, not just measured on purchases the customer makes but across the whole long-term relationship. Customer lifetime value is the total value to a brand of a customer over the whole period of a customer's engagement with the brand.

A general rule of thumb is that 80 per cent of the brand's sales come from 20 per cent of their customers. So it is vital that a brand identifies its most loyal customers and invests in increasing the CLV targeted at those specific customers rather than investing in more scatter-gun-type promotion.

Let me illustrate this by way of a fictitious example. Let's assume a brand invests (through marketing and advertising) £10,000 in acquiring 10 new customers. This gives a customer acquisition cost (CAC) per customer of £1,000.

Let's assume one customer spends £2,000 with the brand every year for a period of five years. In this case the CLV is £10,000. But the brand spent £1,000 to acquire the customer so the net CLV for the customer is £9,000.

Repositioning the value of a customer from a purchase-to-purchase basis to a longer-term relationship is imperative if businesses are to retain customers and convert them from merely purchasers to advocates. Another benefit of prioritizing CLV is that it is far more expensive and takes a lot more effort to acquire a new customer than it does to retain one. According to a report by Econsultancy/ Responsys:

> Attracting a new customer costs five times as much as keeping an existing one. Globally, the average value of a lost customer is $243. 71 per cent of consumers have ended their relationship with a company due to poor customer service. The probability of selling to an existing customer is 60–70 per cent. The probability of selling to a new prospect is 5–20 per cent.[16]

CLV being at the heart of customer engagement illustrates the level of personalization invested by a brand into delivering unique and relevant customer experiences across all touchpoints.

So how do we measure CLV? The *Insider* explains that to calculate customer lifetime value, you need to first calculate the average purchase value, and then multiply it by the average purchase frequency rate:[17]

$$\text{CLV} = \text{Average Value of Sale} \times \text{Number of Transactions} \times \text{Retention Time Period}$$

However, *Insider* points out that it is important to note that the lifetime value is calculated in terms of the revenue generated by the customer and does not take into account the costs involved in acquiring the customer, nor the profit margins. So we need to refine the formula to arrive at the customer lifetime value:

$$\text{CLV} = (\text{Lifetime Value} \times \text{Profit Margin}) - \text{Cost of Acquisition}$$

These are very generic formula and will obviously depend on the type of business and the product service category.

Another way for brands to reposition value is to shift from being a product (or service) owner to being a story owner.

All businesses should become story owners. In this, social media is critical. As I described in Chapter 6, for brands social media is not a broadcast channel, it is a dialogue channel. The extent to which people share the 'voice' of the brand is critical to the success and value of social media to brands.

Social media and brands

In becoming a 'story brand' it is critical that the stories are told not by a faceless corporation but by real people: people within the brand such as the founder or the designer of its products, or people that represent the brand such as a celebrity or influencer. However, the people who are most effective in telling the brand stories are customers. And so it is incumbent upon all businesses and brands to either equip their customers or fans with the stories they can share, or they must create the conditions for those fans to share their experiences and craft the stories that connect with their networks of friends.

INDUSTRY EXPERT
Koral Ibrahim

Koral Ibrahim is the youngest of the contributors to my book. (Full disclosure: Koral is my son.) I have witnessed the rapid growth of his start-up digital and social media strategy and design business, The Ready House. Koral has an intimate understanding of the value of social media to a brand, and explains here how businesses can reposition social media from a communication tool to a strategic platform at the core of any business.

It took Samuel Morse and his team the best part of 10 years to develop Morse Code. The technology and infrastructure were not available at first and so had to be developed from scratch. This was the first time people could communicate and connect instantly at a distance.

Fast forward to 1997 and the birth of Six Degrees – one of the first social media platforms whose driving force (as with Morse Code) was connection. But, again, the technology was not available. The connectivity and accessibility of the internet was not available to support the idea.

Ever since, social media platforms have been about one thing: connection. And with brands this is a key truism. And now the technology is available to support platforms from a brand point of view and access from a customer point of view.

Successful social media strategies focus on building communities of like-minded people with whom a brand can share ideas, and who in turn engage with each other as a community. And no matter where our business is, people all over the world can access these communities; that makes this way of building a brand perhaps the least expensive and most accessible it's ever been.

Being a 'social-first' brand: why it matters

A 'social-first' brand is one that doesn't treat social media as a 'nice to have' or an afterthought, but puts it at the very heart of the brand and its strategic planning and content decisions.

In today's world, people often start their discovery of a brand through digital, and more often than not through a social media platform. Such platforms not only allow engagement with potential new brand advocates but also engagement with current brand loyalists. Social media is a hugely frictionless and cost-effective way for brands to engage with customers, and unlike more traditional forms of marketing, it is one that is constantly in the palm of the hand.

Social media represents an invaluable hat trick of opportunity: to create more retention, more brand loyalty and more of that most valuable of facets: word-of-mouth recommendations. Over 91 per cent of marketers claimed that their social marketing efforts greatly increased their brand visibility and heightened user experience.[18]

Brands must think of social media as a digital shop window into their business to extend reach to a wider audience. But firstly, before defining a retail or social media strategy, it is essential to define the brand's purpose.

Shifting from product to platform and making your customer the protagonist of your brand

Of course, a brand needs a great product or service, that's a given, and cannot be everything to everyone. Consumers are over-exposed, jaded and not fooled by empty promises and businesses that jump on bandwagons (or brandwagons!). They want to follow, engage with and be loyal to brands that stand for something – the same kind of something they stand for themselves.

Whether a brand's purpose is driven by a belief in issues such as sustainable fashion, workers' rights, the overfishing of oceans, clean air, equal pay, homelessness, healthy lifestyles or indeed other specific interests and passions, the point is, there are many issues that affect the daily lives of consumers that can translate into a brand's narrative and engagement with its customers.

Once a brand is clear about what it stands for, and how it aligns its offering to that and what its customer are passionate about, it is then comparatively straightforward to build a brand community. This is the start of the critical shift from a 'product-first' mindset to a 'platform-first' one, where a brand talks less about its offering and more about the life and passions of its customers.

A platform-first brand is about being a truly opinion-rich business. A common misconception is that content, ideas and opinions always need to come from the brand. Instead, it's about creating the right opportunities for the right people to talk about the brand. Brands must provide customers with the tools they need to talk about the issues you stand for and the ideas and activities that interest them: in other words, make them the protagonist of your brand.

As Stefan Olander and Ajaz Ahmed said in the book *Velocity*: 'The customer wants to feel like the protagonist of your brand story, as opposed to the victim of your campaign.'[19]

If a brand values sustainable fashion, it must give customers the 'mic' and let them talk about responsible fashion choices they make in their daily lives. If it's all about travel, give them the space on Instagram to showcase their favourite locations, document their trip, or talk about their favourite places to eat, see, do and be.

'Customers' in this case don't have to be seen in the traditional sense either; they can also be individuals with their own relevant online communities. Influencers are a really effective way to share fundamental brand values.

Nano- (1–10k followers), micro- (10–90k) and macro- (100k+) influencers can spread the message to other untapped communities, encouraging greater reach, followship and engagement. However, it's important to think about influencers in a more engrained way than just purely paying them to post.

Ecosystems need to be set up around the brand for those who start to represent it. And finding the most appropriate influencers to engage with, who will reach your target audience in the most efficient way, will be key. The scouting of the right influencer is not just about followship either. It's about engagement, it's about aspirational and relevant content that aligns to the brand's opinions, attitude and outlook on the world.

Such influencers are critical to successful social media and need to be in constant dialogue with the brand to make sure the latest messages and opinions are being shared, but also utilizing their reach and collaborating with them to also influence the sales of the brand's products and services. This is a true social-first brand.

Influencers can engage in many ways. Perhaps they curate a specific collection? Perhaps they have their own dish on a menu? Perhaps they occupy part of a brand's physical space to stage their own event and invite their own followers to attend? So a brand must provide the right tools to influencers to spread their own message and in tandem advocate the brand.

However, a key challenge for brands is to measure the return on investment in social media.

The value social media to your brand and how to measure it

Brands task agencies or in-house teams to create content and push ads. The return on investment here can be measured in financial terms, but there is also non-monetary ROI that we need to consider.

A purchase decision by a customer can take time, particularly when the price point is high. Before and between purchases, social media can help in organically growing a trusted and loyal following who like, engage, share and discuss your content.

Having this type of connection with customers is priceless.

Up until now, it's been difficult to measure the value of the conversations brands have with their customers online. Social media data-scraping tools can be very effective here. These tools look at the social media footprint specific to each and every person in a given catchment, and perform a very granular 'deep dive' into those that a brand wishes to target.

Social media data-scraping tools can identify those with specific interests, hobbies, the brands and influencers they follow, the places they visit and what they think of them. A brand can then cross reference this information with credit card data and start connecting the dots between customer interests and engagement patterns with the activations and content and opinions of the brand. The brand can then use the insight it has gleaned to inform the curation of bespoke events and hyper-relevant content always with the four Es in mind: enrich, engage, educate and entertain.

This cannot be a one-time activity; data should be reviewed regularly to track changes in activity and sentiment. The more relevant the brand's content, activations and offers are to the local catchment, the more the engagement and spend.

It's a constant North Star by which brands can measure the value of such engagement and how engagement can be influenced with relevant content for the right people.

Key takeaways

• Social media is about connection.

• Being a social-first brand is a highly cost-effective way to engage with audiences.

- Talk less about products or services and more about what the brand stands for.

- Provide customers with the tools to engage in the conversation.

- Create content using the four Es: enrich, engage, educate and entertain.

- Use data to make sure your content, activations and offering is hyper-relevant to your target audience.

- Data must never dictate but guide; otherwise it may stifle your creativity.

The value of place

In Chapter 6 I wrote about 'Fourth Place' as the next iteration of Ray Oldenburg's Third Place. To deliver true added value and make a real difference, it is not sufficient for Fourth Place to be merely a new version of the shop:

- Fourth Place must be a place that really galvanizes communities, a place where people feel they belong, a place whose function is not pre-determined, where people feel free to use how they want for whatever function at whatever time.

- Fourth Place must represent the new 'living rooms of our public realm', distinguished not by function but by etiquette.

- Fourth Place must deliver on-demand spaces to respond to the increasing demand for semi-public spaces whose function will be determined by its audience, whether that function is meeting friends, eating, learning, working, health and wellness, entertainment, etc.

As Professor William Mitchell of MIT said, 'There will be a huge drop in the demand for traditional, private, enclosed spaces and a huge rise in demand for semi-public spaces that can be informally appropriated to ad-hoc workspaces.'

Shops, cafés, museums, hotels, libraries, co-working spaces, cultural centres, train stations, airports and schools are all in a position to create such fourth places, creating spaces and amenities for people to think, meet, work, shop, rest, eat, drink and play.

There is also an opportunity to reposition the value of such places in response to an increasing demand for such places to be 'quantified' in terms of their environment.

The Covid-19 pandemic has prioritized the need to create healthier, safer places. Most critically the extent to which public places are safe and healthy must be communicated to alleviate any concerns or stresses that people may have. The extent to which places are healthy and safe will also increasingly determine its preference.

We must create the tools for measuring, quantifying and communicating the health, wellness and environmental safety of our public and commercial places if we are to encourage people to visit, stay and return.

The environmental aspects of a place that we must quantify and communicate can range from air quality, pollution levels, noise levels, temperature, humidity, air flow, daylight, footfall and information on other people such as their vaccination status.

The communication of such data does not only give value in terms of reassuring people and making them feel safe. It is also an opportunity to present the data in a compelling way as part of the storytelling of a place. Such data could be communicated as part of a signage and wayfinding system or as part of the media strategy. The storytelling data could also form part of art installations and other environmental gestures such as kinetic sculpture, digital interfaces or installations that respond to the environment.

A great example on how to capture environmental data of public places is **San Diego's** new street lights, all connected digitally in the form of an Internet of Things (IoT) network.

The new street lights employ LED lighting to reduce energy. They are also connected to the city's LightGrid infrastructure allowing them to be connected through a wireless network so they can be monitored and managed remotely. The smart street lighting system is manufactured by GE and is part of GE's Intelligent Cities Platform which gives the network of street lamps additional benefits through wider connectivity of multiple sensors that collect and process metadata collected by the sensors.

As well as conventional cameras used to capture activity on the street, San Diego's new intelligent lighting platform includes sensors that can detect air quality, temperature, wind speed and sound. The platform can also detect pedestrian flow and sense the number and location of cars, which allows the city to build an accurate parking and traffic management system. The system's ability to detect and measure sound is even being used by law enforcement agencies to fight serious crime. In the event of a shooting, the system can identify where and how many gunshots are being fired, and even the direction of the shooting.

Another great example of repositioning value in improving the place experience for our audiences is an initiative by the city of **Bilbao**. According to *Design Boom*, the city has treated the advertising banners on its lamp posts and the advertising vinyl on some of its trams with pureti® print, a coating material which turns the advertising banners into active air purifiers. The pureti® print material triggers a natural process of photocatalysis, which causes a purifying effect similar to that of trees. The impact of this outdoor advertising campaign is said to be the equivalent to the air purifying effect of over 700 trees.[20]

In order to reposition value, it is no longer enough to do slightly better than before. Future success will be determined by rethinking and reimagining the place experience.

FUTURE-READY NOTE

It is no longer enough to do slightly better than before. Future success will be determined by rethinking and reimagining the place experience.

I passionately believe that we cannot create compelling places by starting with architecture. We must start with people and culture. We must understand the new relationships people have with place, services, brands and experiences and how this drives their expectations and behaviour.

A human approach to placemaking

During many public speaking engagements, I have spoken at length about the importance of a human-centred approach to placemaking.

However, taking this approach to the next level I believe we must stretch the idea of a human-centred approach to encompass the macro and the micro.

The 'macro' is a much broader *humanity-centred* approach which focuses on repositioning value to deliver environmental, economic, social and cultural value and the galvanizing of communities.

The 'micro' employs a *person-centred* approach which focuses on repositioning value at a personal level to deliver personalized experiences and amenities and personal wellness.

This takes a localism strategy to a new level where the approach is to 'think local and act personal'.

INDUSTRY EXPERT
Vivienne King

I first met Vivienne King when I sat on a REVO committee while she was the CEO. REVO is a UK membership organization that represents the retail, leisure and placemaking real-estate business community. Vivienne is a highly respected and knowledgeable leader in the retail real-estate sector and a specialist in ESG. Her piece below explores why a focus on ESG is critical and how we can reposition the criteria of value in real estate.

Everywhere we look, we are seeing a growing business environment encompassing impact alongside risk-adjusted returns; in the words of B-Corp, aiming to 'balance purpose and profit'.

This is a world where politicians are looking to meaningfully address climate change, investors are demanding integrated ESG (environmental social governance), and purpose-driven consumers are seeking out brands with strong sustainability credentials. For retail and retail property, what this means is that businesses which can successfully anchor ESG in corporate strategy are finding themselves with a commercial enabler that will fuel their long-term success alongside endurance of the planet and its communities.

This tectonic shift has been intensified by recent history. Alongside the human toll of the pandemic, there is the emergence of collective resilience, shared identity, localism and entrepreneurial spirit, but also mass unemployment, the seismic impact of the Black Lives Matter movement and the spiralling refugee crisis.

In our recent past, retail as a sector has been synonymous with big name entrepreneurs who took pride in understanding and influencing their customers as a means of building market dominance and personal fortunes. Today, some of those entrepreneurs have lost touch with the rapidly changing marketplace as conscience and wallets are increasingly aligned and a new generation of entrepreneurs are commanding the space, building relationships through a shared story of positive impact through the value chain. The Federation of Small Businesses talks about there being 'entrepreneurs all over the place' and, if actively nurtured, these individuals have a key role to play in providing innovative and marketable solutions to the local as well as global challenges of carbon control and social equity.

Sustainability, or environmental social governance, is the new 'value metric' for achieving improved comparative performance and a visionary purpose which guides strategy and behaviours for long-term resilience. Larry Fink, Chair and CEO of BlackRock, has been building this narrative in successive annual letters to CEOs. In his 2021 letter, Fink makes the connection between purpose and value: 'The more your company can show its purpose in delivering value to its customers, its employees and its communities, the better able you will be to compete and deliver long-term durable profits for shareholders.'

Value-driven purpose binds each of the key commercial stakeholders encompassed by Fink's message. Businesses want to showcase their own credentials to meet investor and employee expectations. Employees are seeking more than economic returns from their working life. Communities welcome local development where they see shared value from trusted sources. Investors are exercising purposeful capitalism when mobilizing capital, with a lower cost of debt and equity available to companies with high ESG ratings. This is big business. Morningstar, the data provider, estimates that by the end of 2020, total assets held in sustainable funds hit $1.7 trillion – a 50 per cent rise onwhere they started the year.

This is a pan-industry movement and the retail ecosystem, from start-up entrepreneurs to multinationals, from single-unit family owners to property-owning institutions, are increasingly alive to what is being demanded by well-informed customers and through ESG disclosure frameworks. There is a real and rising demand for substantial and authentic change to traditional ways of doing business.

For the retail sector, this means that unsubstantiated claims, false binaries and hyperbole around environmental and social value are called out as 'greenwashing'.

Increasing demand does not mean these changes are easy to make. Sustainability is a multi-layered and relatively immature imperative requiring systematic change throughout the value chain from supplier to customer as well as operations within a company's direct control. The barriers to such transformational change in the retail sector apply across industry and include cost, the overwhelming scale and complexity of the issues and the Milton-Friedman-perceived tension between ESG and commercial performance.

The levers of change include:

- *ESG rooted in core business*. New entrepreneurial businesses are hard-wired to be sustainable, whereas established companies tend to require systemic change to effectively transition to an ESG-aligned model. ESG needs to be rooted in core business as a strategic fiduciary imperative focused on a company's material issues, if long-term risk-adjusted returns are to be achieved.

- *Effective communication*. Companies should find ways to communicate the full breadth of the value proposition, articulated in a way that makes an authentic connection with their stakeholders, both internal and external, through for example, integrated reporting, awards and certifications driving positive reputation.

- *Culture change*. ESG-related changes requires team buy-in from a coalition of motivated individuals led from the top as change agents tackling barriers and driving ESG as a value creator with calls to action, storytelling, upskilling, context mapping and new ways of working. In this way, culture change will start to emerge through the catalysts of personal motivation, corporate loyalty, risk management and reward.

- *Sound measurement.* What gets measured gets done and measuring ESG delivery allows for progress tracking, highlighting weaknesses to improve performance and disclosure. This is fast becoming non-negotiable for investors and increasingly demanded by government, customers and employees. A range of measurement tools, e.g. GRESB/GRI, exist to measure environmental value whereas the full breadth of social value, being less tangible, is more challenging to measure with no universally adopted standard measurement.

- *Entrepreneurial confidence.* A package of support from government to encourage the symbiotic relationship between entrepreneurs and their positive impact on retail places. This can include public realm and infrastructure investment to attract footfall, a flexible, locally curated planning and licensing regime, financial policy incentives including tax breaks, grants and property tax reforms with business rates slashed for entrepreneurs and locally mentored business skills hubs – all signposted through a national PR and marketing campaign celebrating the social, environmental and economic value that entrepreneurs bring to town centres.

Start-ups to well-established brands are grasping the challenges and turning them to early-adopter advantage for long-term viability for themselves, their communities and the planet.

INDUSTRY EXPERT
Jag Minhas

I haven't known Jag Minhas for very long, but when I first met him with his colleague Ajay Kurien their business Sensing Feeling caught my attention. I was particularly interested in how it could add value through insights into peoples' behaviour in spaces. As Jag explains here, the technology behind Sensing Feeling can measure the mood and emotional response of people as they are going about their daily life whether that is in offices, high streets or shopping centres. Sensing Feeling can also measure levels of stress and fatigue and attention levels. Other data that can be captured includes vehicular and pedestrian volume and flow paths through places, crowd densities and crowding behaviour including compliance to social distancing and face-covering rules. Here Jag not only explains Sensing Feeling's capabilities; he also explores other firms in this space. I am sure you will find his piece interesting and insightful.

2020's global health emergency has transformed customers' attitudes in every dimension. People think differently about work and workplaces, commuting and travelling, and buying versus belonging. It is a re-evaluation that touches every aspect of our lives, society and economy. As a sector hit hard by Covid-19 and lockdowns, retailers and operators of physical spaces are responding, redesigning and repositioning value as they welcome visitors back.

Amazon and other e-commerce retailers have revolutionized the shopping experience. Customers' expectations are permanently raised in every aspect of buying: range, discovery, searching and filtering, price, shipping, returns and aftercare. Customers' motivations for shopping remain broadly the same:

- efficiency: to buy something for an immediate need
- entertainment: shopping as pastime, a leisure activity at a retail and recreation venue
- excitement: the psychological effects of anticipation, discovering new products and experiences, securing exclusive, limited items, or returning with a haul of bargains

Customers no longer flow through neat funnels. Instead they experience a series of discrete moments that compound into lasting impressions that become motivations:

- Each moment is an opportunity for brands and retail staff to be helpful and kind, to inform and inspire, to surprise and impress.
- Moments are multimedia in every sense, from traditional display and online advertising to how-to and assembly videos, to access to the founders, makers and designers via podcasts and social media.
- Physical spaces are another medium for delivering memorable, valuable moments: helping potential customers understand products and services, developing affinity with staff through inspiring and entertaining events and activities, and building a welcoming place to tell brand stories.

Metrics like sales per sq ft help analysts measure and compare performance. Before e-commerce, retail stores were stockrooms fronted by staff trained and incentivized to pick and pass goods to customers via the till. How will companies measure performance when customers want physical spaces to be living rooms not showrooms, to be creative and work spaces? How will mall owners, town managers and city councils understand visitors' evolving behaviours and needs?

New technologies and approaches developed by my company Sensing Feeling and other innovators deliver insights beyond ad impressions, click-through rates and footfall counts. I am excited about the leaps in computer vision, machine learning and AI technology that helps businesses understand people as they navigate the world and their lives.

For retailers, understanding who visits has always been more valuable than counting how many. A deeper understanding of visitor segments informs operational decisions, from recruiting strategy and rota management to advertising spend, marketing and activation plans. Traditional passive infrared (PIR) sensors offer crude counting that does not perform with crowds or large objects like shopping trolleys. Visual analytics using AI is a practical and exciting enhancement to existing CCTV systems, replacing simple PIR counters with smart IoT sensors:

- **Hoxton Analytics** has a unique way of counting and classifying visitors, identifying footwear using AI models. The company's system provides estimates of age, gender and height based on the footwear observed. Unlike PIR footfall counters, Hoxton's system is not confused by large traffic volumes or large objects like shopping trolleys. For GDPR compliance, no personally identifiable information is present in recorded video.

- **RetailNext**'s store analytics products use dedicated IoT sensors to measure traffic, dwell and occupancy. Traffic reports include direction and duration, counting repeat visitors and measuring flows across different areas of the store. Measuring occupancy in real time helps stores reopen safely, determines periods of overcrowding or underutilization and can help plan staff rotas. POS logs can be linked with CCTV surveillance for security and loss prevention.

- **Auravision**'s in-store analytics products connect to existing CCTV cameras and systems, performing AI analysis *in situ* to provide visitor demographic data, and movement and dwell patterns for customers and staff.

Customers and visitors have new expectations of retail spaces and leisure domains. Shopping as convenient leisure presents opportunities to enhance and automate inconvenient chores like queuing, carrying shopping or waiting for personal service. Maximizing customer dwell time and minimizing the friction between objectives and outcomes increases customer satisfaction and spend per visit:

- **Quidini** offers customer experience solutions, allowing customers to schedule visits or online appointments for advice or services, join virtual queues for sales or returns with regular updates on waiting time and schedule contactless order pick-up. Nike uses Qudini's appointment scheduling software for its express shopping service and virtual queues to safely serve walk-in customers.

- **The Up Group** delivers a range of services for retail and hospitality businesses. ServedUp is a mobile ordering service where customers choose and order food and beverages from their phones, and pay via the company's PaidUp payments service. It supports customers seated at tables or waiting at bars, ordering takeaways or click-and-collect purchases. ChargedUp offers customers portable device chargers from branded charging stations located in retail and hospitality venues. Chargers can be returned to any ChargedUp station and the service extends visitors' dwell and leisure time by eliminating low-battery anxiety.

Spaces adjacent to retail and entertainment locations are vital contributors to customer experience, increasing dwell time and spend when suitably designed for safe gathering, for social interaction and for entertainment:

- **Outernet Global** is a media and entertainment business developing entertainment districts consisting of live entertainment venues, external art and entertainment installations and internal spaces to showcase fashion, the arts, storytelling, gaming and technology. Situated next to Tottenham Court Road station in London, the Now Building's atrium hosts a vast 360-degree immersive video experience using advanced display panels four storeys high. Sensors in the atrium measure audience reactions to the space and its content and dynamically vary the audio and video in response and to enhance the experience.

- **Quividi** works with digital out-of-home advertisers and digital signage operators to integrate its real-time audience analytics technology into digital signage systems. The computer vision system measures views and attention time in front of the display and estimates the age, gender and mood of dwellers and passers-by. The company worked with Westfield to add cameras and computer vision capability to 450 screens across the mall operator's estates.

As shoppers and visitors return to roads, pavements and buildings after the severest of Covid restrictions, operators of physical spaces need to understand how people and vehicles flow, dwell and cluster in order to deliver safe and comfortable experiences.

At Sensing Feeling, we make software products and services that understand human behaviour at scale in real time, in real-world conditions and with real regard for privacy and ethics.

Working in partnership with a UK utility and civic services company, our technology can monitor traffic and pedestrian flows and can categorize passing vehicles by type, record dwell, speed and average speeds for vehicles and pedestrians on nearby footways, and also produce motion paths showing how physical space is consumed over time. The product adds value for town planners and local authorities by helping them to understand utilization and plan improvements to roads, footways, parking and pedestrianization.

The Sensing Feeling technology also counts visitors by demographic, dwell time and motion paths through spaces, and measures emotional responses from happiness to sadness. We can determine how people utilize work spaces through collaboration indices.

We urgently need to reposition value itself, where we reframe *value* in terms of *well-being*. And so we must focus on creating places that deliver social, cultural, environmental and economic *well-being*.

Reframing value as longer-term, sustainable well-being suggests that well-being must be baked into the DNA of every brand, business and place. It is paramount that the idea of well-being runs through their blood stream.

We must shift from a human-centred approach to a humanity-centred approach, where we don't just consider solutions for the individual but also solutions for wider communities and society. And as designers we've got to think beyond the immediate benefits of our designs to the longer-term consequences to communities, society and the wider world. And so we must progress from the much trumpeted 'design thinking' approach to 'outcome thinking', where we are not just forecasting from the present to the future, but we are *back-casting* by painting a picture of a future experience and defining a trajectory with a series of moves to connect to that future.

We have also seen the gradual evolution of the internet, from the internet of information to the internet of value. The internet has become increasingly decentralized, allowing us to connect directly, peer-to-peer. We are seeing the gradual decline of the dominance and influence of the intermediary.

Designers of place must also reposition their value and shift from designing nouns to designing verbs: from *objects* to *experiences*.

> **FUTURE-READY NOTE**
>
> From crafting of environments to shaping of experiences.

Long gone are the days where a designer's value can be measured only in the physicality, the form, the styling, the aesthetics and materiality of our built environment.

As I have touched on in previous chapters, designers of place must adopt the approach that is driven not by architecture but by people, focusing on the 'software' not the 'hardware'.

By 'software' I refer to the journeys, missions, actions, rituals and experiences that drive interest, engagement, immersion and emotional connection. These are the fundamental ingredients of which architecture must be a by-product and that can create truly authentic places where people want to spend their time and share their experiences.

So if we wish to create environmentally, socially, culturally and economically sustainable places that are compelling and that resonate with people, we cannot just focus on differentiating (in the market) but on making a difference.

> **FUTURE-READY NOTE**
>
> Don't just differentiate. Make a difference!

So in order to reposition value, we need to shift our focus from giving people a return on their money to a return on their time. And we must remember that time well saved is as important as time well spent.

That is the true repositioning of value.

Notes

1 Statista. Share of self-storage users UK 2021, www.statista.com/statistics/1246502/usage-of-self-storage-uk-united-kingdom/ (archived at https://perma.cc/YE64-9HEH)

2 J Becker. 21 surprising statistics that reveal how much stuff we actually own, Becoming Minimalist, www.becomingminimalist.com/clutter-stats/comment-page-3/ (archived at https://perma.cc/Y6JF-4HWA)

3 Fast Company. Why this CEO doesn't own a car: The rise of dis-ownership, 2013, www.fastcompany.com/1681112/why-this-ceo-doesn't-own-a-car-the-rise-of-dis-ownership (archived at https://perma.cc/9HK2-LT3W)

4 L Peake. Why hasn't the sharing revolution taken off?, Inside track, 2017, greenallianceblog.org.uk/2017/05/26/why-hasnt-the-sharing-revolution-taken-off/ (archived at https://perma.cc/M3GY-P2X6)

5 C Petrov. 25+ sharing economy statistics to share in 2021, Spendmenot, 2021, spendmenot.com/blog/sharing-economy-statistics/ (archived at https://perma.cc/TXW2-TY7G)

6 *Global Times*. China's sharing economy expected to grow 10% annually in the following five years grow, 2021, www.globaltimes.cn/page/202102/1216183.shtml (archived at https://perma.cc/P9P6-ZBBQ)

7 *Global Times*. China's sharing economy expected to grow 10% annually in the following five years grow, 2021, www.globaltimes.cn/page/202102/1216183.shtml (archived at https://perma.cc/P9P6-ZBBQ)

8 Schroders.com. The sharing economy, 2016, www.schroders.com/nl/sysglobalassets/digital/resources/pdfs/2016-08-the-sharing-economy.pdf (archived at https://perma.cc/EU92-Q58V)

9 Office for National Statistics. Vital statistics in the UK: births, deaths and marriages, 2021, www.ons.gov.uk/peoplepopulationandcommunity/populationandmigration/populationestimates/datasets/vitalstatisticspopulationandhealthreferencetables (archived at https://perma.cc/WR74-RBU3)

10 Office for National Statistics. Families and households in the UK, 2021, www.ons.gov.uk/peoplepopulationandcommunity/birthsdeathsandmarriages/families/bulletins/familiesandhouseholds/2020 (archived at https://perma.cc/NN2K-DLAT)

11 Eurostat. Household composition statistics, 2021, ec.europa.eu/eurostat/statistics-explained/index.php?title=Household_composition_statistics (archived at https://perma.cc/R62J-CRHH)

12 C McDonald. How many Earths do we need?, *BBC News*, 2015, www.bbc.co.uk/news/magazine-33133712 (archived at https://perma.cc/Y5KM-EG46)

13 N Jeffries. Case studies from the circular home, Medium, 2018, medium.com/circulatenews/case-studies-from-the-circular-home-f7204a741a27 (archived at https://perma.cc/MFN6-3RD2)

14 N Jeffries. Case studies from the circular home, Medium, 2018, medium.com/circulatenews/case-studies-from-the-circular-home-f7204a741a27 (archived at https://perma.cc/MFN6-3RD2)

15 E Chapkanovska. 19+ Uber revenue statistics every traveler should know in 2021. SpendMeNot, 2021, spendmenot.com/blog/uber-revenue-statistics/ (archived at https://perma.cc/R6DT-46J6)

16 G Charlton. Companies more focused on acquisition than retention: stats, Econsultancy, 2013, econsultancy.com/companies-more-focused-on-acquisition-than-retention-stats/ (archived at https://perma.cc/T3RL-7VLV)

17 T Katsabaris. What is customer lifetime value (CLV) and why does it matter, Insider, 2020, useinsider.com/what-is-customer-lifetime-value-clv-and-why-does-it-matter/ (archived at https://perma.cc/2TV3-Z35B)

18 C Dude (2020) *Secret Sauce Of Digital Business,* self-published

19 S Olander and A Ahmed (2012) *Velocity: The seven new laws for a world gone digital,* Vermilion, London

20 *Designboom.* Guggenheim museum Bilbao installs outdoor banners that help purify the city's air, 2020, www.designboom.com/technology/air-purifying-banners-guggenheim-bilbao-pureti-print-06-30-2020 (archived at https://perma.cc/B8Q6-FMJC)

08

Data, new revenue models, new value metrics

In order to survive and prosper, retail businesses in the future will need to become data businesses as well. This will require many to reinvent their physical spaces from shops that distribute products to media platforms that deliver shareable experiences, where data is the core asset. This chapter will cover how retail can develop new rent models and new ways of establishing the value of a physical space (e.g. store and shopping centre) to both the occupier and asset owner.

Retail space as media

As I have already alluded to, the new notion of the store will not only monetize the experiences they offer, but also monetize the data that these experiences generate. In future much of physical retail real estate will be valued on its ability to drive footfall, engagement, sharing and resultant media impression.

At its core, retail has always been and will always be about four things:

- *recruitment* (finding the consumers)
- *transaction* (selling them something)
- *fulfilment* (make sure they get what they have purchased)
- *retention* (make sure they come back)

What's interesting now is that transaction and fulfilment are migrating gradually away from the physical space, so in many cases we are left with the purpose of the physical space being *recruitment* and *retention*.

Although these are quite sweeping generalizations, the trend in this direction cannot be disputed. So, if we accept this prognosis, then this demonstrates the truth that the physical space will increasingly behave more and more like a media platform, because in many cases it's function will be primarily to recruit and retain customers. Its purpose then is to drive customers to the brand's e-commerce and social platforms.

So, in future we must think about physical retail assets not in terms of real estate but in terms of *content*. This changes the game dramatically! If physical retail assets are to be treated as content platforms then this has a far-reaching impact, such as:

- how the place in which it is located is masterplanned
- its physical make-up and how the space itself is designed
- the customer experience and the service proposition that supports it and how this connects with the local community and the fans of the brand
- how and if the space activates the public realm and connects to other offers and the servicing of the place
- the technology employed, the data gathered and the insight from it
- the basis on which the occupying brand pays rent and the form of the lease itself
- and finally, and most critically, how the asset of which it is part of is valued

In order to establish how we can create a revenue and valuation model from this new type of store that will increasingly become a place for customer recruitment and retention, we need to understand and leverage the data that these physical places generate. So, as I have already mentioned, but which needs emphasizing, it is no longer sufficient to monetize experiences; we must take the opportunity to also monetize the data that the experiences generate.

These are some of the reasons why the retail real-estate industry is facing existential challenges, along with changes in customer expectations and behaviour, the speed of which we have never before witnessed in history. This is *Retail Darwinism* whereby consumers' expectations are changing faster than retail businesses and places can adapt. So, if brands use their physical space as a media platform to recruit customers, the challenge for landlords will be to determine how the value of having that presence can be measured.

Value- and data-responsive environments

How do we capture the data that shows us the impact that the media platform has on the brand's social media engagement, online sales and other forms of media impression?

Let's look at this hypothetical scenario. If 10,000 people visit a store and 1,000 of them decide to follow the brand on Instagram because of what they've experienced at the store, that is very valuable. The retailers have achieved this because they've taken a space in the right asset, with the right audience, in the right location and delivered a compelling experience.

The asset owner therefore needs to determine the value of that space in order to determine the rent that is to be paid. However, this will not necessarily be based on the store's sales turnover or on the size of the store. It could be determined by the level of engagement the store experience drives due to the fact it occupies space in that specific asset.

But it is even more complicated than that. If we are determining rent values based on the engagement and sharing of in-store experiences, footfall may be irrelevant, as a customer may photograph and share the experience at a distance, even from outside the store.

Some traditional retailers and asset owners may be able to adapt their business models to this new paradigm; however, many will not. It will be the innovators and new kids on the block who will see this approach as totally normal. The new players occupying physical space will include 'digital first' direct-to-consumer brands and innovative brands in sectors such as entertainment, media, technology, fashion and publishing.

Once we define ways of capturing data from the in-store experiences we can then use this data not only to determine the value of the physical space and the rent to be paid, but also to inform the design, programming and activation of the space.

We need to create data-responsive environments that can be 'edited' quickly and easily. In order to continuously edit physical space we need to create designs that are based on a configurable and programmable 'kit of parts'. This will allow us to approach the physical space in a similar vain to a website.

Imagine the space as a physical website where the 'click-through' is actually 'walk-through'. So we can capture the data that shows us where people are walking, where they're stopping, where they're looking, what mood they are in, whether and where they are engaging with products and staff, and whether they have visited the store and when. From this data and insight we can determine where the 'hot spots' and 'cold spots' are in the space and how customers engaged with specific experiences and events. This data is very valuable in helping to inform how we can adjust the design of the physical space, very much like one would adjust the design of a website according to the click-through data.

INDUSTRY EXPERT
Herculano Rodriguez

I have worked with Herculano Rodriguez and his teams over many years on projects across the globe. Our projects ranged from airports, mixed-use developments, shopping centres and retailers. Herculano is a data specialist, with a background in consumer research. He has an intimate understanding of the value of data in assisting businesses to define the best and most appropriate offers and experiences that should be developed.

Retail has always existed in an analogue world. Shopkeepers used to keep data on their customers in little notebooks to provide personalized experiences. Growing up in South Africa, I recall going to the local fruit and vegetable store run by Ingrid Coetze. And Ingrid would remember me and often ask me to pass her regards to my mum. Now and then, she'd give me a free apple and tell me, 'an apple a day keeps the doctor away'. I remember those moments vividly.

Fast forward 30 years, and the world is going through a digital revolution. Traditional industries have been transformed through advancing technologies, and vast amounts of data are generated at the heart of this transformation.

By the end of 2020, 44 zettabytes will make up the entire digital universe. One zettabyte equals around one trillion gigabytes, or as much data as 250 billion DVDs of information which, when stacked, would be 93,000 miles high (or 13 round trips from London to New York). In 2019, 306.4 billion emails were sent every day, 500 million Tweets were posted and over 65 billion messages on WhatsApp were sent.

With all this data being created (and occasionally captured), it fundamentally and structurally changes how consumers behave in everyday lives. How they shop, how they learn about brands and how they consume information has permanently shifted.

The traditional retail model and brand building was linear. Traditionally, brands would advertise on TV, in print or on radio, and then consumers would go to stores and purchase products from the brands they recognized. Brands would typically target consumers by segmenting them into neat little cohorts of demographic (age, gender, etc), psychographic (consumer's personality traits, values, attitudes, interests and lifestyle) and geographic segments.

Brands had little information to work with and made advertising and product development decisions on assumptions that, for example, all 35-year-old female consumers, with two kids, earning between £35,000 and £40,000 per year, living in a leafy suburb of Leeds, all shopped the same way. But the internet and digital transformation brought richer and deeply insightful behavioural data, allowing brands to separate consumers based on their actions.

Brands are now able to capture data to understand their target consumers in more extraordinary ways than ever before. Data on consumers is being captured everywhere along the customer journey, from digital browsing, IoT devices capturing footfall and movement intelligence, mobile phone movement data, in-store movement through heatmapping cameras, payment data from digital payments or credit cards, and finally through customers leaving reviews, or retailer loyalty programmes capturing even further customer insight.

Data is often called the new oil, and like oil, data itself has little underlying value. The data that is being created can only become valuable if brands, retailers and companies can understand the context of the data and how to stitch it together to make better decisions.

This is driving the new world of retail and commerce. 'Everywhere Commerce' is the concept of no longer thinking about retail in simple channels. Increasingly lines are blurring between commerce channels and content channels. Everywhere commerce, the concept of consumers purchasing at any point, has risen. Consumers don't see digital versus non-digital. They engage with brands/retailers in an ever-expanding number of ways and expect seamless connectivity between them all.

This change has disrupted the traditional retail KPIs of sales per sq ft, average order value (AOV), customer retention, conversion rate, foot traffic, digital traffic and inventory turnover. And in the digital world, site traffic, conversion, cost per click, return on ad spend (ROAS), AOV, etc are still the most used KPIs.

While these metrics are still vital to run a retail business, winning brands of the future will combine on- and offline metrics. The shift will no longer be about invisible shoppers with static KPIs. Still, the most important metrics will be customer acquisition cost (merged on-/offline) and customer lifetime value (CLV) rather than cost to serve.

The ability to unmask your consumers will enable the winning brands to dynamically drive consumers through personalized experiences.

This is helping brands and retailers to think about new revenue models. No longer is the revenue only going to come from the gross margin of individual purchase, but the longer-term value will come from bridging the connective tissue on- and offline. New revenue models such as subscription retail, rental and recycling will be the future models, and retailers are accelerating their advertising businesses to generate new revenue. The channels of the future will remain physical, digital (including social) and an amalgamation of them all, live-streaming being a great example of this amalgamation.

It's incredible to think the experiences that stick with us most are the ones that are personal and unique to us. If I cast my mind back to Ingrid Coetzee, who operated that incredibly personalized grocery store 30 years ago, bringing that experience to life through intelligent use of data will be the difference between brands remaining relevant to consumers or not.

Knowing the amount of data created every day means nothing if we do not know how to use it strategically. Instead, what matters is the actionable insights that can be learnt from it. The winning retailers of the future will be companies who are the most responsive to changing consumers' needs, or better yet, those who can change consumer expectations.

INDUSTRY EXPERT
Burak Capli

Over the past two years I have been working very closely with Burak Capli and his colleagues at Radius. Radius is a very young business with big ideas on data, its value and its translation to actionable strategies. The Radius AI-based technology can unearth the human truths of behaviour and brand engagement through the granular mapping of and insight from social media and influencer activity. As the co-founder of Radius, Burak is frighteningly young when you consider the potential impact that the Radius technology could have on the retail industry, and many others.

Millennials have experienced many significant game-changing events and discoveries in a short period of time. This created a generation that is very comfortable in adapting to change, and is keen on challenging or even disrupting anything that shows a slight resistance to change.

Hereby, as a Millennial, I will share my understanding on how one of the most powerful tools of our time has contributed to the paradigm change in consumption. This articulation might contradict some of the existing and accepted beliefs. Yet, it is this understanding that led me to build an artificial intelligence business, serving some of the biggest commercial real-estate owners, and to grow a women-empowerment NGO with 222,561 Instagram followers that reaches millions on a single social media campaign. [1,2]

Finding yourself on social media

It doesn't matter whether you are on social media or not... because your digital-twin already is! Regardless of who you are, what background you are from or what income-level you earn, there is someone who shares your age, background, socioeconomic status, similar aspirations of life and who is active on social media. In other words, among 4.48 billion worldwide social media users, there is your 'digital-twin'. [3]

Before tapping into why digital-twins are important in understanding new forms of shopping we need to have a look at the fundamentals of social media. From a realist's point of view, social media might look like a cyber-world where like-craving, attention-seeking people expose their personal lives. However, in practice, social media is the most recent tool of the individual for exploring their likes, taste, lifestyle, ideologies and beliefs. Namely, social media is the simplest yet most advanced self-actualization tool of our time.

On a daily basis, social media users are being exposed to masses of content on various topics and interests. Being (over-) exposed to 'user-generated content', social media users become more and more aware of all the alternatives, lives, habits, ideologies and so on. In this vastness, intentionally or unintentionally, users curate their own feed, inputting their preference on types of content that they would like to continue seeing.

Once a user expresses their interest in a certain topic (e.g. political, consumption), social media algorithms start to cultivate it by pushing more of them. This is sometimes referred to as falling into an 'echo chamber'. An echo chamber is an environment where like-minded people and perspectives exchange information or opinions that reflect and reinforce the user's own. Over time, they get more and more familiar, or in other words, get trapped in their own curated feed.

On a typical day, on average more than 500 million Tweets are posted: that's 500 million posts on a single platform.[4] Considering there are many other platforms with even more active users, the amount of content that a single user is exposed to on a daily basis is just astronomic.

This content-load gets social media users exhausted with constant, fast-moving demands on their attention and requirements and decisions to be made about every Tweet, Facebook post and Instagram comment that requires moderating, responding to, reporting, deleting or encouraging.

Loaded with information, more than the average individual cognition can handle, users with a finite resource of willpower and decision-making get tired of making new choices and want to surround themselves with content that nurtures their existing beliefs/preference. This practice increases the tendency to fall into an echo chamber where their cognitive biases will not be pushed as hard.

Finding themselves in their echo chambers, users act according to their confirmation bias: the tendency to favour recommendations that reinforce existing preferences, especially those from powerful figures on social media. In the changing paradigm of social media power, this figure is very unlikely to be a politician or a religious leader, but instead it can be a 15-year-old Twitch broadcaster who uses their bedroom as their studio. This powerful figure is what we call an 'influencer'.

Users start to align themselves with influencers and endorse their opinions and preferences without giving it a second thought. This is inevitable, as exhausted users lose their willpower and cognitive capacity.

And so, the biggest shift in self-actualization brought on by this modern-era tool is that individuals are seeking their *profile-based* identity, rather than the pursuit of *role-based* identity. The major difference between these two definitions of identity lies in the increased perception of 'being an individual'.

Until now, role-based identity was defined by the social class you belonged to and the associated expectations with your status. However, profile-based identity is more associated with how you define yourself as an authentic individual. In the modern era, where anyone can be anyone, individuals find pleasure in 'copying' the traits of an influencer in the most basic and simple form alongside a distorted sense of still staying authentic.

Social media influencers play a vital role in shaping individuals' lives today. Data from MuseFind shows 92 per cent of consumers trust an influencer more than traditional information sources.[5] Another study shows that the users trust influencers more than their family and friends. That's why Kylie Jenner, a 24-year-old influencer with 272 million followers on Instagram, can charge brands considerable sums – $1,490,000 on average for a single Instagram post.[6]

A social media user is very much inclined to become a part of an echo chamber and endorse one or few influencers. This means essentially all 4.48 billion social media users can be gathered under reflections of a couple of archetypes. (An archetype can be a statement, pattern of behaviour, prototype, 'first' form or a main model that other statements, patterns of behaviour and objects copy, emulate or 'merge' into.[7])

Today's most powerful self-actualization tool is creating individuals that can be easily defined, explained and understood. Thus, it doesn't matter whether you are on social media or not. Thanks to your digital-twin, you also fit into a social media archetype.

You are what you consume

According to Harvard Business School professor Clayton Christensen, there are over 30,000 new products introduced every year, and 95 per cent fail.[8] There are many contributing factors to this failure. However, one of the leading factors is the discrepancy between customers' wants and brands' offers.

Research by Acquia states that 60 per cent of consumers express the view that the brands who should know them, don't know them very well.[9] This leaves consumers unsatisfied and frustrated, particularly as today's consumers have never been more willing to share their information and communicate with businesses. In fact, 76 per cent of customers are comfortable sharing their data for personalization and improved services.[10] While some brands are excelling at this phenomenon, some are failing to adapt to changing forms and insisting on keeping the traditional and outdated customer engagement approaches.

Despite the proportion of failed product launches, consumption rates have never been as high. We are not just consuming the goods and services offered by brands, but also the content generated on social media. The best part of this new form of consumption is that it doesn't take place behind closed doors; it's happening publicly, in front of all of us. This lays a golden opportunity for those of us who are trying to understand today's consumers.

Understanding consumers' needs and wants has never been as simple and accurate as it is today. Because let's not forget 'You Are What You Consume!' This is why researchers investigate household garbage when trying to identify a neighbourhood demographic and consumption patterns by looking at the leftovers and general waste. With digitization we can access even richer information without needing to knock on peoples' doors.

A bit of fairy dust, magic and data science

To break down the sorcery that allows us to understand billions of customers, first we need to start with the magical ingredients. Luckily, we don't need to climb the highest mountain or find the rarest flower to gather these ingredients. All we need is an internet connection, a computer and a PhD in data science (or in my case a co-founder with a PhD in data science).

Once all the stars are aligned, we are all set to understand consumers' demographics (age, income, education, etc), preferences and even future aspirations. This rich information becomes available to us by creating the previously mentioned 'digital-twins', using the data from user-generated content, echo chambers and influencers.

Even though this rich data is accessible by everyone, it's ignored by many, based on concerns for managing and processing vast amount of data. This sort of untapped data is referred as 'dark data': the kind of information that is collected but neither used nor thrown out.

According to a professor from Carnegie Mellon University's Heinz College, of all data created online about 90 per cent or so is identified as dark data.[11] It's no surprise that many brand executives fail to fully understand their consumers and even their businesses, while in fact a majority of the available data stays untouched.

This became clearer to us during a leasing pitch to find the best occupier for a vacant unit at a site that had a 20 per cent vacancy-rate and was attracting 3 million visitors each year. As part of the pitch, we were sharing insights on the sales potential of the brand in the catchment area. At the height of the pitch, we had to stop as the prospective tenant interrupted us.

The tenant interrupted us to request a copy of our pitch deck. It wasn't that they needed the deck to work out the numbers to justify their expansion, but that they had realized we were sharing information about their own brand, performance and customers that they had no clue about.

Every data and insights should be taken with a pinch of salt. That's why, to challenge our insights, we shared information on a specific order that was placed by a customer a few months prior and asked them to check it against their own sales data. Once they checked their till to validate our insights, they not only insisted on having our deck but offered to hire us for their remaining eight branches around the UK. Unfortunately, that brand never leased our client's unit as Covid-19 hit a few weeks following the pitch, but we managed to secure the second-best prospective tenant amid the crisis that started to bring the highest footfall in the shopping centre a few weeks after the relaunch.

What makes a brand?

Availability of information has been critical in shaping the shopping dynamics. To understand the role of information within the shopping context, we need to understand how both consumers and brands have adapted to the changing pace in information exchange.

For nearly as long as humanity has existed, goods have been shared, bartered, sold and consumed. The inception of retail stores could be traced back to the 'agora' of ancient Greek towns – an established marketplace with merchants (*circa* 800 BC).[12]

Over the years, there have been game-changing developments which disrupted the supply–demand dynamics in all possible aspects. To have a holistic view on shopping, researchers and academicians have embraced various methodologies to better explain the evolution of shopping. As we are more interested in consumer identification, I will be focusing on how shopping has continued to evolve around the first phase of the shopping journey, *awareness* (i.e. discovery). The awareness stage, the starting-line for any shopping journey, is defined as the stage where the consumer becomes familiar with a brand through channels, including advertising and word-of-mouth.[13]

Just before e-commerce became as widespread as it is now, the awareness stage was linear and simple as consumers were only exposed to brands available in their physical shopping destinations. Product or price alternatives were limited to what was available to them, and therefore, for brands it was critical to have the right product at the right time and in the right location. This allowed brands to adopt product-centric strategies, which mainly focused on having the right product/service in place that would somewhat satisfy the needs of consumers.

In the early 2000s, with e-commerce and especially with the launch of online price and product comparison services that allowed consumers to search for better alternatives, brands found themselves in a more vigorous and competitive environment. Now, they not only had to offer the best alternative but also had to differentiate their brand from other brands with their 'brand-image', which for many at the time was just a fancy marketing buzzword. This is when brands started to evolve from being product-centric to customer-centric.

Today, digital marketing experts estimate that most consumers are exposed to between 4,000 and 10,000 ads each day.[14] This excessive number is way beyond the number of inputs any human cognitive system can handle. Thus, brands realized that having superficial brand-image strategies in place would only leave them unnoticed in this overload of brand/ad exposure.

Personifying their brand was the only way to differentiate themselves, which would be possible by aligning their brand's values and messages to those of their consumers – evolving into a lifestyle brand, rather than a product brand. What does this actually mean? In a way, this was a step backwards to re-forming the brand–customer relationship to more of a 'tribal' relationship, in which the brand is the leader. Therefore, the new success metric of a brand wasn't sales any more. It was loyalty and conformity – i.e. the sense of belonging to a stronger group, the pride of being one of them.

The most fundamental challenge in embracing this transformation was in understanding how to form a group, how to infuse it with the sense of belonging. This obviously wouldn't be possible by only selling a pair of high-quality shoes. Brands had to look deeper into their consumers' values and respond by evolving towards a values-driven brand.

To form a loyal customer base, brands had to target specific consumer archetypes, more commonly referred as 'personas' by marketeers. Identifying the archetypes is the first and most simple step. This is what brands have been doing to a certain degree for decades with one-dimensional brand-image strategies. Now, these archetypes had to be explained through 360 degrees alongside their demographics, psychographics, preferences and, most importantly, their values.

The recipe

To identify and explain archetypes we can listen to echo chambers. Paying close attention to influencers allows us to understand those digital-twins that actively use social media, and therefore understand today's proclaimed ambiguous consumers.

A great example of how applying this methodology can grow a brand's sales is from one of our clients, a sustainable brand. They were exploring effective ways to strengthen their relations with their consumer base, attract new ones and identify new locations for expansion. Their brand-tone was on sustainability and ethical production.

We first started by finding their existing consumers online and started to listen to them more closely. They were 30–35 years old, professional workers, married with kids. Indeed, they were concerned about sustainability and ethical production. However, what is more important is to understand the reason for their concerns as there were many other brands advocating the same values on sustainability. We had to look at the types of content they were consuming, books they were reading, movies/documentaries they were watching.

As a result, we realized it wasn't their conscious or ethical values that were fuelling their motivation to support sustainability or ethical production. Actually, at the core of their ethical concerns and their main motivation for buying from sustainable brands was to leave a better future for their kids. In the end, we advised the brand to link their brand story more strongly with future aspirations by creating a utopia, by finding look-alikes of their existing customers with similar demographic traits, purchasing power and values. As a result we listed locations around the globe that had similar consumers and hence the highest potential sales.

Growth with ripple effect

This new way of identifying consumers and positioning brands has disrupted brand–consumer relations. Whether it's a product-centric brand, focusing on product availability, or a customer-centric brand with its image as a differentiator, or a values-driven brand with stronger bonds with customers, at the end of the day the brand needs to sell its product/services to keep the lights on. Sales take place by guiding a customer from awareness to purchase, which is called customer conversion. With the evolving shopping journey, the ways brands convert their customers have also been disrupted.

Brand executives developed various conversion techniques tailored specifically to the nature of their businesses and customer behaviour. In this modern era, values-driven brands see that their consumers are not customers but *community members*, where the brand sits in the centre of the community representing the shared values, while bringing a definition to the community identity. Values and identity are intangible entities. Yet, most of the brands are profit-oriented businesses staying afloat by charging for their products or services. The responsibility of values-driven brand executives is to convert these intangible commitments into tangible commitment by encouraging consumers to purchase their products or services.

This new form of customer conversion can be viewed as levels with a similar structure to the capillary waves of ripples in water. Just like the ripples, there are inner and outer circles of the community. Inner circles consist of already devoted community members that fully embody the values, embrace the community identity and engage with the brand in tangible forms, while also being strong advocates for the brand. Whereas outer circles consist of consumers that are inconsistent with their commitments but still have high tendency to become a part of the inner circles, but haven't been motivated enough. Profitability caused by higher conversion rates is directly linked to success in motivating these outer circle members to move inwards.

Thus, to sustain and grow sales, brands need to engage and nurture the community. Essentially, to give the needed nudge to motivate the outer circle to join the inner circle of the community, fuelling participation and showing commitment by engaging actively with the brand and buying its products/services.

This level of engagement could only be possible by understanding the existing community and explaining the characteristics of both outer and inner circle consumers. This will allow brands to make the most out of 'pulling forces'. These pulling forces are what encourages consumers to move inwards, such as new product launch, promotions, influencer or brand collaborations, store expansions, design, etc. Referring to the previously mentioned sustainable brand case with identifying core consumer values, resonating the message around 'sustainability' wasn't enough to move consumers inwards. They had to collaborate with pioneer influencers in sustainability who had a reputation for being great parents. Endorsement from these specific influencers was much more effective.

All these efforts need to be very carefully tailored and linked back to the community characteristics.

The dark data and available data sources shed light not only on understanding customers but also on estimating the potential impact of any commercial, operational or marketing effort. Essentially, the predictive use of data supports brand executives in explaining the effectiveness of each nudge of a moving force before execution.

Harmonic retail

A consumer is the same individual with the same values and preferences both offline and online. So, brands should also be consistent on all channels and treat them as one. For this reason I don't think 'omnichannel retail' is valid any more.[15] It is a single channel that exists directly from brand to the customer.

Indeed, there are many operational channels, thousands of products and millions of customers. The numbers add up to a level where it gets impossible for brand executives to make effective decisions by relying purely on their intuition. Intuition-driven decision-making will always be relevant; however, it needs to be backed by data. With the right data management strategy in place, data can present a fact-based reality in an unbiased way. It tells you both the upsides and downsides of previously employed strategies and efforts. With regard to predictive data approaches, everything is a matter of probability. There is no all-knowing data set as well.

However, there is indeed the perfect balance between intuition-driven and data-driven decision-making, which allows brands to minimize risks and maximize the gains from opportunities.

For all I know, in this fast-moving world with new technologies, ideologies and habits emerging every day, consumers will always adapt to these changes, while business success will rely on achieving stability and consistency. However, seeking stability and consistency shouldn't be understood as resistance to change. Instead, brands should sustain a stable growth by being consistent in keeping up with the latest trends and changes. Brand executives who become more comfortable with using data as a tool to understand the current dynamics and explain the future, by shedding light on both yesterday, today and tomorrow, will be able to shape the new consumer and retail landscape.

INDUSTRY EXPERT
Alex McCulloch

In the short time that I have known Alex McCulloch I've had many interesting and provocative conversations with him and his colleagues at CACI. It quickly became apparent that they were thinking deeply about the future of retail and the new paradigm of data-driven revenue and valuation models, for which they created the models shown in Figures 8.1 and 8.2.

Following on from our conversations, Alex and I participated in a podcast on the future of high streets where I was struck by his eloquence and clear thinking, and his assertions on the urgent need to explore new ideas around the basis of physical retail rents and real-estate valuations. Here Alex explains his ideas and the CACI model.

FIGURE 8.1 Quantifying the value a store generates

Quantifying the value a store generates

An approach to value every store on its real value to the brand, regardless of channel

Influencing Impressions

Not all footfall is equal, some is more valuable and relevant to a brand than others. CACI objectively quantify these 'Influencing Impressions', when a store has the opportunity to influence a customer's behaviour

Online Uplift

The impact the presence of a store has on online sales within the centre's trade area. Varies by category, brand and location, but it is the impact of 'showrooming', whereby the presence of a store triggers a purchase online

Customer Service

There is value in any face-to-face contact in a store, whether that being answering a product query, returning items or a genius bar. There is a benefit to having a conversation with a customer on the brand.

Click & Collect

The instore fulfilment of an online commitment to purchase, either transacted already, or reserved online, and transacted in-store.

Store Sales

The historic method of valuing stores, often still the major contributor to turnover, this is a decreasing volume as point of purchase transfers to digital channels

CACI's Halo model reflects the true contribution stores make to turnover.

Reflecting the multi-layered role of the store to objectively measure contribution for every store and category.

CACI

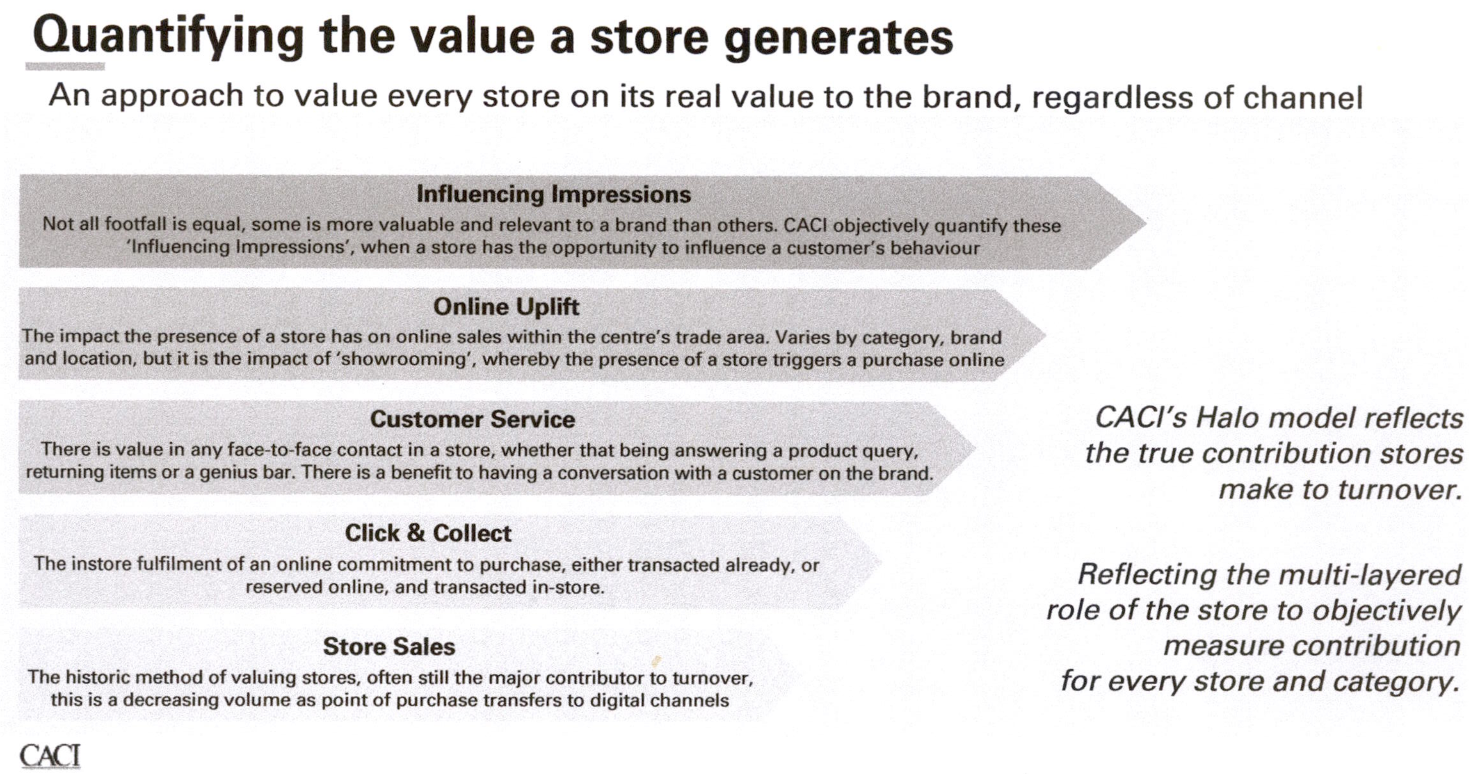

SOURCE CACI

FIGURE 8.2 An objective, data-driven, collaborative approach

An objective, data driven, collaborative approach

A model that uses actual performance data to quantify performance

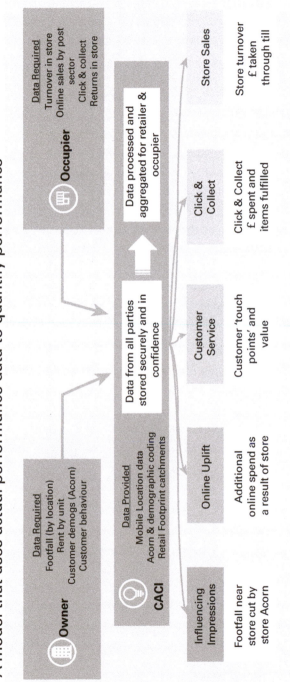

Output that can be flexed to reflect the unique context of every brand in every location

CACI

SOURCE CACI

The CACI Performance Lease was created on the premise that a store's rent should be valued on the basis of what benefit it brings to the occupier. Before the internet this was pretty straightforward. Almost all transactions took place at the point in which the retailer physically handed the item to the customer over the counter and rang it up in the till.

Without the till and the store it sat in, the retailer would have struggled to reach the customer. As such, stores were valued on the basis that they were the only point of contact the retailer had with the customer and so were the source of most of the retailer's income. Laid out like that today it seems deeply anachronistic and old-fashioned. So a rental model that is still based on the pensionable 1954 Landlord Tenancy Act (introduced when we still had post-war rationing) is clearly not fit for purpose.

Today, retailers engage their customers through multiple channels: they transact on- and offline and they fulfil via at-home delivery, collection boxes, local convenience stores, click-and-collect and indeed, on occasion, via an in-store.

The customer path to purchase today is infinitely more complex. In this world, then, valuing stores must become more complex. So we started with what value the store brings to the brand, and we believe there are five elements, reflecting the fact that the role of the store is now more complex:

- the 'old-fashioned' transaction hub remains extremely important...

but they do so much more today:

- they are fulfilment hubs for transactions made elsewhere (e.g. Argos)
- they are customer service hubs (look at Apple's temples of branding)
- they are there to maintain brand awareness (mobile network stores)
- they grow market share through creating experiences (e.g. Niketown)

Crucially all these functions will vary in importance by location and by brand. Note that even in all the examples here these stores also simultaneously play in the other 'channels'.

Valuing this objectively is therefore complex, but crucially, with all these added touchpoints of the customer, we have data. Our model works on using CACI's data-handling skills, independence and relationships to bring the occupier's data environment (which captures all the sales by channel and customer experience touchpoints) together with the owner of the store's data (who see footfall outside). We pull these through with CACI's data (using Acorn classification to describe the relevant customer and the Retail Footprint model to describe the store's sphere of influence) and analytics to produce an objective model of store performance, in any location. Crucially, putting CACI in the role of data processor we remove issues of confidentiality (protecting the detail for both parties), auditing (we see the whole data universe) and independence.

This gives both parties a data-led solution that clearly and objectively values a store around which both sides can then negotiate a rent. A turnover rent deal provides lower risk to the retailer as rent is tied to performance, and it also incentivizes the landlord to offer longer deals. This in turn allows retailers the security of tenure to invest in stores as they can amortize costs over a longer period. But perhaps most important of all, it gets both retailer and landlord to pull together – a store that boosts sales for the brand by any means necessary is in everyone's interest and in an uncertain, changing world that security cannot be over-valued.

A key challenge for the retail real-estate industry is the plummeting valuations they are experiencing. Retail real estate has historically been a very safe investment with predictable and stable returns; hence it attracted investment from institutions such as pension funds.

As consumer behaviour, demands and expectations changed and many retailers and inflexible retail real estate could not adapt, store vacancies increased. As valuations plummeted the market became attractive to private-equity investors whose main objective was to make short-term moves to increase values and exit relatively quickly.

We are now seeing the emergence of a different type of investor, one that prioritizes sustainability, community building, regeneration and long-term placemaking. These can include institutional investors, local government and specialist funds that focus on ESG (environmental and social sustainability and governance).

In some of these cases we are seeing the return to longer-term investment that involves root and branch repurposing of assets, recalibration of the commercial mix and reinvention of the customer experience. Often the investment in the asset will form part of a larger regeneration strategy or development opportunity.

It is clear from Burak's and Alex's pieces how critical data is in guiding strategy and design, and how in the future data will play an increasingly important role in determining the value of physical space and the content therein for a brand, operator, owner and investor. The data will be the key asset.

It is worth repeating then, that in future the physical space will not only monetize experiences, but also the data that is generated by those experiences.

Notes

1 CORDIS EU Research Results. European Commission, Innovative AI algorithms promise to revitalise the retail industry, cordis.europa.eu/article/id/421520-innovative-ai-algorithms-promise-to-revitalise-the-retail-industry (archived at https://perma.cc/4TMN-HJSV)

2 S Kasap. Turkish university ranks 2nd in Facebook competition, Anadolou Agency, 2018, www.aa.com.tr/en/science-technology/turkish-university-ranks-2nd-in-facebook-competition/1210721 (archived at https://perma.cc/N6LF-LMJU)

3 Wearesocial. Digital 2021: The global overview report, wearesocial-cn.s3.cn-north-1.amazonaws.com.cn/common/digital2021/digital-2021-global.pdf (archived at https://perma.cc/CE37-5P4R)

4 Internet Live Stats. Twitter Usage Statistics, www.internetlivestats.com/twitter-statistics/ (archived at https://perma.cc/8PHG-GDHJ)

5 J Chiang. Influencer marketing latest trends and best practices: 2018 report [blog] Muse Find, 2018, blog.musefind.com/influencer-marketing-latest-trends-best-practices-2018-report-a508540ad625 (archived at https://perma.cc/KGM9-8QXQ)

6 BBC. How much does Kylie Jenner earn on Instagram? CBBC Newsround, 2019, www.bbc.co.uk/newsround/49124484 (archived at https://perma.cc/AV5X-S5R6)

7 Wikipedia. Archetype, en.wikipedia.org/wiki/Archetype (archived at https://perma.cc/Y2XN-5K73)

8 S Menn. 3 questions from the oracle of Harvard Business School that changed my life forever, Inc.com, 2016, www.inc.com/slava-menn/3-questions-from-prof-clayton-christensen-that-changed-my-life-forever.html?cid=search (archived at https://perma.cc/YH7W-DLSG)

9 Acquia. Deliver the CX they expect: Customer experience trends report, www.acquia.com /resources/e-book/deliver-cx-they-expect-customer-experience-trends-report (archived at https://perma.cc/2K7Q-7SNX)

10 Kearney. Privacy and personalization: The paradox of data in consumer marketing, www.kearney.com/consumer-retail/article/?/a/privacy-and-personalization-the-paradox-of-data-in-consumer-marketing (archived at https://perma.cc/6FS9-UVDC)

11 T Taulli. What you need to know about dark data, *Forbes*, 2019, www.forbes.com/sites/tomtaulli/2019/10/27/what-you-need-to-know-about-dark-data/?sh=11c2f9332c79 (archived at https://perma.cc/BS9Y-D4AZ)

12 D Roth. The history of retail in 100 objects: Greek agora [blog] David Roth, 2014, www.davidroth.com/2014/06/10/history-retail-100-objects-greek-agora/ (archived at https://perma.cc/5MGA-ZTCH)

13 Chartered Institute of Marketing. Five stages of your customers' buying journey, CIM Exchange, www.cim.co.uk/content-hub/blog/five-stages-of-your-customers-buying-journey/ (archived at https://perma.cc/33YY-35B8)

14 J Simpson. Council post: Finding brand success in the digital world, *Forbes*, 2017, www.forbes.com/sites/forbesagencycouncil/2017/08/25/finding-brand-success-in-the-digital-world/?sh=41173ddd626e (archived at https://perma.cc/YG8A-KKXR)

15 T Roberts. What is omnichannel commerce? Definition, benefits and trends, Bloomreach, 2019, www.bloomreach.com/en/blog/2019/07/omnichannel-commerce-for-business.html (archived at https://perma.cc/H6A6-EL4P)

09

A people revolution

In retail, owners, operators and investors can develop lots of new initiatives, strategies and designs, all supported with sufficient funding. But this is a waste of time and money if they do not have people with a diversity of backgrounds and the rights skills, approach and attitude that will be required to deliver the initiatives. And critically, they need to be directed by a leadership with clarity, insight and an eagerness to encourage their people to 'think new' and flourish.

People first

So it all boils down to people. And the new art and science of place-making will require 'a people revolution'. By a lack of diversity, I am of course referring to ethnic or gender diversity, but also to a lack of diversity in skills and culture.

As I have described somewhat rhetorically in previous chapters, 'The future of retail will no longer be about property, it will be about content, where property is a by-product.' So as retail increasingly shifts to being driven less by property and more by content it will need to attract people from new industries with new skills.

If we can agree in a broad sense that this is a truism of the future then a people revolution is urgent. And to ensure that the sector is truly 'future-ready' it will need more people from the culture, entertainment, hospitality, tech and creative industries.

If we can introduce more of these skills and cultures into the retail real-estate industry and combine them with traditional skills, then we can move beyond seeing retail assets as mere concrete boxes with glass fronts that just sell stuff. We will be able to identify the future-ready brands, offers and amenities, and curate them to deliver a compelling blend of experiences that will bring back the excitement and the crowds.

The need for diversity

Considering this in more detail, the industry needs people from the culture, entertainment and hospitality industries: set designers, curators, stage managers, directors, storytellers, writers and technicians. They can help demonstrate that the way forward is to be a host who delivers experiences that are constantly refreshed and that encourage participation beyond transaction.

The industry needs trend forecasters who understand how to research and identify key trends that drive consumer behaviour, and data scientists who can analyse and unearth the insights to provide evidence on what value the physical space has to a brand in recruiting customers and driving engagement on social platforms and e-commerce, i.e. the value of media impressions and online sales driven by experience in physical space.

We need people from the media industry who understand physical space as a media platform and how to monetize it with new revenue models. We need social media experts and social and cultural influencers who understand that social media must be a dialogue channel and not a broadcast channel, where stories are shared with communities of interest. We need ethnographers who understand the importance of going beyond the traditional market research of surveys and focus groups, who understand audiences through observation, by digging deep into people, communities and cultures to unearth the human truths.

The retail industry also needs to respond to the fact that consumers are much more knowledgeable about what they are buying. They have access to information and the power to choose like never before.

Shopfloor associates also must be able to go beyond product information and sales. According to recent research by Tulip Retail, about 83 per cent of shoppers believe they're more knowledgeable than retail store associates. However, almost 50 per cent said they would be encouraged to shop in-store if they could talk to knowledgeable store associates who could suggest products based on their purchase histories. And about 73 per cent said they would be interested in having a store associate text or email them about order status.[1]

INDUSTRY EXPERT
Jacqueline Welbers

In my 30 years or so working as a consultant in the retail sector I have never come across anyone who understands how to develop successful store associates and brand advocates as well as Jacqueline Welbers. She is the founder of Lovelyday, a consultancy that 'links purpose and people'. Before that she held senior management positions at de Bijenkorf and IKEA Group. Jacqueline is also a visiting lecturer at the renowned Design Academy Eindhoven. Here she explains her approach with a narrative and diagrams which she has honed over many years.

From ticking the box to lighting the fire!

Have you ever experienced a staff member who is truly connected to their brand when you talk to them in a store? Their energy lifts you and you get inspired. The staff member is really committed to helping you.

People buy from people, and retail is THE example of a human-centred industry.

The influence of your staff connecting with the customer is of great value. They can make or break the relationship and therefore have responsibility for the financial results.

Why?

Nowadays we can buy nearly everything online. There is no longer a necessity to go somewhere to buy a product. The need we have to meet other people, to feel the energy, to get inspired is always there. People want to connect with brands that add value to their life. Brands that are well aware what is important in the life of human beings. To connect with other human beings. Brands that use digital to the max but put humans first. Humanity with a digital touch.

How does this work?

It all starts with your purpose (Figure 9.1). Purpose is the one thing in your organization that's a must. It's the reason your organization exists. It's the value you add to people's lives. It's the flow in your organization. It's the guiding line that connects everything and explains everything.

It's the starting point for your strategy. How do we make the purpose work?

It's the starting point for your business concept. What are we going to do to prove our purpose in practice?

How will our purpose look when we translate it into product, planet, price, people, promotion, etc?

Who can bring our purpose to life? How do we want to work together and how do we inspire others with our purpose?

FIGURE 9.1   The building process

SOURCE © Lovelyday

Your vision on staff

What is your vision on staff? Do you share the vision about their influence on the customer? Are you convinced they can light the fire and inspire the customer? Do you see yourself as the one who is creating the right circumstances for the staff, so they can inspire customers? Most important is to put your staff first, tell them and act on this with all the power you have. Is your culture ('the way we do things over here') supportive?

Are the processes developed from a customer's point of view? Or are you looking at staff as a number of functions who cost money?

To have staff who can light the fire you have to develop three steps:

1   *Do they understand the purpose of the brand?*

2 Did you just tell them or did you explore together with your staff what it means? What strategy fits the purpose and how will you all deliver the purpose with the products, price level, etc. All people know why, not only the managers. All people are involved!

3 *Do they love the purpose of the brand?*

4 Is it just a job or do they 'belong' here? (Figure 9.2) What do they feel about the purpose? Are they proud to work with this challenge? Do they feel connected?

5 *Do they live the purpose of the brand?*

6 Can they inspire others? Team-members, customers and even strangers get inspired by their energy, their stories. They own the purpose! (Figure 9.3)

The magic happens when the customer meets the staff!

FIGURE 9.2 To belong

SOURCE © Lovelyday

FIGURE 9.3 Living the purpose!

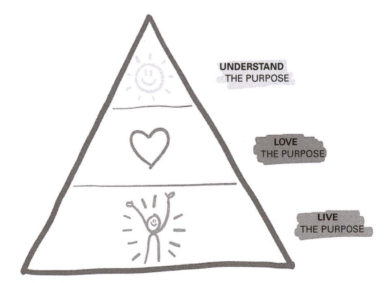

SOURCE © Lovelyday

Human motivation

But how do you know if your current staff or staff you want to hire have the right attitude to understand, love and live the purpose?

There must be a common ground before we develop the specific skills they need for the purpose (Figure 9.4).

FIGURE 9.4 McClelland's iceberg

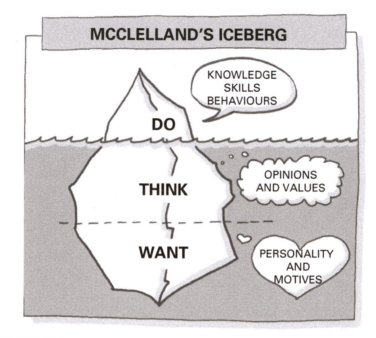

SOURCE © Lovelyday

It all starts with the human motivation. What motivation do we need to be able to live the purpose?

And how do we need to build the teams to have the best mix of people to support each other and to develop the organization.

First we have to agree on what we need on an individual level. Next step will be the structure and mix of the teams.

Attitude is more important than skills. Skills you can train. Attitude is something different...

How?

Do we need curious people? Do they want to connect? Or are they more driven by their own need for status? Do they have a fixed mindset or are they flexible and open to explore new challenges? By using these 24 motives (Figure 9.5) you can decide which ones are important and why.

FIGURE 9.5 Motivation spectrum

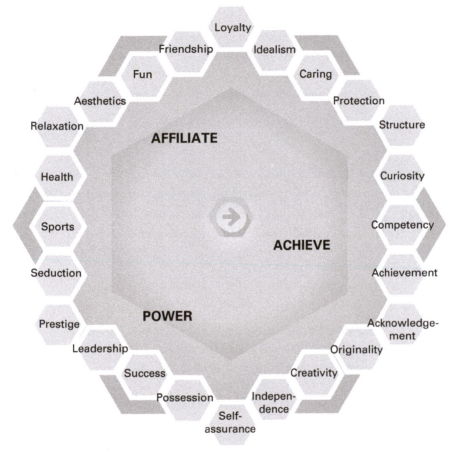

SOURCE © Lovelyday

Once you have decided which motives are important you can use a test that takes three minutes to get insights on the human motivation of the people you want to hire or who you already have as staff.[2]

It does not tell you about behaviour, but everything about what they really want.

What makes them tick!

Now you have a common ground (attitude) to start and develop the skills that are needed to understand, love and live the purpose.

Working with human motivation is a vision on organization development.

This vision puts people in the centre of the organization as the most important asset.

People who know their own motivation have more energy because they are aware of the things that bring them energy or cost them energy. They can create their own flow.

You can imagine what will happen if customers can connect to people who have the right flow and can inspire others.

This is a basic need of human beings, to connect with other human beings.

The moment you connect and get inspired, people are more than willing to buy from you![3]

I hope this has helped in understanding how retailers and brands need to respond to the increasing knowledge and information that consumers have on the products they sell. How to develop individuals and create teams that embody the brand and connect with consumers.

Notes

1 D O'Shea. Survey: 83% of shoppers think they know more than store associates, Retail Dive, 2017, www.retaildive.com/news/survey-83-of-shoppers-think-they-know-more-than-store-associates/438307/ (archived at https://perma.cc/KLQ9-FJED)

2 For more information, see www.my-buttons.com (archived at https://perma.cc/2YRE-6UAQ)

3 Lovely Day. Change fixes the past, transformation creates the future, llday.nl/ (archived at https://perma.cc/95D9-P7FE)

10

The future of our high streets

As a board member of the UK government's High Streets Task Force, I care deeply about the future of our high streets. Our high streets are the glue that binds our communities, and they have the potential to galvanize these communities with truly relevant, localized experiences and amenities.

My deep involvement with high streets, both as a member of the Task Force and in my day job running Portland Design – a design business that works with retailers, developers, operators, landlords, investors and local authorities – has exposed me to both the problems and also the enormous opportunities our high streets have.

For too long high streets have been neglected and abused. We have allowed too many out-of-town developments that have killed many high streets. More recently we have created an uneven playing field with online businesses in respect to business rates and taxation.

Although many high streets have created their own problems by being increasingly irrelevant, they still have the opportunity to prosper again if they can adapt to the new demands and expectations of their communities, and if they can think beyond a 'me-too' clone high street that allows domination by international and national chains who blindly roll out their concepts without (mostly) giving any consideration to the local context and community.

A love letter

Over many years I have felt anger, sadness and hope in equal measure, but I truly believe that we can all fall in love with our high streets again. And so, as the Covid-19 pandemic lockdown was beginning to ease, I decided to write a love letter to the high street:

Dear High Street
Being in a relationship with an addict has been tough. Although I haven't visited you as often as I used to, when I did several times earlier this year, there seemed to be a blankness. You were physically present, but very quiet and somehow lifeless.

I remember the times when we used to have so much fun, even though you were like all the others.

I am really looking forward to seeing you again now that the Covid restrictions are being eased. I am sure we'll have a good time and do some fun things again, now that you have realized the need to kick your addiction to 'shops', that drug you get from those dealer agents you call friends.

After your long period of inevitable cold turkey, it is so good to see that you are finally looking to the future again and feeling a little more optimistic. I know it will take time to turn things around, particularly as you've had so much of the drugs for so long. And I know how difficult it is to find the money to pull yourself out of the rut you have been in.

As I advised you, the way forward is to abandon some of your old, toxic acquaintances and find new friends with different interests and outlooks. Surround yourself with friends with fresh thinking and who look to the future. Maybe you will find a group who can see the potential in you. They may even be willing to invest in your future and some of the new ideas you have.

As you embark on your transformation I am looking forward to being introduced to your new friends and to having a fun time again. I look forward to meeting those lovely events and markets – they will be such fun to be with. To enjoying engaging with the yoga classes or going for a run now you are planning to plant lots of trees and create little parks. It's important you keep healthy, and those vacant spaces you are planning to fill with your new health-conscious friends, the wellness clinics, health food stores, athleisure stores and spin classes will help you achieve this.

You also need to learn new skills by getting to know those new kids on the block, the bearded makerspaces with their hipster coffee bars and 3D printers.

I see there is a chance of introducing low-cost flats in that block of empty shops you have. That would be a great addition that will give you new energy.

To ensure you don't go back to your old ways I will be introducing you to a new bunch of guys who can support you and show you a new way of life, and a new future. I've got to know this new group recently. They come from different sectors but they are interested in getting to know you. They include great storytellers, hospitality guys, curators, stage managers, set designers, social media specialists, influencers, programme managers, media buyers, data scientists and even ethnographers – oh, those are the guys who can tell you lots about the new people who will visit you in the future.

I am looking forward to seeing you make these critical changes to your life, and I hope you continue to make steady progress.

Just as a last word of advice, you have been through a torrid time, and looking forward, the 'do nothing' strategy is not an option. You must rethink your lifestyle, make decisions and take actions for the long term. Short-term easy fixes are not the answer, and if you think they are you will only go back to your old ways.

I have known you for long enough to have total confidence in you, and so I am really optimistic for your future. I have no doubt that there will be brighter days ahead.

Good luck my love,

Ibrahim xx

Although the retail sector is experiencing tectonic shifts and going through a very challenging time it will continue to play an important role in and contribution to the health of the wider economy.

According to UK Office for National Statistics (ONS), the retail sector's economic output was £97.0 billion in 2020, which represented 5 per cent of the UK's total economic output. However, this was a 2.5 per cent reduction when compared to 2019. This was obviously as a result of the impact of the coronavirus pandemic.[1]

How will the rapidly changing retail landscape impact the future of our town centres and high streets (main streets). And what role will developers, local authorities and communities play?

Since the retail sector still represents a considerable component of the UK's GDP and the jobs that the sector supports, the government must take urgent action before the current challenges impact the economy and our communities irreversibly.

The key macro-economic reason for a potential crisis is that we are experiencing a generational time bomb whereby most of the wealth of the country resides with the elder generation who engage least with retail. The younger population have increasing costs, more uncertainty and decreasing wealth but are the key consumers, particularly in important retail categories such as fashion, beauty, electronics and household goods.

As Mark Pilkington points out in his book *Retail Therapy*:[2]

> If something is not done, consumption of many retail categories is going to collapse. More and more spending power is going to be channelled into areas such as travel, healthcare and old-age care, as people prolong their lives into their eighties and nineties, and less is going to be available for the categories of spending that support the retail sector.

Mr Pilkington goes on to point out that governments are not incentivized to change anything because they need the votes of the elderly, who tend to vote more than younger generations.

However, to address this problem, governments can adopt strategies to ease the burden on younger generations. The cost of higher education could be reduced. The elder generation could be incentivized through the tax system to pass on more of their wealth through inheritance. The tax system could also be used to reduce the cost of buying a first home.

Of course, the increasing cost of goods discourages the young to consume. Although this is a complex area, the government could take action in helping retailers reduce their costs. The government must urgently address the imbalance in corporation tax and business rates.

Protectionism is another cause of rising cost of goods. Mr Pilkington addresses this point very poignantly:

> Wherever protectionism has the upper hand it has had a devastating effect on retailing. As we have seen, one of the prime reasons why the UK retail sector is so badly affected is because of Brexit, which caused the collapse in the pound from nearly in 2015 to under US $1.30 after the referendum. This raised the cost of the goods imported by UK retailers by 20 to 25 per cent and has put a substantial squeeze on profit margins.[3]

He goes on to point out that 'The US government's policy of placing tariffs on Chinese and other imports will almost certainly have a similar effect. The consequences for the US retail industry, already staggering under multiple pressures, could be devastating.'

Finally, Mr Pilkington makes his most far-reaching point:

> For every manufacturing job saved by protectionism, there are three retail (and brand) jobs at risk. Governments (and voters) need to draw back from the precipice of protectionism and understand the huge benefits that have accrued to them from free trade.

As well as seeking help from governments, the retail sector must address how it appeals and relates to consumers and communities and what role it is to play in the future of our town centres, high streets and main streets.

So there is a sense of urgency and no time to waste in addressing the dichotomy between the dependency on physical retail and its decline. In previous chapters I have described how shops must change and how we can create a new blend of experiences and amenities to recharge and transform our high streets and main streets.

As I have emoted in my love letter, to tempt the crowds back high streets and main streets must firstly kick their addiction to transactional retail.

The internet has taken business away from physical retail. But I passionately believe the internet will not kill physical shops. It will liberate them! To be released from the shackles of transactional retail where they cannot compete with online players, to developing offers and experiences that cannot possibly be delivered online and so make them relevant again to their customers and wider communities.

A place with a community rhythm

There is a case for optimism if we grasp the opportunity to reimagine our high streets and main streets as compelling places for communities to gather, enjoy and share. As I have already emphasized, we must shift the emphasis from a 'shopping rhythm' to a 'community rhythm'. And urgently rethink old siloed 'mixed-use' into connected 'blended-use' to bring together a compelling mix of shops, and a broad blend of experiences and amenities to create the 'connective tissue' that can activate the public realm and encourage new and sustainable footfall, while also driving value above ground.

I have already, rather provocatively, spoken about the future of high streets and main streets being about content and not real estate. To deliver the shift from siloed 'mixed-use' into connected 'blended-use' and make our high streets and main streets alive again we will need to adopt a 'community curation' approach that transcends 'leasing boxes'.

This approach progresses well beyond commercial leasing to the identification, selection, organization and presentation of programmed physical and digital content that delivers a blend of occupiers, both ephemeral and longer term, national and regional retail and food brands, leisure and entertainment brands, local independents, influencers, individuals and community groups. All blended with workplace, hospitality, healthcare, education, makerspaces and residential to create truly authentic places with a new rhythm, a new feeling and a new relevance to their communities.

Mariam Saltzman suggests in the book *Next Now* that we have entered the era of the surprising, the spontaneous, the unplanned and the serendipitous.[4]

In order to imbue our high streets with engaging experiences, interest and surprise, we need to bring 'back-of-house' activities 'front-of-house'. Activities and experiences such as making, education, workshops, theatre, artisans, etc, which have been hidden from view, should be brought into the public sphere to create interest and intrigue in our public spaces. We should expose communities to the inner workings of the city, activities and goings-on that are normally hidden from public view.

This approach and thinking applies well to education. In order to meet the future expectations of students, local communities and visitors, university campuses must be more than a series of building where people teach and learn stuff.

A future-ready university masterplan must imagine a campus with a range of blended experiences and offers with an activated public realm that is connected to community. A campus that includes a permeable and connected 'programmable platform' will enable a series of services, amenities and curated commercial offers to deliver newness and surprise with a blend of physical and digital experiences. And it can form a critical part of the masterplan, creating the 'step-stones' for journeys of discovery, engagement and community.

Two good examples of university campuses that form an important part of community connection and activation are the Central St Martins art college and Kingston University.

Central St Martins (CSM) is part of the Kings Cross and Granary Square development. As the public walk along the small intimate streets past shops and restaurants they are able to look through openings into the CSM workshops and studios while observing the art students participating in drawing, painting and making work.

The CSM building creates a sense of discovery, interest and intrigue for shoppers, workers, visitors and the local community alike. It gives a 'change of pace' to the journeys that link the plazas and streets and presents a very different type of experience for those shopping, eating, drinking and playing.

Kingston University won the recent RIBA Stirling Prize, displaying new thinking in the design of higher education buildings. Named the Town House, this important building clearly demonstrates the value of a 'blended' approach to development, an education building that is permeable and meaningfully connected to community.

In their design of the Town House, Grafton Architects have created a deliberately democratic, inclusive, open space. The name 'Town House' suggests a building with a civic role that offers students and the local community alike a place where they can feel at home, one that is welcoming, democratic and that creates a sense of belonging.

The project expands the public realm because it is set back and connects with the street, blurring seamlessly with the pavement and so being inviting to students, locals and visitors alike.

The Town House sends a message to students and the local community that university life and learning no longer just happens behind closed doors in isolation of local people and activities. It demonstrates that education and related amenities can activate public realm, form part of the streetscape and tapestry of urban life while connecting to the day-to-day rhythms of the town and its people.

RIBA describes the Town House as:

> … a building that has no barriers. A 200 m-long, six-storey, deep colonnade offers shadow and shelter, with terraces and gardens above creating shelves of connected public space. The facades are permeable: open and transparent at the lower levels – revealing views to the passer-by of the engaging activities taking place. Equally open and spacious inside, users and visitors are greeted by the public forum, leading to an amphitheatre. From the ground floor, eyes are drawn up through the building – through voids and staircases – to complementing social and study spaces. Exemplary acoustic design enables the bustling public forum, quiet library, archive, dance studio and theatre to co-exist, and enrich the experience of the users… this highly-adaptable building will stand the test of time and provide an inspiring environment for students, residents and visitors for years to come.

Speaking on behalf of the 2021 RIBA Stirling Prize jury, Lord Norman Foster, said:

> Kingston University Town House is a theatre for life – a warehouse of ideas. It seamlessly brings together student and town communities,

creating a progressive new model for higher education, well deserving of international acclaim and attention.

Kingston University's Town House sends a critical and far-reaching message that this is a place for everyone: students, visitors, local residents, young and old – everyone is welcome and valued.

To accommodate a diversity of occupiers it is essential to have diverse revenue models. These can include fixed rent, turnover rent, footfall-based rent, subscription models, 'halo rent' based on the impact of online engagement and media impressions.

In the case of retail, this will be an inevitable development as many physical shops shift from being focused on transaction to customer recruitment. They will increasingly behave like media spaces, and so fixed, longer-term leases are often not fit for purpose. New data-driven lease models will need to be developed to demonstrate, prove and measure the value of physical space to a brand and a landlord.

So, in order to prosper, our high streets and main streets must embrace these new models and experiences, all driven, not by the old priorities of the real-estate industry, but by the new priorities of consumers, citizens, communities.

Successful high streets in future will be those that deliver not only commercial value for their occupiers, owners and investors. They will also deliver social, cultural and environmental value for its individual citizens, its wider communities and our planet.

In implementing new strategies to regenerate our high streets, we must find ways to measure social, cultural and environmental value. Of course the metrics may vary for each high street, but can include:

- the change in the proportion of the community that visit, who visits, when and how long
- how they get there
- the amount of community participation, and what they are participating in
- the sentiment that it drives
- the level of sharing on digital platforms

- the comparison between visits to the high streets against other destinations
- the proportion of cultural experiences, community services and amenities as compared to commercial offers, and the number of visits to each and time spent
- the proportion of green space and pedestrian areas, air quality and levels of noise pollution
- the impact on crime and the type of crime, how safe citizens feel during the day and night, etc

---

INDUSTRY EXPERT
Mark Robinson

I discussed these and many other issues with Mark Robinson, a good friend, client and my chairman on the High Streets Task Force. I posed four questions which Mark eloquently and quite robustly addressed. Here are his thoughts.

WHAT ARE YOUR THOUGHTS GENERALLY ABOUT THE HIGH STREETS AND REAL ESTATE?
I sometimes wonder whether the generic word 'high street' is helpful. Fundamentally, a high street is a row of shops in a town centre. Some people refer to the high street as anything to do with retail, so sometimes the definition itself holds us back I think.

High streets always involve commerce, where you are buying stuff and fulfilling a need or want. And that's what retail is. And you know, I think the distinction between retail and leisure is breaking down. So a high street is just somewhere you go to exchange cash, to feel better about yourself and to come together with other people.

We are cultural animals and like to come together in places to do stuff together, and yes, in future there will be less exchange of goods, but there will still be lots of 'exchange' happening.

As the Chairman of the High Streets Task Force, I'll know that we've succeeded when people stop judging high streets in purely retail terms. You know it used to be that success for a high street depended on what it was anchored by and it went up in scale from Woolworths, BHS to M&S and on to John Lewis, for example. This whole hierarchy is no longer valid or fit for purpose and that's a good thing.

We need to judge our high streets and town centres by their vitality and whether they fulfil their community needs. And of course sustainability is key, and I'm not just talking about environmental sustainability. I'm talking about places that have resilience and adaptability. To not be obsolete once a certain modality or use is no longer valid. At its heart sustainability is resilience, where something can be adapted and reused.

Also, if you say 'landlord' it conjures up an image of a twiddly moustachioed guy with a top hat on the monopoly board. And it's the tenant who is always nice and the downtrodden part of that relationship. And that has been true for millennia.

Almost uniquely in the UK, and for complex historical reasons, the legal framework over-complicates matters and gets in the way of what is a very simple relationship between a supplier of a good and a consumer of a good. It's worse than that because of the way the 1954 Act was set up to protect landlords. And a lot of the legislation that is in place was predicated on this idea that lease renewals and lettings happen once every 25 years. It has infantilized the relationship in the UK between owners of real estate and occupiers.

I think we need to move beyond the language of 'landlord' and 'tenant'. We have owners of real estate and we have occupiers of real estate. And nowadays an occupier could be occupying space for an hour, a day, a week, a month or for 10 years.

The legal system needs a complete overhaul, and the government does seem to recognize that. The over-superannuated value in retail property drove out all the other uses (in high streets) that we now really want to get back in our town centres.

In France and other places where leases might typically be 3–5 years, people still build shopping centres, still build shops. And people still lend on them. The world doesn't come to an end just because we don't have 25-year leases or even 10-year leases any more.

So we need to promote investment, dynamism and change, because what the consumer wants has changed. Nobody wanted these clone towns we created full of the same shops that never change. And that's why people fell out of love with our town centres.

Everything is telling us we need to change and as a consequence of Covid-19 we have seen 10 years of change in 10 months.

HOW DO YOU SEE THE IMPACT ON VALUATIONS? AND WHAT DO YOU THINK ABOUT DATA THAT DEMONSTRATES THAT CONSUMERS ARE ENGAGING WITH A BRAND, NOT JUST IN THE SHOP BUT REMOTELY AS WELL?

I hear a lot about valuations driven by data, but I'm very sceptical whether that is something that's going to be taken into account any time soon. But there is some interesting work being done about performance leases by CACI.

If I'm really honest, one of the problems we've got with the valuation of retail real estate is that the occupiers don't know what it's worth to them. Because of the market dynamics at the moment, the value of the shop is 'how little I can pay for it'. Which in many scenarios it's very little indeed, but that's not the true value of the shop.

There is every possibility that we might end up with some turnover provision, as long as it is based on affordability for that tenant. Because affordability for a discount retailer is wildly different to a high-margin retailer.

We can just over-complicate things. This thing (a shop) has a front and a back in two sides, and it's worth something to somebody now and it depends on what their business is. But the one thing it isn't worth is what some idiot paid next door. And traditionally, the value of retail space has been based upon what the idiot next door paid for it, good or bad.

CAN YOU SHARE YOUR THOUGHTS ON GOVERNANCE, PLANNING AND REGULATIONS IN RELATION TO HIGH STREETS?
I think the UK government clearly has a pro-growth agenda in its planning policy. Which is to be encouraged, and I think the flexibility around asset classes has been a very good thing.

Covid has also driven what is called 'tactical urbanism', albeit sometimes on a temporary basis. This happened almost overnight, and it made change happen that would have taken a decade to get through planning and licensing. It has been one of the brilliant things to take away from the impact of Covid.

However, I am worried about taking away communities' and local authorities' right to protect vibrant retail uses in their high streets by allowing PDR (permitted development right) for changing retail to residential use. Many of our retail places in our high streets should be protected and PDR as it could currently be implemented is a real-life concern to most people in the placemaking industry.

Class E is great, as a hairdresser can change to a bookkeeper which can change to a tattoo parlour and then into a really cool bookshop over a 10-year period. And that's great as they're all commercial users. But if they change to residential use they tend to stay that way; changing back to commercial use is very difficult.

WHAT IMPACT DO YOU THINK THE COVID-19 PANDEMIC HAS HAD ON HIGH STREETS?
Covid has inflicted awfulness upon the world but what good can we take from it? Well it has energized people to care about their local places in a way that wouldn't have happened otherwise.

What was going wrong with our town centres and high streets had been going on for many years before Covid. You know, the High Streets Task Force was put in place in 2018 to stop a declining trend trajectory! Covid has really energized people to being closer to home and really made people engage with their local places and feel passionate about them. People don't want to commute into cities all the time, so that's been a massive boost for the suburbs and small towns.

The government sees the challenge; there are votes in rescuing town centres. They are pouring high-street fund money into various parts of the UK because there are votes in saving our high streets and that might not have happened in the same dramatic way without Covid.

Putting wellness at the heart of what everybody wants from place is central to all this, and it's something we saw from the Ellandi Real Shopper survey. We saw that health and well-being is something people want from their high streets. It's one of the biggest increases in consumer preferences, and I don't see that going away any time soon.

Where high streets don't work, they make people feel bad about themselves. If you live near a run-down town centre you don't feel any civic pride. When you go into your town you feel worse about life.

The opposite is true if high streets provide people with their wants and needs that they can't get anywhere else. And it might help some fall back in love with high streets again.

So, for too long commercial returns in high streets have been prioritized at the expense of everything else. And this approach has proven to deliver unsustainable value. We must now urgently balance commercial value with social, cultural and environmental value, and if we do this, it will result in more sustainable commercial value.

High streets and main streets must encourage and incentivize occupiers who create community spaces. Occupiers with offers and experiences that are participatory and bring people together around common interests and passions. These types of occupiers along with community services and amenities will deliver true social value to a high street and its communities.

So, let's make sure we introduce a broad range of experiences and amenities to our high streets and main streets, and ensure that all stakeholders work together to rediscover the highs of our high streets (and main streets).

Notes

1   G Hutton. Retail sector in the UK, House of Commons Briefing Paper, 2021. researchbriefings.files.parliament.uk/documents/SN06186/SN06186.pdf (archived at https://perma.cc/8CQE-Z3DW)
2   M Pilkington (2019) *Retail Therapy: Why the retail industry is broken and what can be done to fix it,* Bloomsbury, London
3   Z Wood. Brexit likely to raise cost of clothing and food, warns Next boss, *The Guardian*, 2016, www.theguardian.com/business/2016/jun/25/brexit-raise-cost-of-clothing-and-food-warns-next-boss (archived at https://perma.cc/8L3L-EKS5)
4   M Salzman and I Matathia (2007) *Next Now,* Palgrave Macmillan, New York

11

Post-pandemic reality

As in other spheres, the Covid-19 pandemic has exposed many fault lines in retail. It has brought forward the day of reckoning for many retailers and has accelerated many trends that were emerging. Some changes have proved to be transient while others will prove to be systemic.

Changes: transient or lasting?

One significant acceleration has been the polarizing of retail, with autonomous, hyper-convenient, zero-touch experiences at one extreme ('fast experience'), and experiential, participatory, immersive learning experiences at the other ('slow experience').

One of the lasting legacies of Covid-19 in public life will be an acceleration of 'zero-touch' environments and experiences. As well as well-established, zero-touch digital payment, we will see the growth of gesture recognition and voice technology in physical retail to enable customers to avoid making physical contact with surfaces.

The gesture recognition and touchless sensing market is projected to reach $37.6 billion by 2026 from $13.6 billion in 2021; and it is expected to grow at a CAGR of 22.6 per cent from 2021 to 2026.[1]

According to Business Wire:[2]

> The gesture recognition in the retail market is expected to grow at a CAGR of 27.54 per cent over the forecast period (2021–2026).

As e-commerce pioneers provide exceptional online consumer experiences, experiential retailers are reinventing the in-store experience, creating environments that attract and delight consumers.

With physical stores remaining at the hub of modern retail, and with most consumers still choosing to end their journeys there, retail is getting digitized. This includes multiple smart devices working together on a single IoT platform to deliver hyper-personalized, adaptive and context-specific experiences. While much of the technology is to be invisible to the consumer, shoppers will have the opportunity to interact digitally within the physical store environment.

While Mordor Intelligence reports:[3]

> In addition to the adoption of gesture recognition in digital catalogues, retail owners are able to monitor the success of a product with shoppers, by monitoring their facial and hand gestures. And data gathered through this could reveal a whole new set of insights, which may not be realized by using numerical data alone. For instance, an Italian retailer, Coop Italia, teamed up with Accenture as it wanted to transform the customer shopping experience. The company integrated digital capabilities into the store atmosphere to create the supermarket of the future. However, limited numbers of recognizable gestures along with inaccurate and inefficient systems are certain factors hindering the growth of the gesture recognition market globally.

We will also see the growth of virtual concierge services, virtual learning environments, and the explosion of brands and experiences that focus on wellness, mindfulness and experiences that have nature and biophilia at their core.

The rise of the appointment economy

Covid-19 has also accelerated the 'by-appointment' economy. Due to the fear of crowds, many retailers, particularly in the luxury sector, grew their 'by-appointment' offer. However, these 'one-to-one'-type experiences are also being introduced by many mainstream retailers. Please allow me to give you a small anecdote that illustrates this well.

A while ago I built a workshop where I spend many hours making furniture and sculpture. Over the years I have bought my wood from a local timber merchant. The merchant has a very large timber yard with a small shop in the centre, which I can best describe as a small tin shack.

My usual routine before the Covid-19 pandemic was that I would arrive at the yard and park my car on uneven ground in a random spot as there were no car park markings. I would then make my way to said tin shack and wait in a queue outside until there was enough room for me to proceed into the small space allowed for customers. After the two very expert gentlemen had finished their conversation, I would then hesitantly interrupt them to give my order. They would then hand-write a receipt, and after paying for the goods, I would take the receipt to another gentleman in the yard, and then help him carry my goods in my truck.

However, it was a very different experience during the Covid restrictions. During that period I arrived at the yard to be greeted at a new barrier by the daughter of the owner. After a few minutes wait, she raised the barrier and directed me to one of the designated and numbered car parking spaces, each with a fresh even gravel floor. I was requested to stay in my truck whereupon an assistant came over to take my order. My goods were then brought to my truck and loaded into the back. I paid for my goods and left, a very happy and unstressed customer.

This is a great example of a retailer changing the way they serve customers due to Covid-19. And in the process transforming the customer experience from a very unsatisfactory mainstream service into a concierge-type premium experience, for which I would have been prepared to, but didn't, pay a premium.

FUTURE-READY NOTE

Covid-19 has caused the 'mainstreaming' of premium experiences.

In a recent piece by Brian Solis for *Forbes* entitled 'The rise of the appointment economy: The last mile of customer engagement will be scheduled, optimized and personalized' he noted that

> As a result of the pandemic and its acceleration of digital adoption, more and more customers are starting to expect innovative and personalized services that value their time. This is giving rise to an 'appointment economy' and it can quickly become a competitive differentiator in earning customer relationships and ultimately, loyalty.[4]

The piece went on to explain that 'Within the first 90 days of pandemic disruption, customers were starting almost every buying journey on a digital platform, which influenced new routines and expectations in the experiences they preferred.' These customer expectations were listed as:

1 they move faster, across multiple touchpoints
2 they seek clear, contextually relevant and visual information
3 they rely on peer reviews
4 they expect all touchpoints – across both physical and digital – to be integrated, convenient, intuitive and frictionless, experiential and personalized
5 they are increasingly impatient and expect outcomes on their schedule, and
6 they demand that companies expedite and enhance digital engagement and also introduce new types of experiences

The Economist has identified some key aspects of the by-appointment economy and the impact of Covid-19 as follows:[5]

- Appointment and queue-management technology lets businesses open that otherwise could not. At reduced capacity, many businesses simply aren't viable. Appointment technology allows businesses to better predict and manage customer flow and serve people more quickly, making up for lost capacity.
- Customers can book visits in advance via an app before shopping, (e.g.) at Brown Thomas, a department store in Dublin... walk-ins can join a virtual queue by scanning a QR code by the entrance...

- Virtual queuing technology for restaurants, like that built by Atlacarte, also lets customers pre-order meals while they wait. That makes life easier in the kitchen and dramatically streamlines the at-table experience, says Onur Simsek, Atlacarte's founder. 'The ordering process is 87.5 per cent faster,' he claims.

In the same piece *The Economist* goes on to explain that

- For many (businesses), appointments are a survival tactic, made necessary by social distancing requirements. But some firms are looking at appointments as a longer-term opportunity to improve or transform their offering.

- Interest in reservation and queuing technology is booming. 'We're seeing a lot of retailers using this as a catalyst for projects they already had on the roadmap,' says Imogen Wethered, chief executive of Qudini, a firm providing virtual queuing software for big British retailers including Tesco, O2 and Dixons Carphone.

Appointment technology has got smarter. Gone is the receptionist's notebook or even the vibrating puck: next-generation booking systems make use of smartphones, are powered by whizzy data analytics and can integrate with inventory management, point-of-sale and customer relationship management software. The piece then described the benefits of the by-appointment economy that firms can grasp for a competitive advantage. These benefits are endorsed by various business leaders in the piece and are defined as:

- Optimizing resources. At the individual store level, appointments let shops prepare the right stock or staff to handle the particular needs of the day, says Bill Clark, chief executive of TimeTrade, the market leader in America for appointments software. This capability is even more powerful when applied across multiple branches, and is real-time. 'It's not only about setting appointments, but allowing enterprises to optimize resources,' he says.

- Building a digital-first relationship with customers. Appointments offer an opportunity to capture customer data and build a digital relationship with in-store shoppers, says Mr Clark. Shops can use queuing apps to engage customers with content, reminders, offers and personalized service, and tie offline behaviour to online shopping profiles. You're seeing this great emergence of the omnichannel retail concept, agrees Ms Wethered.

- Rethinking revenue models. Tock, a restaurant-reservation app, has pioneered the introduction of dynamic pricing for restaurants, encouraging in-demand restaurants to offer meals at different prices at different times, which guests pay for in full in advance. 'Surge' pricing at times of peak demand cuts waste and brings in more revenue. The same approach could be used by hairdressers, spas and other service retail.

- Add to these benefits the fact that appointment customers spend more, it's easy to see by-appointment shopping gaining popularity in retail sectors previously unaccustomed to it.

And according to *The Economist* in the same piece, 'Appointment shoppers spend three times more than walk-ins because they tend to have done their research and are primed to buy.'

The desire for well-being and safety

Covid-19 has also accelerated the focus on wellness, and as a result wellness has transcended being just a commercial category. Physical and mental wellness must now form part of the DNA of all places and businesses, including high streets and main streets.

We must approach the development of places with a 'wellness mindset'. A biophilic approach to the design of our public spaces is now a priority. This extends beyond 'greening', to a wider connection to nature with the use of natural materials, water, light, open spaces with the sounds and aromas of nature, and with environmental sustainability at its core.

Another Covid-driven future consideration will be 'design for distance'. This is a new paradigm in the development of places. We are well versed in design for sustainability and design of experience; now we must give consideration to 'design for distance'.

A key part of the post-pandemic reality is that our audiences will demand reassurance that the places they visit and engage with are safe and promote wellness. To meet these new expectations we must capture and communicate data that demonstrates that the environmental conditions are not harmful. This includes data on air quality, no exposure to antigens, clean and safe surfaces, zero-touch operations, voice- and gesture-control technologies.

To avoid skin contact, we have seen a move towards replacing traditional manually operated door handles with foot-operated mechanisms. It seems that we will see the adoption of range of similarly 'zero-touch' ideas.

An alternative approach to zero-touch door opening is a door handle by Tweaq. This is the world's first self-disinfecting door handle and is a good example of a door handle that demonstrates a focus on safe surfaces. Each time it is used, virucidal liquid is sprayed on the handle from a replaceable cartridge.

Building back better

Covid-19 has also been the catalyst for the UK government's 'build back better' initiative.

The UK government's High Streets Task Force provides the encouragement, tools, skills and training that communities and local government need to transform their high streets. As part of this remit, the task force has published a Covid-19 recovery framework in partnership with the Institute of Place Management.

The framework is designed to help local authorities and leaders in the regeneration of high streets in both the short-term recovery and the longer-term transformation of their specific high street. The framework is formulated as four phases: crisis, pre-recovery, recovery and transformation.

The first phase, *Crisis*, outlines the need to start actions immediately by setting up a crisis team structure to co-ordinate all strategies and actions and point the way forward and reassure all stakeholders. The next step is to collect and communicate all relevant data that gives insight into the extent of the crisis.

Pre-recovery is the second phase which focuses on building capacity for recovery and transformation. It involves imagining and defining the vision supported by new ideas for recovery including digitization, and from these setting out a specific and clear recovery plan. During this phase it is recommended to build networks and plan ongoing communications.

The third phase is *Recovery* and involves getting businesses operational and people back to the high street, safely. The key to this phase is crafting and communicating the story of recovery backed by data-based evidence. This phase also involves the practicalities of managing footfall and social distancing and introducing a safety-driven cleaning regime.

The final phase is *Transformation*. The priority here is to support the place leaders in transforming their high streets. Fundamental to this is funding, so helping with researching and accessing specific funding and investment opportunities. This phase involves identifying potential partners and building strong partnership bodies that are driven by clear determination to deliver the vision.[6]

Notes

1 Markets and Markets. Gesture recognition and senseless touching market, www.marketsandmarkets.com/Market-Reports/touchless-sensing-gesturing-market-369.html (archived at https://perma.cc/3N6R-7JCD)

2 Business Wire. Global Gesture Recognition in Retail Market 2019-2024, 2019. www.businesswire.com/news/home/20190624005610/en/Global-Gesture-Recognition-in-Retail-Market-2019-2024---Anticipating-a-CAGR-of-27.54-Over-the-Forecast-Period---ResearchAndMarkets.com (archived at https://perma.cc/AU7M-UH4S)

3 Mordor Intelligence. Gesture recognition in retail market: Growth, trends, Covid-19 impact, and forecasts (2022–2027), 2021, www.mordorintelligence.com/industry-reports/gesture-recognition-in-retail-rfid-touchless-displays-interactive-screens-window-display-screens-industry (archived at https://perma.cc/D2XZ-V3AK)

4 B Solis. The rise of the appointment economy: The last mile of customer engagement will be scheduled, optimized and personalized, *Forbes,* 2021

5 *The Economist.* Welcome to the 'appointment economy', 2020, applied.economist.com/articles/welcome-to-the-appointment-economy (archived at https://perma.cc/P7VR-PCYL)

6 High Streets Task Force. Covid-19, www.highstreetstaskforce.org.uk/covid-19 (archived at https://perma.cc/R5WZ-NC44)

12

Final thoughts

As I write this, Facebook has announced that it is changing its name to Meta. This is a reference to the 'metaverse'. Facebook sees this as the next chapter in its evolution of connecting people whereby connections and engagement, it predicts, will take place in a hybrid physical/digital world:

> The metaverse is the next evolution of social connection. Our
> company's vision is to help bring the metaverse to life.

We have seen the evolution of augmented reality (AR) that overlays digital objects and content onto the physical world. This experience enhances the real world with digital components such as images and text. In an AR experience users are in the real world and are aware of what's going on around them physically.

In virtual reality (VR) users are fully immersed in a digital environment with a 360-degree experience of an artificial world and are not aware of what's going on around them physically.

We are now seeing the development of mixed reality (MR) where physical and digital objects co-exist in real time in a hybrid world where the user can interact with the digital objects in a physical world.

The metaverse will be driven by extended reality (ER). This is also a hybrid world, but here the experience is multi-sensory and users cannot easily distinguish between physical and digital objects.

If I were to predict what ER will mean in the future for retail, I can imagine a physical shopping centre or high street occupied by digital shops, environments and activations. I could also imagine a customer in their home doing online shopping whereby the shop is a digital environment that the customer inhabits, engages with and from which he or she buys products.

Notwithstanding the development of MR and ER, we are still witnessing rapid and existential changes to retail, specifically in our shopping centres and high streets.

So, in this rapidly changing retail world, safe is risky. And incremental improvements don't work in a world where change is not incremental.

Businesses, organizations and institutions do not fail because they do the wrong thing. They often fail because they continue to do what used to be the right thing for too long.

There are three types of people in this world and three types of leader:

- those who make it happen
- those who let it happen
- those who wondered what happened

So in a world where change happens at warp speed and in tectonic shifts, if you are a leader, don't 'wonder what happened'.

Try new ideas, test them rapidly and understand why they succeed or fail.

And if you are going to fail, fail successfully.

Do and learn, don't wait and see.

INDEX

CPSIA information can be obtained
at www.ICGtesting.com
Printed in the USA
JSHW061227290622
27633JS00009B/251

9 781398 603349